Speaking of Books –
and Life

Books by J. Donald Adams

The Shape of Books to Come
Literary Frontiers
Copey of Harvard:
A Biography of Charles Townsend Copeland
The Magic and Mystery of Words
Speaking of Books—and Life

Edited by the Same Author

The Treasure Chest:
An Anthology of Contemplative Prose
The New Treasure Chest:
An Anthology of Reflective Prose
Triumph Over Odds:
An Anthology of Man's Unconquerable Spirit
Poems of Ralph Waldo Emerson

J. DONALD ADAMS

Speaking of Books–and Life

Holt,
Rinehart and Winston
New York Chicago San Francisco

Published simultaneously in Canada by Holt, Rinehart
and Winston of Canada, Limited.

Library of Congress Catalog Card Number: 65-22458

First Edition

Designer: Ernst Reichl
80090-0216
Printed in the United States of America

Contents

Speaking of Books – and Life

Foreword

THE RIGHT TO CHANGE one's mind is unfortunately more readily accorded the sex misleadingly and somewhat hypocritically referred to as the "weaker" one, although every man half in command of his senses knows that his is the less realistic, and in some respects, the less tough of the two. Men have conceived all the harebrained schemes for human betterment, all the utopias; they are the cloud-treaders. Women cling more closely to the earth. They had to, both in self-protection, and because without their restraining influence, Homo sapiens would have joined the dinosaurs long before. He may still do so.

No human being, male or female, likes to admit he or she was wrong, but I truly believe the admission comes more readily from the derivatives of Adam's rib. Difficult to deal with as men have found them, they are, aside from propagation of the race, close to being indispensable, whatever bachelors may think to the contrary. A good case might be made for the war between the sexes as greater in its ultimate consequences than either World War I or World War II, and like no other war, it has never ceased. For untold centuries, man was the aggressor, although there are those who think he is now surrendering the initiative.

But I am letting an intriguing question tear me from my moorings; what I am really concerned about here is that flexibility of mind which women are more commonly permitted than men. The book that follows is largely made up of opinions I held during a period when everybody's mind, if it was functioning at all, was necessarily subjected to forces, new in the world, that demanded a reassessment of one's attitudes.

Certainly I have had to reconsider some of mine. More than

twenty years ago I wrote *The Shape of Books to Come;* the title was something of a cheat, because except for its concluding chapter, from which the book derived its title, it was a brief survey and assessment of American fiction and poetry from the closing years of the nineteenth century down to the year of its publication. Some of it was drawn from my "Speaking of Books" columns in the New York *Times Book Review,* and a few of the pieces so used are included in this book.

No man should be able to pass through almost a quarter century of his life without changing some of his opinions, and I am happy to confess that I have modified certain ones I held when that first book was written. I am equally glad that others have not altered. Wherever the changes of attitude were marked I have added postscripts in explanation of the change. These alterations in my point of view are not confined to the opinions expressed in *The Shape of Books to Come;* a few of them concern statements made in the column during recent years.

Between the summer of 1943, when "Speaking of Books" first appeared in the center of Page Two, flanked by the "Treasure Chest" and the "Poets' Column," and the fall of 1964, when I retired from the *Times,* more than 900 columns appeared under my signature; Of these 125 are included here. The selections are not chronologically arranged; they are segregated under various group titles, each group headed by a brief foreword. The bulk of them were written in the column's later years. A few were woven into earlier books, like those incorporated in *The Shape of Books to Come.* Such columns as were worked into *The Magic and Mystery of Words* (1963), are not included. For the most part, the selections appear in their original form. I have made some deletions and corrections.

I wish to take this opportunity to thank the readers of "Speaking of Books" for the interest, encouragement, and stimulation their letters gave me. I can truthfully say that this correspondence considerably widened my own horizons. The letters came from all fifty States, all the Provinces of Canada, and from nearly thirty countries abroad. Not only did they teach me much; they sometimes furnished me with that windfall prized by all columnists—a topic.

My special thanks are due to Mr. Samuel Stewart, managing editor of Holt, Rinehart and Winston, for his help in winnowing whatever wheat there may be in this collection, from the chaff that accumulates in any long-conducted column. In pleading guilty to having sometimes repeated myself, I recall with some comfort that Don Marquis, whose "Sun Dial" has unfortunately no counterpart today, used occasionally to reprint "by request," for the entire length of his column, those memorable verses entitled "Noah 'n Jonah 'n Cap'n John Smith."

I wish also to thank the New York *Times* for permission to reprint the copyright material herein contained.

New York City, March, 1965.

—J. D. A.

I

Truth Isn't Always Stranger . . .

FICTION, LIKE POETRY, in this century of ours, is perennially in a state of turbulence and siege. Biography, to be sure, passed through what might variously be described as its muckraking era, its Freudian phase, its emphasis on debunking. Beginning with Lytton Strachey, we were for a while intent on reducing famous figures to life-size or less. Like the revolution in poetry and in fiction, this was a normal reaction: in the case of biography, against the solemn obsequies over reputations that characterized the dutiful but dubious biographies of the Victorian period; in poetry, against the tired prettiness of post-Victorian echoes of Tennyson; in fiction, against the refusal to admit that the sexual drive is a prime determinant in human behavior, and that there are necessary interpolations between the meeting of boy and girl and the concluding words, "They lived happily ever after."

The novel, in our time, has surely lived up to the protean quality that has accompanied its history. In the Thirties, it nearly foundered by succumbing to propaganda; our so-called proletarian novels matched in their dismal dedication the state-directed literature that has brought Soviet fiction sharply down from the heights attained by the Russian novelists of the nineteenth century.

Today the novel flounders about in strange convulsions which some observers mistakenly regard as its death throes. For my part, I doubt the novel will ever die, sick as it may be. Recurrently despaired of, it displays remarkable powers of recovery. Just now, it resembles nothing so much as the hydra-headed monster. There is the grinning head of sex minus love, the stolid head of clinical observation, the swollen head of giant-sized novels with little or nothing to say, the self-pitying head of complete introversion, the hopped-up head of spot-news fiction, the faceless head of the non-novel.

In spite of the monster's menacing aspect, good and near-great novels occasionally appear, and there are times when I believe they will increase in number. One branch of contemporary fiction in which excellence is frequently achieved is the historical novel, and my former colleague, Orville Prescott of the New York *Times,* deserves credit for drawing repeated attention to its resurgence. This fiction is so superior to the cloak and sword romances which flourished around the turn of the century that I am surprised more notice has not been taken of it by reviewers and critics in general. The term "historical novel" had come to be accompanied by a smile of condescension or a sneer by those forgetting that it includes some of the greatest fiction yet written.

There has been a revival of the novel of manners, led by Louis Auchincloss. The novel of suspense has been carried to a high pitch of skill. There has been an awakening realization of man's duality, a recognition of his capacity, in a world torn by tensions greater than ever before, for aspiration as well as degradation. If the trend toward a better-balanced realism has not reached the full swing of the pendulum, I mistakenly predicted in *The Shape of Books to Come,* the movement upward is at least intermittently perceptible.

Thumbnail Survey

Today I am asking myself the question, What is the present state of American fiction? Our losses have been heavy in the last few years; since 1960 three major novelists have passed into literary history: Marquand, Hemingway, and Faulkner. We were well into the century when we lost Dreiser, Lewis, Ellen Glasgow, Willa Cather, Sherwood Anderson, Edith Wharton, Margaret Mitchell, Elizabeth Madox Roberts, Fitzgerald, and Wolfe. What names now are of comparable distinction? Are there any that give promise of achieving it?

Suppose we begin this brief survey by considering those living writers whose reputations—whatever their degree of merit—have for years been fully established. Such appraisals as I shall make are personal; some of the writers I shall name enjoy greater esteem than I can grant them, some not as much. One of the older group, Pearl Buck, was the second American novelist to be awarded the Nobel Prize. It came to her in consequence of her first book—the only instance of the kind, I believe, in the history of these awards. *The*

Good Earth was an excellent novel, but it seems likely to remain Mrs. Buck's best performance; certainly her excursions into American life have not matched in depth of understanding her sensitive approach to the Far Eastern world. She exemplifies perfectly the importance of early background in the novelist's equipment. So too does James T. Farrell, a heavy-handed truth teller whose debt to Dreiser was also his misfortune; his importance will be of a documentary kind.

Older still is Henry Miller, who, as I see it, is not a novelist at all, and unfortunately, outside his cult, known to the public only as the author of the cheaply meretricious Tropic books. The better Miller, the writer of *The Colossus of Maroussi,* is a passionately sensitive man, full of exaggerated attitudes, but with occasional deep perceptions, and at his fervent best, with a remarkable power of expression. Then Katharine Anne Porter, one of the best short-story writers we have produced, whose *Ship of Fools* has been the most extravagantly praised American novel of the century. I resent its pretension to be an allegory of human life; I see it as the product of accumulated venom, born out of disappointment in human relations.

The same age group includes Thornton Wilder and Dos Passos; also, approximately, Steinbeck, Cozzens, Glenway Wescott, Conrad Richter, Jesse Stuart, and Robert Penn Warren. Wilder, one of the most variously gifted writers we have, and Dos Passos, appear to have abandoned fiction as a prime interest—Wilder for the theater, Dos Passos for history—though both made solid contributions to the American novel.

Steinbeck, whose *Grapes of Wrath* was, with the possible exception of *Uncle Tom's Cabin,* the most eloquent novel of social protest written in this country, has not equaled it since. Cozzens, a writer of fine potentialities, seems caught in a web of too great detachment; he gives the impression of avoiding human involvement. Wescott, after a brilliant beginning, appears to have lost self-confidence. Richter's performance has been sustained; recently he accomplished the difficult feat of writing an interesting novel about a good man. Jesse Stuart, good as he can be, remains strictly a regionalist; so too, though not as markedly, does Warren.

I suppose John O'Hara belongs in this group. He is one of our most popular contemporary novelists. In the short story he continues to write with pungency; as a novelist he has become, to my taste, after a strong beginning, a bore; he never knows when to leave off his documentation, inside the bedroom or out of it. He and Mary McCarthy are obsessed by the smaller social distinctions and, in their overemphasized knowingness or exaggerated sophistication, appear to write out of an inner insecurity. Both are totally lacking in taste; why is it that second-rank writers of Irish extraction invariably vulgarize everything they touch? As one whose blood is half Irish, I feel privileged to ask.

Among the younger people, A. B. Guthrie and Wallace Stegner have done much to strengthen our novels about the West. Truman Capote, Eudora Welty, Carson McCullers, Flannery O'Connor, Shirley Ann Grau, and most recently, Harper Lee, have contributed substantially to the South's literary revival. Howard Fast has done brilliant work in the field of historical fiction. John Hersey, whose reportage was the best produced by World War II, has steadily given promise of further development as a novelist. On Michener and Wouk I reserve judgment; both have skill, but what will they do with it?

Next, a still younger group in whose future I have little confidence: it would include Norman Mailer, James Jones, Saul Bellow, Vance Bourjailly, William Styron, Paul Bowles, J. D. Salinger, John Updike, and James Baldwin. It is here that I am most out of step with current approval. These are writers, so it seems to me, without the seeds of growth in them. They are mostly the beneficiaries of overpraised first books. Some of them have power, but few of them have a sense of direction. In most cases their work has weakened as they go on. All have ability, but ability is not enough. Our literary history is strewn with casualties of this kind.

P.S. I am adding a few notes to this thumbnail survey. Certain of the novelists named are discussed at greater length elsewhere in these pages. I wish to say a little more about some of those who are not thus treated.

In retrospect, I think that Willa Cather's claim to the title of "best American woman novelist" cannot be challenged, although Edith Wharton and Ellen Glasgow are close competitors for that distinction. In any case, I believe that with them, she ranks among the few first-rate writers of American fiction, whether written by men or women. She had weaknesses, to be sure—but I can think of no novelist without them. She lacked humor and irony, those essential ingredients to any full representation of human life, but so did Tolstoy, a much greater novelist. She had, too, an aversion to the contemporary scene that proved crippling to her development. But what she did, she did supremely well, and I think *The Lost Lady* is the finest novella in American fiction, subtler even than Mrs.

Wharton's *Ethan Frome.* If there are any other comparable American achievements in that genre, I do not know them.

Such admiration as I have for Dreiser has always been grudging. His value, it seems to me, was that of a liberating force; unquestionably he widened the horizons of American fiction, but I have never been able to overlook his verbal clumsiness, his muddled thinking, his myopic naturalism. I regard *An American Tragedy* as based on false premises and as the most overpraised novel of its period. Sherwood Anderson, for all his gifts, could think no more clearly than Dreiser. The revival of Fitzgerald's reputation strikes me as one of the most overstated efforts of that kind in our literary history; his was a thin and febrile talent, and if it survives its current inflation, it will be by virtue of *The Great Gatsby* and a scant handful of short stories. Wolfe does not wear well; had he lived longer he might have achieved the transmutation of personal experience into universal terms, but to gauge the probability would be idle conjecture.

Of the writers named in the concluding paragraph, a few have published new books since my brief survey was published in 1963. None has altered my lack of confidence in the future of these novelists. I remain bored by what Salinger has written subsequent to *The Catcher in the Rye,* and I still find it difficult to interest myself in the work of Saul Bellow. That *Herzog* should have received a National Book Award in preference to *The Rector of Justin* seems to me a miscarriage of justice; I consider it a vogue book, but little more. Norman Mailer I can see only as a disintegrating writer. Updike's *Centaur* I thought a pretentious and befogging marriage of realism with myth. These are harsh opinions, but I stand by them.

Finally, I wish to add one name, unaccountably overlooked, to the list of older American novelists who have ably reflected man's dualism in their fiction. It is that of Paul Horgan, whose reputation as an historian of the Southwest, largely secured by *Great River,* now overshadows his distinction as a novelist.

Louis Auchincloss and the Novel of Manners

To me the most interesting distinction that can be made between the sciences and the arts is that although both achieve truth, only the sciences can prove that they do. You cannot demonstrate an artistic truth as you would a proposition in geometry. You cannot prove that one novelist offers psychological truth while another does not, although the critic may be wholly convinced that this is so, and may be able to convince others that he is right in his contention. Was Pilate jesting when he asked, What is truth, and did not wait for an answer?

When I say, for example, that no good novel can be written unless its author has the ability to tell a story and has also not only a consuming interest in human behavior, but the power to project reality in his description of it, I believe I am stating an obvious truth; yes I cannot, no matter how many supporting arguments I may include, append a Q.E.D. This is why there is no such thing as scientific criticism applied to the arts. A biologist may make objective criticism of another biologist's theories, but no writer can do the same about another writer's work. He must see it through the prism of his own personality.

I would like to prove that Louis Auchincloss is the best living American novelist, but of necessity I cannot even prove that he is a good one. The best I can possibly do is to persuade you that he is. Even the angle from which I approach the matter is necessarily subjective. I happen to share Mr. Auchincloss' belief that the most interesting form of fiction is to be found in what is called the novel of manners—the novel as written by Fielding, Jane Austen, Thackeray, Balzac, Turgenev, and Tolstoy, Galsworthy, Henry James, Proust, Edith Wharton, Ellen Glasgow, John Marquand, and today by John O'Hara and Mr. Auchincloss himself. That list is not comprehensive, nor are the writers it includes of equal merit. Neither is my appreciation of the novel limited to writers like them. I would not, for example, describe Willa Cather as a novelist of manners, although I consider her superior as an artist to Mrs. Wharton.

The novel of manners is to me a preferred form because in it our attention is most sharply focused on human beings in relation to one another, and to the form of society in which they move. It need not be a society of the most exalted level, as it is in Proust, and as it is not in Jane Austen, in Galsworthy, or in John O'Hara, to name three totally dissimilar writers. But man is primarily a social animal, and it is in the relationships with which the novel of manners is concerned that he is most fully revealed. When we are shown him at war, we see him in a very special situation, in which certain of his qualities are exaggerated, and some of them submerged. War may be a natural state into which he relapses, but he is a different creature when he is engaged in it. This is the handicap suffered by all "war fiction"—even so eminent an example as Hemingway's *Farewell to Arms.*

Although Mr. Auchincloss' novels and short stories have been well received by the critics and have won a good measure of popular approval, he has nevertheless been handicapped, so far as reputation goes, by current concern with the lives of the underprivileged. It has been fashionable to write about sharecroppers and bums, social outcasts of one kind or another with the tacit assumption that in such lives we find human nature more nakedly evident—the wrappings removed. I believe this to be a basically false assumption; it may take a little more probing to get at the truth about the people whose world Mr. Auchincloss inhabits, but at their core they suffer from fears and compulsions comparable to those of people not so fortunately placed, just as they savor comparable joys and rewards. The depiction of human nature has little to do with class.

One of Mr. Auchincloss' assets has been his career as a practicing lawyer. We platitudinously think of the lawyer as a rather desiccated man, forgetting that in certain areas, at least, of his profession, he has opportunities, matched only by those of the physician or the politician, to observe human motivations at their most exposed level. I find in Mr. Auchincloss' novels (and I recommend particularly *Sybil, Venus in Sparta, The Great World of Timothy Colt, The House of Five Talents,* and *Portrait in Brownstone*) a shrewd and yet compassionate understanding of why men and women behave as they do, that I do not find equaled in the work of any other contemporary American novelist.

He far outdistances any of his contemporaries in his understanding of women. Both in *Portrait in Brownstone* and *The House of Five Talents* he has accomplished the real feat for a man of writing convincingly in the feminine first person singular. Considering the importance of women in American society, his perceptions here are of the greatest value in describing the world of which he writes. He knows too—for his *Reflections of a Jacobite* is excellent literary criticism—that the novelist's first concern must be to entertain; if he also adds to our understanding of life, he becomes a great novelist. I think Mr. Auchincloss is on his way to achieving that stature. He may fall short of it, but I am convinced that he has the essential qualities.

P.S. With *The Rector of Justin* in 1964, I think that Louis Auchincloss further confirmed the expectations I expressed in the foregoing column. The book has, in its delineation of the central character, portraiture of a depth and width of perspective which this novelist has not attained before. I can think of only one other recent novel that approaches it in the probing of character, and that is Morris West's *The Ambassador*. Superficially, that book derives from the news of the day, but its true concern is with the psychology of guilt, as that of *The Rector* is with the psychology of domination.

Sex and the Novel

There are two major weaknesses in contemporary fiction, and they are closely allied. Both have their roots in an attitude toward life which is essentially sterile. It is a kind of inverted ethics, the nature of which I have seen best expressed by Robert Elliot Fitch, who in *The Decline and Fall of Sex* has written what I believe to be the most penetrating study of sex in our society that has yet appeared. That brief book is worth a carload of Kinsey reports; all that Kinsey did was to pile up a mass of questionable data regarding the sexual habits of American men and women. He never got to the root of the matter.

The inverted ethics which reveals itself both in the treatment accorded sex in current fiction and in the "new compassion" has produced a crop of writers who are, in the words of Mr. Fitch, moralists without being moral. Frequently the new compassion, which is not compassion at all, and its allied approach to sex are combined in the same writer. You will find them both, for example, in the work of James Jones and Norman Mailer.

The best spokesman for their point of view, observes Mr. Fitch, "is Schopenhauer—whose teachings are implicit in much of Herman Wouk, explicit in Norman Mailer. The pendulum of pain and ennui: desire unsatisfied yields pain, desire satisfied yields satiety and ennui: this is the meaning of life. The escape into a compassion that is defeatist, into an asceticism that is hopeless, into an aesthetic contemplation that is emasculated: these are the permitted modes of salvation. But an Aristotle, or a Christ, or a Shakespeare, can tell us of a better way. This is to live, not for desire, but for creation. Not to think, what pleasure can I find? What can I get for myself?—but to think, What can I make? What can I do? What can I give? Such creating is life, is love."

And this I might add, is what Tolstoy had learned when, at the age of thirty-four, he sat down to write *War and Peace*. It is also one of the reasons why that novel holds in its embrace a fuller content of life than any other. Not because of its length: we have had novels as long in recent years which contained nothing. Not because of its pictorial skill; we have writers who can convey things or persons seen as deftly as Tolstoy, but they cannot give them meaning. Tolstoy, no more than Shakespeare, excluded evil from his vision of life. Both saw it in its relation to the whole, but what we have to remember is that this perception of theirs is not the prerogative of genius. It is within the reach of every writer.

Mr. Fitch is getting a respectful hearing for his views on contemporary attitudes toward sex because his book makes it abundantly clear that he is not a prude, because he has wit and the willingness to call a spade a spade. He does not rant; he is master of a cool logic, and he has really studied the evidence. He sees that the root of the trouble is that too many writers, absorbing the attitudes about them, have separated sex from love, with unavoidable results. When that happens, the writer, in treating of sex, takes one of two courses. Either he achieves the unrelieved obscenity of a *Peyton Place* or the cold and clinical content of a Mary McCarthy. Even in as good a writer as John Cheever, the scenes devoted to sexual encounter are devoid of human feeling—almost as much as those in Edmund Wilson's *Memoirs of Hecate County*.

There are also the writers in whom the dehumanization of sex is carried so far that it reaches the inevitable end of absolute boredom. That is what happens in such a book as Norman Mailer's *The Deer Park*, in which the procurer remarks: "So he would separate the soul from the body by teaching the body that it may never attain the soul, and the greatest sin is to believe the two may live together." This is also where young Françoise Sagan arrives. As Paul Pickerel remarked of her second book, *A Certain Smile*, "here everything is soiled, everybody is bored, nothing happens for the first time."

Then, as Mr. Fitch points out, when sex is divorced from love, "and the tedium becomes unbearable, our next impulse is to spice it with cruelty. Sadism is the first sign of the frustration of the proper fulfillment of sex in love. It is part of the genius of Hemingway that, with all his pleasure in bloodletting and in bullfighting, he never really succumbs to sadism—which is a vice for humans rather than animals—and so remains faithful to his portrait of man on the level of the strictly biologic."

Sex can, and should be, in its proper human conjunction, one of the greatest, if not the greatest, energizing forces to which the writer, like everybody else, is susceptible. But too many novelists are, in Mr. Fitch's phrase, putting it in the deep freeze.

Social Purpose in Fiction

That was a wise and suggestive observation of Somerset Maugham when he remarked that "Much pessimism is caused by ascribing to others the feelings you would have if you were in their place." There, it seems to me, he put his finger on much that has been false to life in the sociological novel, from the day of Dickens down to Steinbeck and our own. As Mr. Maugham so pointedly observed, the novelist who is betrayed by his own sensitiveness, by the very quality which makes him an artist, falls into the error of constructing a public world out of his private one.

The irony of his situation is obvious, for no writer, however skilled, can hope to escape entirely from the bounds of his own sensibility. Zola and the naturalists whom he sired have made a conscious attempt, and it may be argued that they have succeeded, but if they have, it is the success of the man who cuts off his nose to spite his own face. For what they have produced is not art, but a literal transcription of life; and even so, it is life seen from a restricted and fixed angle of vision. Thus, when Mr. Farrell, let us say, writes his *Studs Lonigan* trilogy, it becomes necessary for him to write a tetralogy—the story of Danny O'Neill—in order that the balance may, in a measure, be restored.

Naturalism is no solution of the novelist's problem, when he is trying to present a deeply veracious picture of human society which illuminates as much as it reflects. To continue with Mr. Farrell as an illustration: His own naturalism is diluted by reason of his sensibility, by the tenderness and compassion which he is unable to exclude from his contemplation of his characters. A writer must be devoid of feeling, as detached as a laboratory worker watching his test tubes, if he is to achieve the logical consummation of the naturalist's objective.

Heaven help us if it were ever possible to hold literature to such a level. Then indeed it would be time to burn the books, and to quote with approval the bitter words of Disraeli, "Books are fatal: they are the curse of the human race. Nine-tenths of existing books are nonsense, and the clever books are the refutation of that nonsense. The greatest misfortune that ever befell man was the invention of printing."

In Mr. Maugham's reflections you will find the key to that solemn and dispiriting procession of autobiographical novels that streamed across the country during the Twenties and after, in which a host of young American writers of both sexes bewailed the hardness of the fate which caused them to be born in the little prairie towns or on the farms of the Middle West. Because they were endowed with a degree of sensitiveness greater than that of the sons and daughters of their neighbors or, it might be, of their parents and brothers and sisters, they saw their surroundings in deeper shadow, and with less of the contrast and beckoning horizons which their more imaginative natures craved. They fled to Greenwich Village and to Paris, for they could not bear the prospect of living out their days in the environment which the others accepted, but which they could not.

Of course there were other reasons as well. They were influenced by their reading too; by the irritations and yearnings which had crystallized in Sinclair Lewis's *Main Street* and in the tales of Sherwood Anderson; but their response to these was also the measure of that same sensibility which provoked them to lamentations over the places of their birth, and to invest them with tediums and terrors which did not exist, or at least, were nothing like so pressing, in the minds of those who were less sensitively composed. In one way or another, they played the variations on Mr. Maugham's theme when he points out that because we prize privacy ourselves, we pity the very poor for lacking it, when, as a matter of fact, it is one of the last things they desire.

The existence of such inescapable limitations as these does not, of course, invalidate the novel of conscious social purpose. It can be made, and frequently has been made, an extraordinarily effective instrument of humanitarian propaganda. Dickens made it precisely that, and the indignation which he poured into his work bore tangible fruit in betterment. The most obvious example in our own literary history is Harriet Beecher Stowe's *Uncle Tom's Cabin;* its most recent counterparts have been such books as Steinbeck's *The Grapes of Wrath* and Lillian Smith's *Strange Fruit.* The "proletarian" novels of a few years back defeated their purpose because they were nine-tenths propaganda and one-tenth art, whereas in the effective books which belong in this category, the proportions have been more evenly mixed. This was true to a very considerable extent of *The Grapes of Wrath,* some of its pages are among the best Steinbeck has written, and the poorest are those in which either his anger runs away with him or in which his sensibility slops over into sentimentality.

What we have to remember, of course, is that just as soon as a novel undertakes to prove something, to right a wrong or to plead a cause of any kind, it necessarily surrenders something of its value as a work of art.

Jesse Stuart, Regionalist

Four weeks ago this column made a thumbnail survey of contemporary American fiction. In the course of it I remarked of Jesse Stuart that "good as he can be, he remains strictly a regionalist." Since then I have been thinking a lot about regionalism and about Jesse Stuart, and there is more I would like to say about both.

Let me say first that I think "regionalism," in its literary sense, is a tricky and unfortunate word. Mostly it is applied to writers in rather a derogatory way; it implies the absence of universal values, or, you might say, of universal truths. Actually, the majority of novelists and short-story writers, including most of the greatest, can be called regionalists because, more often than not, their work is rooted in and reflects the environment which nurtured them, or that to which they became adapted. I think it fair to say that the eighteenth-century fathers of the English novel were all regionalists; so, certainly, were Jane Austen and Dickens; so were Balzac, Tolstoy and Dostoevski, Proust, Hawthorne, and Henry James. So was Joyce.

Recently I expressed the opinion that Louis Auchincloss is the best living American novelist—a regionalist if ever there was one, so too, before him, were Ellen Glasgow, Elizabeth Roberts, Sinclair Lewis, Marquand, and Faulkner. Much as Hemingway ranged the world, however often he used settings foreign to his birth, his attitudes were fixed by the experiences of his Midwestern boyhood. They controlled and determined his whole course as a writer, as much as Faulkner's Southern inheritance controlled and determined his.

No, something needs clarification here. There is a term, once frequently used, which has almost disappeared from literary criticism—"local color." To write regionally is not necessarily to be a local colorist, who relies chiefly for his effects not only on the manner of speech peculiar to his region, but on local idiosyncrasies of behavior. He does not use big themes; he relies on the little things that separate the people of his region from those of another, although he makes them share the basic human aspirations and frustrations. When I say "big themes," I mean those that rest on tragic conflict of one kind or another. There are no others.

To clarify my position: I think Jesse Stuart is a local colorist of the first rank—probably the best we have produced in the United States. I have known him and his work for nearly thirty years, and I respect him highly both as a writer and as a man, which is more than I can say of some writers whose work I respect. He has made the people of his region—the hill country of eastern Kentucky—live for us, in the novels and short stories he has written about them. They owe him an inestimable debt for his books and for what he has done for them as an educator. Small wonder that October 15, 1955 was proclaimed as Jesse Stuart Day by the Governor of Kentucky, and that a stone marker bearing his name was unveiled on the courthouse lawn in his native town of Greenup.

Jesse Stuart's work, both poetry and prose, derives from the most intense love of place of which I am aware in any American writer. It is so genuine, so deeply felt, that one overlooks the lack of those subtleties and symbolical suggestions that an oversophisticated period seems to demand. Jesse Stuart has attempted no great themes, in the sense in which I have defined them, but he has made real for us the people and the land he loves. The acres on which he was born and grew up are still his home, though he has probably traveled farther afield than any man in his native county.

It was his good fortune to have had a father and mother whom he honored and loved. I met them both in 1939, in the house in W-Hollow that Jesse helped to build when he was a boy of sixteen and they first acquired land of their own; before that they had been tenant farmers. Jesse's mother might have sat for a statue of the pioneer woman, and she had an unforgettable dignity. His father could not read and could write only his own name. Perhaps the most moving book his son has written is the portrait of his father called *God's Oddling*, the story of an unlettered poet who lived a life of physical toil; he passed on to his son a deep sensitivity to the natural world about him, and an indomitable courage.

Jesse Stuart was handed a hoe at the age of six, put behind the plow at eleven. For a year he worked in a steel mill. He went to college with $29.30, and during his years there all his family could send him were two crumpled dollar bills. He began writing in college and kept on writing as he farmed and taught. As a schoolteacher he walked miles with a suitcase full of books so that his pupils might come to care for them. As a high-school principal and county superintendent he fought for and won reforms in the local school system. *Man With a Bull-Tongue Plow*, a book of poems, introduced him to the American public in 1934. Since then there have been more than twenty others.

If you do not know his work. *A Jesse Stuart Reader* provides an excellent introduction. He has written autobiographical notes for each of the selections.

Plea for a Balanced Realism

No word in the reviewer's lexicon is more commonly abused than "realism." Constantly it is applied to work which is factually accurate only for that restricted aspect of life which the novelist would have you see; if he admits to your view only the debit side of human nature, he is no more a realist than the sentimentalist who prettifies life. For surely there can be no realism which does not accept and reflect life in its entirety. I do not mean, of course, that each novelist must present us with that total picture of the human comedy at which Balzac aimed; that would be asking more than we can reasonably expect.

What we may reasonably ask, however, is this: that in the particular segment of experience which any novelist takes for his province, no matter how small, no matter how rigidly confined its boundaries may be, he will take into account the full complexity of human nature, whether he deals with its manifestations on a high or a low level of human intelligence and character.

He will take into account the inner life of his people, however dimly lived, as well as their outward acts. He will recognize that man is essentially a creature torn between satisfaction and aspiration, for these are the basic and controlling urges of human nature. It is seldom indeed that both are not to some extent present in every man or woman. The proportions of their mixture are, as we all become aware as life goes on, of an infinite variety. The saint becomes as free from the urge of satisfaction as any animate bundle of appetites, Homo sapiens included, can ever be, though his freedom can never be absolute, so long as he draws breath; and all but the most brutish or moronic of men contain within them impulses which rise above the satisfaction of physical and material needs.

Yet you would never guess the existence of this unalterable condition of life from the writings of too many novelists who have in our time been hailed as realists, as honest and objective commentators on human life. They have chosen to ignore the reality of that inner world of which I have spoken; they have denied the existence of man's aspiration, however blunted and aborted in its form. And so, whatever the vividness and the reportorial exactness of their documentation, the truth is not in them.

Nothing in the failure of recent American novelists to achieve a true realism is more obvious than their prevailing inability to treat with truth and insight the relations between men and women. From the time of Howells, in whose novels the deeper emotional currents between the sexes found no easy passage, there has been up to now almost no creative writing about the central relationship in men's and women's lives that can be compared with the best in British and Continental fiction. And what little there is, is chiefly the work of women.

Think back for a moment. In the novels of Dreiser, women seldom have any entity other than as objects of a man's desire; in Sherwood Anderson's, they are confused symbols in the minds of baffled and thwarted men; in those of Sinclair Lewis, they are projected dream girls; in all of Faulkner, there is not a normal relationship between a man and a woman; in Steinbeck, with the exception of Ma Joad, they must be prostitutes to be respectable.

Scott Fitzgerald, until he came to write his unfinished *The Last Tycoon*, saw them still in the terms of the flapper who was to become the glamour girl; in the novels of John Dos Passos they assume reality only, as John Chamberlain recently pointed out, when they are bewildered young women dedicating themselves to social service; in those of Thomas Wolfe they are merely disturbing factors in the life of a young man who is trying to discover himself. In Hemingway, they are, for the most part, interchangeable girls with whom the young man goes to bed.

Even in the work of John Marquand, who is writing with a greater maturity than most American novelists of his generation, women, unless they are museum pieces like Miss Sarah in *Point of No Return*, have little independent life, with one notable exception; for Cousin Bella of *Wickford Point* is the most engaging and veritable hussy in fiction since Becky Sharp, even though she must reckon with a young woman named Scarlett O'Hara as a possible contender for that dubious honor. And then, of course, there was also Lady Ashley of *The Sun Also Rises*.

So there you are: you have your choice between these and the heroines of what has been the prevailing mode in recent historical fiction: those full-bosomed lasses who are about as credible as the average heroine of Hollywood's picture of the month. In the names of Flaubert and Maupassant, of Turgenev, Balzac, and Tolstoy, in the names of half a dozen more recent French and British novelists, why cannot the American novelist write of women and the relationship between men and women in such a manner that the adult reader can say, This is true, this is the common experience that we all share, and that we all know?

From Here to Eternity

The literary year, like that of the theater, customarily begins with the end of summer. *Gone With the Wind*, to be sure, was published in August, but that was an exception. So far the current literary year has, for the most part, revolved about two topics; the first was Hemingway and his *Across the River and Into the Trees* or in E. B. White's version (a shining example of the almost defunct art of parody), "Across the Street and Into the Grill." The second was Scott Fitzgerald, providing the most remarkable revival of a literary reputation in recent years. Like most reactions, it has swung to the extreme; Fitzgerald, it is true, for a time suffered unmerited neglect, but the revival has magnified him beyond his actual dimensions.

Now a third topic seems likely to take over: a new author, James Jones, and his novel, *From Here to Eternity*. Not for a long time has a publishing house introduced a new writer with such extravagant claims for attention. The impulsion to do so is quite understandable. Our fiction has been marking time; publishers and at least a part of the reading public have been waiting for the emergence of an exciting new talent. The house of Scribner is convinced that it has found one in the person of Mr. Jones. The blurb for *From Here to Eternity* confidently introduces a writer who "will take a commanding place in American literature."

The reviews so far—I have seen about ten—support the publishers' contention. All the same, let's hold on to our hats. I would say that within certain limits Mr. Jones's novel is the most impressive performance in fiction that we have had for several years. It has vividness in a superlative degree. It has an ear, so far unmatched, for army talk. That will be apparent at once to anyone who has ever served however short a hitch as an enlisted man. The language may offend you, but it is army language, and no other. The story is full of gripe, and so is the army, particularly the Regular Army; most of the action in Mr. Jones's story takes place in Hawaii before the attack on Pearl Harbor, and his chief characters think of themselves as "thirty-year men." All the same, let's hold on to our hats.

Most of the reviews seem to me punch-drunk, bowled over by the undebatable vitality of Mr. Jones's novel. It is, in the first place, 860 pages long, and the vitality is maintained throughout. It is the longest sustained gripe in print; the consistency of that attitude is astounding, and it is best illustrated, perhaps, by a small thing. Rarely do Mr. Jones's characters smile or laugh, but they grin interminably; they grin "wolfishly" and "savagely" and otherwise, but almost always, they grin; they bare their lips. Though this it not actually a war novel, the gripe of enlisted man against officer has never been so fiercely emphasized.

This, I think, is one of the minor weaknesses of Mr. Jones's book—the lengths to which that particular gripe is carried. It is one thing to give expression to a prevalent feeling; it is another to load the dice. For one reason or another, all of Mr. Jones's officers are contemptible, not only as they appear in the eyes of the men who serve under them, but as they appear in the book. Incidentally, perhaps the only writer about the last war who gave the officer a fair break was Ernie Pyle, in spite of the fact that his interest and sympathy were centered upon the enlisted man. But he wasn't writing fiction.

Let us turn to something more important, so far as the craft of fiction is concerned. Mr. Jones's book is weakest where the American novel in general is weakest: in its handling of the relations between men and women. I am amazed that this aspect of *From Here to Eternity* has not received more attention in the reviews. There are two such relationships which are given extended treatment in the novel—the loves of the two principal characters, Prewitt and Warden—one a prostitute, the other a captain's wife. I have seldom read anything quite so preposterous or incredible as either of these two affairs. They simply won't wash. So long as Mr. Jones is writing about men among men his work rings true, granted its attitude; when he writes about men emotionally involved with women his realism turns to fantasy so inept that the effect is painful.

That is not strange, because he is definitely a masculine writer, and the markedly masculine writer, from Fielding and Scott down to Lewis and Hemingway, has been notably inept in his handling of the relations between men and women. I don't mean that credible work of this kind is done only by members of a third sex or by women. Tolstoy, who wrote of women as credibly as he did of men, and was always convincing in his handling of the relations between them, was far from belonging to a third sex, but he had that tincture of the feminine mind which the completely masculine writer lacks. I don't think I need press the point that the possession of this capacity is essential to a rounded representation of life. You will find it in all novelists of the first rank; one might say, in all artists of the first rank.

First and Last Pages

There were several aspects of the art of fiction touched on by Elizabeth Bowen in a recent British broadcast, for which I had no space last Sunday. I was particularly interested and pleased by her emphasis on the manner of a novel's opening. She confessed herself "tremendously influenced for or against a book" by the character of its beginning. She believes it essential that a good story should take off well, either actually, from a promising situation, or at least with the suggestion that such a situation is in the making. She admitted it would be unfair to judge all novels, even the best, by their opening pages, yet we are all prone to do so, and for good reasons.

Their nature is, I think, obvious, and I shall do no more than mention them. As a work of art, the novel gains when a keynote is immediately struck; afterward, our sense of form is pleased, and the illusion of truth is strengthened. We have not been tricked. Also, we have been brought at once, without meaningless meandering, into the world which we are temporarily to inhabit.

Miss Bowen chose three examples of eminently successful openings, each of which in a different way sets the tone of the book from which it is taken, and even foreshadows the novel's theme. First, the opening paragraphs of Thackeray's *Vanity Fair,* in which the satirical tone at once emerges, the theme, worldliness, is indicated, and the stage is quickly set for the entrance of the book's chief character, Becky Sharp. Next, on the first page of Graham Greene's *Brighton Rock,* the atmosphere of danger in which the tale is to be enveloped is created at once. The first sentence alone does it: "Hale knew, before he had been in Brighton three hours, that they meant to murder him." And then, in the remainder of the first paragraph, powerfully etched, and preparing us for the tenseness that follows, the dramatic contrast between the man and the carefree scene upon which he is looking.

For her third choice Miss Bowen selected Charlotte Brontë's *Jane Eyre*. On that first page, she observes, "We see the child Jane as life had already made her—solitary, somber, isolated, unyielding. Charlotte Brontë, like Graham Greene, has used contrast to build up immediate drama. The exiled child on a bitterly cold day against the cozy, glowing family group in the firelight. This exile from happiness is to repeat and repeat itself throughout the novel."

It is easy to multiply such examples: Not only the first page of *Moby Dick,* but those first three words, "Call me Ishmael," with their immediate Biblical connotation; the drawing room conversation which opens *War and Peace;* the first page of Maugham's *Of Human Bondage,* with its foreshadowing of pain to be endured; the opening of Dostoevski's *Crime and Punishment,* with the book's psychological theme suggested before we have read more than half a page. Or think of that marvelous opening paragraph of *A Farewell to Arms,* or that almost equally fine one in *For Whom the Bell Tolls.* Such keynotes may not be struck in all great or good novels, but I would venture the guess that they occur more often than not.

The pleasure we derive from craft of this kind is heightened further for me, at least, when such a novel makes a full circle, and we come at the end to a passage which repeats or suggests the opening chord. Among the books I have mentioned, this is true, you will note, of *For Whom the Bell Tolls,* in which, at the close, we leave Robert Jordan, stretched out once more on the pine needle floor of the forest, but waiting, this time, for death. I don't mean to insist upon this closing of the circle as a requisite of the well-made novel; I say only that for me it adds to the pleasure I take in the sense of form, possibly because I dislike loose ends of any kind.

I have left little space for other matters discussed by Miss Bowen, and I shall only briefly refer to them. Having mentioned several character novels, she observed that there seemed to be fewer of these today, and wondered whether that was because we are today less concerned with the individual's destiny, or because the social novel, raising certain questions, or the action novel, concerned with clear-cut issues, "appeal more to our kind of imagination?" That is not a question one attempts to answer in a sentence. I would suggest only that one answer may lie in Van Wyck Brooks's contention that the Victorians were more interested than we in character as such; ours is an interest in psychology.

I like, too, her emphasis on the importance of theme in a novel, and her insistence that the theme must have a moral element, "because it's through the theme that the novelist makes his evaluations or shows some new aspect of truth," and that this theme must be submerged in the story, because "If a theme or idea is too near the surface, the novel becomes simply a tract illustrating an idea."

The Continent of Islandia

Years ago, in Richmond, James Branch Cabell showed me a map he had made in his boyhood of that imaginary land of Poictesme with which he peopled his medieval romances. My interest that day was no greater than what any guest who, like myself, was not enchanted by Cabell's fictional world, might show. For the past few days I have been living in an imaginary land created by another writer, far less known, but whose fabricated country and its people have held me enthralled.

It is my belief that Austin Tappan Wright's *Islandia* is a book unparalleled not only in American literature, but in that of any other with which I am acquainted. I speak of its uniqueness; but I think also that it is a masterpiece of imaginative conception and execution. Those are tall words, and I must do my best to substantiate them.

Islandia is not a new book. It was first published in 1942. The time of its original appearance was unfortunate; we had plunged into a great war and the last thing we could feel at liberty to do was to immerse ourselves for more than a thousand pages in a world so far removed from the demanding realities we were facing. Nevertheless, such was the book's obvious power, that it received for the most part a glowing press; its sales mounted to 30,000, and then misfortune descended: the wartime paper shortage, and worse still, a misinterpreted order resulting in destruction of the original plates. "Islandia" should have been revived before this, but the hesitation is understandable, in view of the cost of a new investment.

We have grown used, in recent years, to seeing novels of comparable length, though I could count on a hand from which some fingers were missing, the number I could read without prodigious skipping. I have been finding it impossible to skip a page of *Islandia*. It is a book that casts a spell from which I, at least, could not escape, because the land it describes and the people who live there have become as real to me as one of the several regions of my own country which I know and love.

Let me first fill in my statement that *Islandia* is unique. Many other writers, from Plato and Sir Thomas More down, have given us their visions of Utopia, but Islandia is not precisely a Utopia in the sense that these others were. It is part of a continent in the Southern Hemisphere whose society and way of life differ greatly from any in the modern world, into which Austin Wright projected his imaginary land. Its values are contrasted with ours and you, the reader, are invited to make your choice, just as the Islandians themselves, faced with the decision whether or not to open their country to foreigners, had to make theirs.

Islandia is unique because no writer has ever lived so completely in the land of his imagining as Wright did in his. This book and his still unpublished manuscripts dealing with Islandia stemmed from a private life he lived outside his family and his successful career as a lawyer and teacher of law. Before writing the novel he wrote a several hundred-page history of Islandia; he mapped the country; he devised a language for it and a detailed peerage; he wrote a bibliography of the literature dealing with it; he wrote specimens of its own literature; he even compiled statistical tables for it, province by province. No one ever conceived an imaginary land in such meticulous detail.

If this were all his achievement, Austin Wright would be merely a literary curiosity. But he did far more. In the novel (published eleven years after his death by an automobile accident in 1931), he made all these things a credible part of the story. We are introduced to Islandia through the eyes of a young American who goes there as the first consul admitted to Islandia from the United States. Through his friendship at Harvard with the son of one of Islandia's leading families, John Lang comes into much closer contact with Islandian life than his mere official position would have made possible.

He comes to love the country, to understand it as no foreigner has ever done; he plays a part in the struggle between opposing factions over the question whether or not to end the country's isolation; he finds himself faced with a choice between a life there or at home. He falls in love with an Islandian woman, complicating his difficulties further: to realize how much, one must learn, as one does, reading the novel, how deeply separate are Western and Islandian attitudes toward life and what we call love—a word which for them has several meanings, inadequately or not at all expressed in our own tongue.

All this is told in a prose that rises frequently to distinction, in a narrative sparked by the conflict of opposing ideas. I am still in Islandia, and I think I shall be for some time to come.

P.S. Since the foregoing column was written, I have reread *Islandia* at least once in its entirety. It stands the test.

Imperial Russia and the Old South

Back in 1934, when budding novelists were carefully tending their social consciences, and that bastard creation, the proletarian novel, was enjoying its brief, inglorious heyday, Stark Young published a nostalgic, autobiographical tale of the deep South. *So Red the Rose* was a well-written novel, deft in its characterization, but unashamedly scented with magnolia. Strangely enough, at a moment when it was literary high treason to dwell with affection upon the habits and customs of the upper classes, the book had a large sale, but, naturally, a mixed press. Your correspondent, who reviewed it on the front page of this section, gave it high praise—but no higher than he would give it now.

In the course of the review, I remarked on the close parallel between the life of the ante-bellum Southern planter and that of the landed proprietor in pre-revolutionary Russia. The similarities were many and marked. Both economies and cultures rested on a slave base, strikingly alike in character. (In Russia, emancipation anticipated Lincoln's proclamation by nearly two years.) In both, among humane masters, a similar affectionate relationship developed between master and slave. In both, hospitality was lavish; kindred came for a month's visit and stayed a year, or until death overtook them.

A few days after the review appeared, I received a letter from a bookseller in the Middle West, who wrote me that he was a Russian who had fled the Bolshevik regime, and that my recognition of the parallel had greatly interested him. That was the beginning of my friendship with Nicholas Wreden, who died the other day at fifty-three; naval cadet, bookseller, publisher, translator, editor, and writer: a man of such enormous zest, energy, gaiety and vitality that it is difficult to believe him dead. Read, if you have not, his unusual autobiography, *The Unmaking of a Russian*.

Thinking of Nick Wreden, I suddenly realized that the parallel I have mentioned was not confined to the social structures of Czarist Russia and the ante-bellum South; it may be traced also in the literatures of the two peoples; more particularly, where the South is concerned, in the writing of recent years which is commonly, but somewhat loosely described as the "Southern literary renascence."

The Russian literature is, of course, incomparably the greater, and by no means all of it had the deep tinge of morbidity with which it is so often associated; writers like Pushkin, Gogol, and Lermontov were free from any such taint; they did not dwell in the melancholy recesses of the mind. Neither, for the most part, did those later giants, Turgenev and Tolstoy. The kinship between Russia and the latter-day writers of the South is most patent in the work of Chekhov and Dostoevski. They are the literary blood-brothers of Faulkner and company; and Chekhov, at least, is close kin to such a comparatively cheerful writer as Eudora Welty.

Over some of this Russian literature hangs the identical miasma and the same preoccupation with guilt that we find in Faulkner, Capote, and others. Dostoevski's man-God, man-beast, walks again through the pages of the somber Mississippi moralist. You can search other literatures in vain, save in some of Hawthorne, for an obsession with sin as intense, for as deep a brooding over guilt, as haunts the work of these literary kinsmen. And you could take Chekhov's *Three Sisters* or *The Cherry Orchard*, or many of the short stories, change the settings to Georgia, Alabama, or Mississippi, and leave the mood and temper of the work identical and unchanged.

As for humor and a lightsome heart, they are as infrequent in the writers of the "Southern renascence" as they are in the powerful fictions of nineteenth-century Russia or in the deadly earnest wastes of the State-dominated fictional tracts of the U.S.S.R. Along with romance and nostalgia, they were sometimes present in the earlier writers of the South; of late, for anything heartier than a tremulous, wistful smile you can turn only to the earthiness of Erskine Caldwell, or to the healthy, hill-country robustness of Jesse Stuart.

Ellen Glasgow, to be sure, was richly endowed both with wit and humor, but she was a Ruth walking amid the alien corn. There is a glint now and then in young Mr. Capote when he is up a tree and not down in the swamp, but my lips never twitch and my abdominal muscles are quiescent when I read (which is not too often) Mr. Faulkner. No one, I imagine, has ever been left breathless with merriment by Tennessee Williams.

I suppose it is my duty to mention Thomas Wolfe, though a North Carolinian can scarcely be accredited to the deep South. Be that as it may, though gargantuan laughter echoes down his endless corridors, we do not laugh ourselves. Even Caldwell's humor is sometimes hamstrung; that of *Tobacco Road* issues from human relations too pitiful for whole-hearted laughter, while they are at the same time so innately ludicrous as to preclude a true emotion of pity. The quest for a healthy, balanced view of life in the literary precincts of the deep South makes me think of the man who was asked why he was poring over the map of the U.S.A. Turned out he was looking for Dixie.

P.S. As if to confound me, several years after this column was written, Faulkner published *The Reitors,* a book so much more humorous than anything he had written before, that most critics found it hilarious. I was amused, but not enough to finish it. Faulkner's reputation will not rest on his sense of life's comicality.

The Conrad Richter Trilogy

This year's [1951] Pulitzer award in fiction is particularly welcome because it calls attention to a truly major achievement in the American novel. I refer not merely to Conrad Richter's *The Town,* for which the prize was given, but to the trilogy of which it forms the concluding part. These three novels, *The Trees, The Fields,* and *The Town,* taken together, form, in my opinion, the finest creative achievement we have had on the theme of the westward movement in American life. It would be a pity if those readers unfamiliar with Mr. Richter's work turn only to the book named in the award; for while it is true that each volume of the trilogy can be read for itself, much is lost if *The Town* is not approached as a part of the whole.

Some time ago, in this column, I expressed the opinion that the West had only recently been receiving the kind of treatment it deserves from our novelists, and that Mr. Richter, in company with A. B. Guthrie and Walter Van Tilburg Clark, had been pointing the way. But Mr. Clark, though he has written of the West from a fresh approach, has not concerned himself with the westward movement, and Mr. Guthrie has not dealt with the complete cycle of the pioneer experience.

That cycle in its entirety, from wilderness life to town life, forms the framework for Mr. Richter's trilogy. Through each of its phases —the nomadic life of the hunter, the turning to the soil, the building of a settled community, we follow the fortunes of a family up to the coming of the fourth generation. Wisely, I think Mr. Richter chose as the central figure of his story, not a man but a woman, because it is the woman who stands, so to speak, at the center of life, and when you are dealing with successive generations, what happens is most fully observed through her eyes. The world that Mr. Richter re-creates for us is viewed chiefly as it was looked upon by Sayward

Luckett, a child in the opening chapters of *The Trees,* an old woman on her deathbed at the end of *The Town.*

Sayward is, to my mind, the fullest and most living portrait of the pioneer woman that has ever been drawn. The picture is not in the slightest degree sentimentalized. At its core is the quality of enduring strength, and if that quality had not been multiplied thousands of times over in women like Sayward Luckett, the history of this country would have run a different course. Their story is one of the greatest in the world's history, and it is one that has never been told in the factual detail that it merits. No women ever lived a harder life; none ever met it more bravely. And it has never been imaginatively projected as convincingly as in Mr. Richter's trilogy.

These books are an extraordinary achievement in bringing the past close. One hesitates to call them historical novels. They have nothing of the synthetic quality that ordinarily is found in that form. From the time you enter the forest with the Luckett family you live in the world they knew. You see it with their eyes. Why do these books achieve such complete reality? The answer does not lie entirely in Mr. Richter's craftsmanship, skilled as it is. It lies also in the intensity of his identification with his material, about which he is explicit in the "Acknowledgments" which preface *The Town.*

"Finally," he writes, "the author wants again to set down his obligation to those men and women of pioneer stock among whom he lived both in the East and West, whose lives and whose tales of older days gave him a passionate love for the early American way of thought and speech, and a great respect for many whose names never figured in the history books but whose influence on their own times and country was incalculable."

And what was the meaning of the pioneer experience? Sayward's youngest son sits by her bedside as she dies, and reflects: "Hardship and work, that's what his mother always harped on. Once when at home he had refused to work on the lot, she had said, 'You're going to live longer than I do, Chancey. Watch for all kinds of new-fangled notions to take away folks' troubles without their having to work. That's what folks today want and that's what will ruin them more than anything else.' Could there be something after all in this hardship-and-work business, he pondered. He had thought hardship and work the symptoms of a pioneer era, things of the past. He believed that his generation had outlived and outlawed them, was creating a new life of comfort, ease, and peace. And yet war, the cruelest hardship of all, war between brothers, was on them today like a madness. Did it mean that the need for strength and toughness was to be always with them, that the farther they advanced, the more brilliant and intelligent they became, the more terrible would be the hardship that descended upon them, and the more crying the need of hardihood to be saved?"

That was a century ago. And now?

P.S. I do not wish to leave the impression that Mr. Richter's worth as a novelist is to be measured solely by his trilogy on the westward movement. He is a writer of greater range than such an assumption would indicate. His *The Sea of Grass*, which may owe something to Miss Cather, is a superior novella, and his more recent books attest the width of his range.

Women as Novelists

Of all the arts, the one in which women have achieved the greatest distinction is the art of fiction. In poetry, although their record is impressive, it is less so than in the novel; in painting and sculpture, they have consistently fallen short of greatness; in music, there is no woman composer of the first rank. There have been numerous good plays by women, but no great woman dramatist. There has been no great architect among women.

We observe today the steadily widening occupation by women of the field of fiction. There is no branch of the art which they have not entered with success. Even in such specialties as the mystery and the Western story in which men might be expected to preempt the field, women have been among the most able practitioners. They are numbered among the most accomplished writers of the short story. They have excelled in the field of historical fiction. They have done some of the best regional writing in the American novel, some of the best social commentary in our fiction. We have reached the point where the author of the season's most promising first novel is as likely to be a woman as a man.

Yet the capacity of women to excel in the art of fiction is by no means new; it is, indeed, almost as old as the history of the novel. Women were among the founders of one of the earliest forms of fiction, the historical romance, and the most celebrated, in its time, of seventeenth-century French romances, was Madeleine de Scudéri's *Grand Cyrus*. What might be called the first psychological novel was Madame de la Fayette's *La Princesse de Clèves*, published in 1678.

During the same period Mrs. Aphra Behn, in *Oroonoko,* wrote what literary historians have described as the first humanitarian novel in English. And in the next century, when the novel was taking shape in England, Fanny Burney followed hard on the heels of Richardson and Fielding. And after Miss Burney, who, for the first time, really, depicted in fiction the world as it appears to a woman, came the deluge! Steadily, since then, women have played a larger and increasingly important part in the writing of fiction.

It is, after all, very natural that this should be so. Why, nobody has stated more clearly and succinctly than G. K. Chesterton, in that keenly perceptive little book, *The Victorian Age in Literature,* which in the space of 250 small pages has more illuminating things to say about the writers of that period than any other book with which I am acquainted. Chesterton touches on the subject of women in fiction in his excellent chapter on the great Victorian novelists.

The modern novel, he remarks, "is a hearty and exhaustive overhauling of that part of human existence which has always been the woman's province, or rather kingdom; the play of personalities in private, the real difference between Tommy and Joe. . . . People put the matter wrong when they say that the novel is a study of human nature. Human nature is a thing that even men can understand. Human nature is born of the pain of a woman; human nature plays at peep-bo when it is two and at cricket when it is twelve; human nature earns its living and desires the other sex and dies. What the novel deals with is what women have to deal with; the differentiations, the twists and turns of this eternal river. The key of this new form of art, which we call fiction, is sympathy."

Certainly the contribution of women to fiction has not been merely in the direction of introducing a woman's point of view. Was it not Jane Austen who, more than any other single writer, rescued the English novel from the maudlin romanticism into which it had sunk during the closing years of the eighteenth century? And was it not, in our own time, another woman, Ellen Glasgow, who delivered the fiction of the South from its immersion in rosewater and the scent of camellias?

And, curiously enough, both these women, whose art was definitely on the side of realism, lived "the sheltered life." Chesterton, incidentally, pauses to remark, in writing of George Eliot: "Jane Austen was born before those bonds which (we are told) protected woman from truth were burst by the Brontës or elaborately untied by George Eliot. Yet the fact remains that Jane

Austen knew much more about men than either of them. Jane Austen may have been protected from truth: but it was precious little of truth that was protected from her. When Darcy, in finally confessing his faults, says, 'I have been a selfish being all my life, in practice *though not in theory*,' he gets nearer to a complete confession of the intelligent male than ever was hinted at by the Byronic lapses of the Brontës' heroes or the elaborate exculpations of George Eliot's."

Indeed, I think it can be said that, with notable exceptions, the women novelists have been more acute in their handling of male characters than the men have been in their delineation of women. For one Becky Sharp, for one Madame Bovary, how many feminine creations of the male novelists have been insubstantial projections of some ideally visioned creature of the wishful imagination? In fiction, as in life, the women are more often the truer realists in the matter of relations between the sexes.

One other random reflection on the subject of women and fiction. Is it not strange that in the two literatures other than English where the modern novel has been most highly developed—the French and the Russian—there have been no women novelists of outstanding stature, with the exception of Colette?

Women in Fiction I

One of this department's correspondents has some interesting observations to make in connection with my recent remarks on memorable women in fiction. Concerning Catherine of *A Farewell to Arms* and Maria of *For Whom the Bell Tolls,* she observes that they have always seemed to her to be "pure wish-fulfillment fantasies, the expression of a craving which apparently quite often afflicts otherwise intelligent men: the craving for a woman who is beautiful, passionate, sweet-tempered, and sufficiently intelligent to do what she is told, but who has no desires, interests or ideas apart from her man, who lives solely for and through him."

My correspondent expresses doubt amounting to conviction that any such creature ever existed save in the novels written by men who dream of her, and makes the not unreasonable assumption that if by some miracle she should materialize, they would probably soon become very bored with her. Whatever the degree of her improbability, there is no doubt at all about the frequency of her appearance in the fiction written by men; and it is equally true that she is encountered much more rarely in the novels by members of her own sex. I cannot, as a matter of fact, bring to mind at the moment a single well-known and shining exemplar of the dream girl who was the creation of a "serious" woman writer.

But her name is legion in the novels written by men, and if a comparative count were to be made I have no doubt that she would be found to appear more often in American fiction than in any other. For satirical or dispassionately realistic portraits of women in the American novel you must read the women themselves; you will find them in the work of such writers as Willa Cather and Ellen Glasgow. Among the men, Louis Bromfield, it seems to me, shoots nearer the mark in this respect than his contemporaries.

Henry James, in a bloodless fashion, was at home in the intricacies of feminine psychology; and Howells, within the bounds of his taboos and his natural reticence, maintained his balance. David Graham Phillips, a novelist who might have gone much farther had he lived longer, gave token of his capacity in *Susan Lenox: Her Fall and Rise*. But beginning with Dreiser, whose women are little more than the objects of male desire, the dream girl occupies the center of the stage in the work of American men novelists, unless, like Thomas Wolfe, they draw their portraits straight from life.

My correspondent throws out a suggestion for what seems to me a very fruitful subject for study by some literary historian, and that is the tracing, through literature and mythology, of two constant figures in fiction—the angelic heroine and the demoniac lover. She took exception to my mention of Rhett Butler as a synthetic character on the grounds that although we have met him before, usually in novels written by women, we must regard him as typical of the "dark, demoniac lover, who in other incarnations has been named Heathcliff, Rochester, and Lord Byron—not the real Lord Byron, of course, but the fictitious character created by that gentleman in collaboration with a number of infatuated women."

She thinks that in creating such characters women novelists do not steal from each other or fabricate them out of synthetic materials; that on the contrary, the "demoniac lover" springs from "much deeper, more obscure and more interesting roots than the male writer's angelic heroine." For the first appearance of both she goes back to antiquity: "The dark lover would surely go at least as far back as the Greek worship of Dionysius—essentially a woman's religion, you will remember. And we find the angelic heroine full-blown, waiting for Odysseus, under the name of Penelope."

Certainly most Ph.D theses in English literature and many literary studies more popularly aimed have dealt with far less interesting material. I hope that somebody may feel impelled to do the necessary spadework. In proper hands there is the making here of a fascinating book. I find myself puzzling, though, over my correspondent's belief that the symbolic figure which women novelists have so often projected, from the Brontë sisters down to Margaret Mitchell, springs from "much deeper, more obscure and more interesting roots than the male writer's angelic heroine." Perhaps that is because I am a man and my correspondent is a woman, but it seems to me that both projections have their origin in an identical longing to find the perfect complement to either the predominantly masculine or feminine temperament.

Imaginative literature has served many uses in its long history, but none has been more insistently exemplified than its use to release the inner demands for which these two figures stand as symbols. How many stories would have been left untold were it not for the personal frustration which made fingers grasp the pen or tap the typewriter! I would not go so far as to say that we would have no literature if all of us lived in a state of inner equilibrium, but certainly there is no doubt that we would have far less.

Women in Fiction II

From one of our younger novelists, Vance Bourjaily, comes a vigorous rebuttal of certain statements of mine about the portrayal of women in the fiction written by American men. I said that it has always been prevailingly weak, that the bitch and the dream girl were standardized types in our novels, and that if there have been any notable exceptions to these shortcomings during recent years, they had escaped my attention. Mr. Bourjaily thinks I was indulging in one of those "out-of-date generalizations about literature which really ought to be challenged every time they come up." These were not critical observations, he adds; they were merely the repetition of "old saws."

By-passing the fact that old saws commonly express established truths, let us note that this weakness in American fiction has, to the best of my knowledge, been pointed out only in the course of Mr. Bourjaily's lifetime, and that the statement of it hardly qualifies as an old saw. Nevertheless, so far as the history of American fiction is concerned, I don't think it can be questioned that the most memorable portrayals of women in American novels have been the work of women: to be specific, in the novels of Edith Wharton, Willa Cather, Ellen Glasgow, Elizabeth Madox Roberts and Margaret Mitchell. Hawthorne's Hester Prynne is a wraith; Cooper, Mark Twain, and Melville were not concerned with women in their fiction; Henry James and Howells dealt with them in a bloodless way. When we come to such more recent writers as Dreiser, Lewis, and Hemingway, whatever their several virtues, we find the dream girl or the bitch taking over. Where are the equivalents, in objective observation, to Flaubert's Madame Bovary, Tolstoy's Anna or Natasha, Balzac's Cousine Bette, or Thackeray's Becky Sharp?

Enough of the past. Mr. Bourjaily thinks I have underestimated what is now being done. "Actually," he writes, "fiction since the war has been full of female characters who are neither bitches nor dream girls, but, in my view at least, thoroughly convincing females, sympathetically seen and scrupulously rendered." I am not impressed by some of Mr. Bourjaily's instances. How much this negative reaction depends upon the fact that I find current fiction increasingly uninteresting to read, how much that in turn depends upon the fact that the more we see of life, the less we are ready to accept fictional representations of it, I don't know.

Be that as it may, Mr. Bourjaily says this in support of his contention: "As full portrayals I would suggest the title characters of Evan Connell's *Mrs. Bridge,* Vladimir Nabokov's *Lolita,* Calder Willingham's *Geraldine Bradshaw,* and Louis Auchincloss' *Sybil.* As less central, but, to me, equally vital figures, I would add such women as Eloise, in J. D. Salinger's story "Uncle Wiggily in Connecticut," Denise in Norman Mailer's story "The Time of Her Time"; Stella, in Bernard Malamud's *The Assistant;* Brenda, in Philip Roth's *Goodbye, Columbus;* both Jacqueline and her mother in George Eliot's "Parktilden Village," and since pride has some part in the composition of a letter like this one, I would be willing to defend the reality of Ellen and her daughter Sheila in my own novel, *The Violated.*"

Mr. Bourjaily's first two titles, cited as central to the issue, make me wonder what his criteria can be. I am quite ready to grant that Mrs. Bridge is neither a bitch nor a dream girl. She is a faceless character; worse than that, she reminds me of those people to whom Mr. Connell refers in his novel, the characters in one of Grimm's fairy tales who are hollowed out behind. After reading *Mrs. Bridge,* I knew nothing about her except that she was kind, and was disappointed in what marriage had brought her. Certainly she is not memorable, and soon I will have forgotten her.

What Lolita has to do with this discussion, how she is "central" to it, I can't imagine. What I was talking about was the relations between supposedly mature men and women, and the representation of that relationship in our fiction. Some of the other books mentioned by Mr. Bourjaily I have not read: some that I have did not imprint themselves on my memory as they did on his. If what I wrote left with Mr. Bourjaily and others the impression that without exception the women portrayed in the novels by American men are dream girls or bitches, that was not my intention. What I had in mind was that those who are not are few in number, and chiefly the creation of women writers.

Mr. Bourjaily suspects that "the real nature of Mr. Adams' complaint is not that such figures are stereotypes, after all, but rather that they do not conform to his personal stereotype of what American women are like and of what, by extension, American life is like." The implication is that my personal stereotype of the American women is a happy creature, undisturbed as the women in the novels he mentions are not. Nothing could be further from the truth, and my chief complaint against the delineation of American women in our contemporary fiction, is that the crux of their dilemma has not been adequately handled in our novels, either by men or women.

P.S. Although I cannot budge from the general position against which Mr. Bourjaily protests, I cheerfully grant that *Sybil* constitutes a notable exception to my contention. I had not read it before I received his letter. There may well be other exceptions, but I still believe that the portraiture of women by male American novelists has always been one of the weaknesses of our fiction, from Hawthorne down. The phenomenon is not a strange one, nor is the ineptitude confined to novelists. What else is one to expect of a nation in which so many men are so little attuned to feminine psychology as to address their wives as "Momma"?

Howard Fast

Three weeks ago I had what was for me an uncommon experience; I read through a book at a sitting. I have done this before, but rarely. True, the book numbered only 184 pages, which means that the reading took something less than three hours. Another kind of book of the same length might well have taken me longer, but this was one of compelling narrative power, of unflagging interest. It was Howard Fast's *April Morning,* a story of the battle of Lexington as seen through the eyes of a fifteen-year-old boy. When I had finished it, I said to myself, "This is an even better book than Crane's *Red Badge of Courage.*" I still think so. All prophecy is dangerous, and literary prophecy in particular, yet I readily wager that *April Morning* will some day reach the standing of an American classic.

My interest in the book was heightened by the fact that only a short time before, I had written a column in which I regretted that the War for Independence had received less attention in our literature than the one whose centennial we now commemorate. In that column I remarked that the best history of the Revolution had been written by an Englishman, that Shaw was the author of the only enduring play based upon it, and that the only memorable fiction written about it was in the novels of Kenneth Roberts. In making that statement I may have done an injustice to some writers I had never read, including Mr. Fast, who throughout his writing career has shown a more than ordinary interest in the struggle from which we emerged as a nation.

Curiously, although I had known about him, he is a writer whom I had somehow bypassed, and this, I can truthfully say, was not because of his one-time identification with the Communist Party; I have prejudices, but they do not go that far. Anyhow, having read *April Morning,* I was impelled to acquaint myself with his earlier work. In the intervening weeks I have read several of his other books —not all, for he has written about twenty—but I have found time to read *Freedom Road, The Last Frontier, Spartacus* an unpublished and as yet unproduced play about George Washington, and *The Naked God,* a book published four years ago, in which he told why he got out of the Communist Party.

I was especially interested in *The Last Frontier,* because the American Indian and the Far West are something I know about first hand. The book was a remarkable achievement for a young man who had never been West before he went out to Oklahoma, fascinated by the epic story of the Northern Cheyennes. Few writers, I think, equal Fast in the power of historical re-creation.

This reading left with me the conviction that he belongs in the top group of living American writers. He has weaknesses—as what writer has not?—and I shall speak of them, but he has a force, a vividness, a moral tone, that I find in few of his contemporaries. He is a writer driven by deep and honest emotion, so strong that it sometimes distorts his thinking, but he is nevertheless a powerful and often illuminating writer. In this respect it is pertinent to remark that his books have been translated into eighty-two languages; I doubt whether any other contemporary American writer is as widely read. I know that some of this distribution can be accounted for by his former affiliation with the Communist movement; a book like *Freedom Road,* for example, naturally appealed to colored and underprivileged peoples all over the world—but writers are not read by so many millions unless they are interesting.

What lies at the heart of Howard Fast's writing is a passionate concern for human freedom; it was that belief which took him into the Communist Party, and out of it. That belief lies at the core of everything of his that I have read. As I have already hinted, his emotion sometimes betrays him, as it did when he entered the Communist Party; as it did, I think, in *Freedom Road,* when it led him to believe that there could have been a firm and fruitful alliance between the poor whites and the Negroes in the post-Civil War South. Men are capable of being as good as Howard Fast thinks they can be, but they rarely are, and they were not, save for such notable exceptions as he uses in *Freedom Road,* during the decade or so following the Civil War, in what happened in the Southern states.

After reading *April Morning* I met Mr. Fast. Much of our talk turned on the American Revolution, and on George Washington in particular, for whom we found we had in common an intense admiration and a regret that as a human being he had been frozen into an unrevealing image so soon after his death. Mr. Fast told me he had written a play that dealt with Washington's decision to cross the Delaware and attack the Hessians at Trenton. I asked to see it. It is the only piece of creative writing I have read that makes Washington come alive as a man. The play may be produced next winter, if anybody can be found who would be credible in the role of Washington. That is a real hurdle, and he is a courageous actor who attempts it. It is a much harder assignment than playing Lincoln, who escaped being frozen. Physically, that actor must approximate the image of Washington we all have; as an actor, he must be able to penetrate beyond the image, and into the man, who was much more human than the books have let us know.

P.S. The play has not yet been produced. Judging by present trends in the theater, the best we can expect is Washington enshrined in a musical.

II

The Proper Study of Mankind

ALEXANDER POPE may have been waspish, and in character as small as in physique, but it is with good reason that he is one of the most quoted writers in English. Of all his memorable statements, none is more prized than his pronouncement concerning the proper study of mankind. For my part, no field of human inquiry exceeds in interest the effort to understand the impulses, the compulsions, and motives by which men, and women in particular, are governed. Its fascination grows with the passage of years. When we are very young, unless we are precocious in an uncommon way, we incline to accept people at face value, but the wider and more varied our human contacts become, the more questioning and skeptical we grow.

The flesh and bones of good biography, it was maintained by the late Hesketh Pearson, that most prolific and readable practitioner of the art, are found in what he called "singularity of character." What we relish even more than the great deeds of men, he contended, are the oddities of human behavior. This may not be the most profound approach to the potentialities of biography, but it is one rooted in awareness of normal human curiosity. In support of his contention, it must be granted that Boswell's attention to these peculiarities accounts in part for the perennial appeal of his life of Johnson, as it does for the lasting fascination of Aubrey's *Brief Lives.*

In a period when so many readers find too much of our contemporary fiction, drama, and poetry unrewarding, there is compensation in the high level attained by so much current biography and history. "There is properly no history," said Emerson; "only biography." It was a typically Emersonian statement. Whatever its measure of truth, few historians, naturally, would subscribe to it, especially those of our own time. Contemporary chroniclers put their faith not in the force engendered by certain individual men, but in forces as impersonal as tidal ebb and flow, of which, they maintain, men are the mere instruments. I confess that I cling to the great man theory of history. How could it be more strongly buttressed than by the career of Sir Winston Churchill? Was it a mere instrument that made victory possible in the Battle of Britain, that great turning point in the history of World War II? Were Marx and Lenin merely the embodiment of a current by which they were enveloped, or were they the creators of that current? True, Hitler gave voice to the frustrations and compulsions that every German felt after World War I, but could they have bloomed as hideously as they did were it not for a magnetic psychopath who had the driving force to give them motive power?

To me, biography, whether written by the subject himself or by an outside observer, is one of the most fascinating of literary forms. The story of a man's life, well told, never disappoints us. The pieces that follow record some of my reactions to a form of writing that can be as truly creative as a great novel or poem.

Richard Le Gallienne and the Literary Life

Anyone familiar with English literature of the Eighteen Nineties recalls the name of Richard Le Gallienne as one in the circle whose center was Oscar Wilde, and any admirer of Max Beerbohm's caricatures will remember a drawing of that group in which the young Le Gallienne's great shock of raven hair floats like a thundercloud in back of the other figures. His is one of the sad stories of the literary life; if he did not, like Ernest Dowson, die of dissipation in his youth, or miserably, like Wilde, in a shabby *pension,* his end as a writer was nevertheless a diminishment of his beginning. For a few years he flourished as one of a glamorous coterie, but these were followed by decades of vexation and disappointment. He lived to be an old man of eighty-one, weary with hackwork, his name vaguely legendary.

Had Le Gallienne's gifts been greater, what happened to him would have been tragic; as it was, the adjective must be "pathetic." Yet that word, though applicable, is not sufficient, for he fought with unwavering courage against his destiny, and kept to the end a razor-edged delight in living. Because he had savored so much in a lifetime almost equally divided among England, America, and France, because his capacity for delight remained so keen throughout his struggles, he cannot be wholly an object of pity, even though the fame he sought so ardently was to fade before him.

Little or nothing of what he wrote so copiously and indefatigably will be long remembered, yet his life commands our interest, lived as it was with courage and with zest. The tough strain of his seafaring Guernsey forebears almost redeems the sentimentality that rotted his fiber as an artist. It was inevitable that his story should be written, and this has now been done by two Englishmen born, as he was, in the drab streets of Liverpool. Richard Whittington-Egan and Geoffrey Smerdon call their book *The Quest of the Golden Boy*. It is published by the Unicorn Press of London, specialists in the literature of the Nineties.

It is a book of nearly 600 pages, in which there are many selections from his correspondence and occasional excerpts from his other writing. Although its length seems disproportionate in view of Le Gallienne's minor stature as a writer, there is, I think, a measure of justification. If its flow as narrative would have been quickened by some cutting of extraneous matter, there is as much to be said for such detailed examination of the comparative failure of an interesting human being as there is for a similar treatment of greater achievement. I say this with some hesitancy because I knew Le Gallienne, and my interest in the book is necessarily heightened by that fact.

For obvious reasons *The Quest of the Golden Boy* is not a critical biography in the literary sense, though its authors make passing judgments on Le Gallienne's work. What they have striven to portray—and have succeeded in doing—is the passage through life of a man who, however shallowly at times, loved much, suffered much and who never surrendered to the blows that were dealt him. His behavior as a sick and nearly starving old man when the Nazis overran his beloved France is a fine example of human gallantry.

His biographers have shown us the apprenticed accountant who dreamed of living a totally different life than the one planned for him by the loving, but not too understanding, completely Victorian father against whom the son revolted. They were interested, too, in divining the reasons for his literary decline. Why did this passion for the written word, this consuming delight in the visible world, and this innate capacity for expression, produce so little that is memorable?

They were fully aware of the pertinence of these questions and took note of them in their prefatory remarks. Surely the reason is not to be sought, as Mr. Whittington-Egan seems to suggest, in Le Gallienne's long residence in "streamlined America"; he lived here during the first quarter of this century, a period to which we now look fondly back, at least in its later years, as one of strong literary excitement, of concern with literary values.

Mr. Whittington-Egan refers also to the fact that Le Gallienne was a sporadically heavy drinker—surely a weakness which has not prevented many men from doing memorable work. But he comes to the heart of the matter when he observes that Le Gallienne was the "victim of an uncontrolled passion for romance." He persisted in wearing rose-colored glasses throughout his life, both in his personal relations and in his reflection of the world in what he wrote. This failing, together with the "fatal facility" mentioned by Mr. Smerdon, destroyed him as a writer, because the feeling for romance, however much it has enriched the literature of the world, is a sensibility that must be kept within bounds. Of such a restriction, Le Gallienne was incapable. His passion for romance, to which, given his sensitive nature, his childhood had conditioned him, led him into morasses of sentimentality and nostalgia.

It is for such considerations as these, so painstakingly made evident by his biographers, that Le Gallienne's life takes on a pointed interest.

Henry James the Correspondent

In his introduction to *The Selected Letters of Henry James,* Leon Edel reminds us that reading the correspondence of famous men is, after all, "a socially acceptable form of eavesdropping." We must always remember that the words were not addressed to us. Those letters are the best reading which admit us to the full flavor and range of the personality they express. It is not surprising, then, that the correspondence of literary men sometimes makes an illuminating supplement to their published work.

The letters of Henry James are a case in point. They afford frequent glimpses of a warmth of nature which is much less readily discernible in his fiction. He was an extremely self-conscious writer even in his correspondence, yet in letters to intimate friends he was often able to achieve a directness and spontaneity which were seldom present in his public writing. You do not need, on the other hand, to go beyond the novels of Dickens, let us say, for evidence of his human warmth, because he allowed it to spill over into his public as well as his private writing.

Henry Adams, who was one of James's correspondents, is another case in point. The *Education* is one of the most readable and remarkable of autobiographies, yet it acquaints us more with a mind than a man. In the striving for detachment by which its writing was accompanied there are facets of Adams' personality which remain submerged in the autobiography. To be aware of them, to sense the gaiety, the affection, and even the enthusiasms of which he was capable one must turn to the two volumes of the letters. They are, incidentally, among the best that American writers have left us, vivid in their pictures of places and people, seemingly effortless, always with the quality of good talk.

It is spontaneity, of course, that lies at the core of all good letter writing—like the amusingly casual portrait that Adams sketched of his fiancée for his friend Charles Milnes Gaskell: "She is certainly not handsome, nor would she be called quite plain, I think. She is 28 years old. She knows her own mind uncommon well. She does not talk *very* American. Her manners are quiet. She reads German—also Latin—also, I fear, a little Greek, but very little. She talks garrulously, but on the whole pretty sensibly. She is very open to instruction. *We* shall improve her. She dresses badly. She decidedly has humor and will appreciate *our* wit. She has enough money to be quite independent. She rules me as only American women rule men, and I cower before her. Lord! she would lash me if she read the above description of her!"

Because spontaneity came more easily to William James than to his brother Henry, he is a more readable letter writer. They make, indeed, an interesting study in contrasts—one so circuitous, the other so direct, one so addicted to the intangible, the other so avid for the concrete. I have always been fascinated by speculation as to the outcome if their roles had been interchanged, if Henry had written the philosophy and William the novels. It is difficult to guess how the philosophy would have fared, but I think the novels might have profited.

It is, again, the quality of unpremeditation that makes the letters of Theodore Roosevelt so readable. His was not, as he was well aware, an original mind, nor, as Elting Morison observes in his introduction to the eight stout volumes of his correspondence, which by no means comprise the whole of his incredible epistolary output, is there much of that "speculation on the larger questions of existence that gives so many famous letters profit by the possession of enduring vitality."

But Roosevelt's letters do give us the man—every aspect of him.

You would never guess from his public acts and speech the reservations which he sincerely held regarding his own capacity. Yet in the letters to his intimates they are plainly stated time and again. He frequently speaks of his mediocrity as a writer (curiously enough he combined a tendency to platitude with a gift for phrase-making); he confessed ignorance about financial and economic matters; he put a low estimate on his critical capacity, and, what must have been hardest of all for him to do, he spoke slightingly of his horsemanship and readily acknowledged his mediocrity as a marksman.

Nevertheless he poured himself unreservedly into everything he did, and it is because this characteristic carries over so completely into his letters that they are almost always entertaining. To the end of his life, Mr. Morison observes, he kept, as most men do not, the sense of curiosity and wonder, and the ability to lose himself completely in the moment. That is why his letters to his children are among the best of their kind. More, perhaps, than any other form of writing, letters profit by the possession of zest in life, and it is for this reason Roosevelt's may be read long after his other published works have been forgotten.

The Letters of Theodore Roosevelt

As the successive volumes of Theodore Roosevelt's letters appear, it becomes increasingly evident that he belongs among the most readable of letter writers. His are, as all good letters must be, the spontaneous reflection of a personality. Like all good writing, good letters must come alive. The quality in Roosevelt's personality which we think of first is, of course, his extraordinary vitality, and it is fully reflected in his correspondence. He once remarked that he had difficulty in writing about anything which did not interest him; reading the letters, one wonders if anything did not.

Actually, there were definitely insensitive areas even in that remarkably expansive and responsive temperament. He had no taste for abstract thought, and he was notoriously bored by economic theory and, even, economic practice. His interest in literature was intense and surprisingly wide in its range, but there, too, his mental hospitality had sharp limitations. His moral dogmatism made it impossible for him to be just toward certain writers; Chaucer's plain-spokenness, for example, offended him deeply. There are times, indeed, when one wonders if he did not conceive of every piece of serious writing as primarily a tract.

Good letters, Lytton Strachey once remarked, "are like pearls; they are admirable in themselves, but their value is infinitely enhanced when there is a string of them. Therefore, to be a really great letter writer it is not enough to write an occasional excellent letter; it is necessary to write constantly, indefatigably, with ever-recurring zest; it is almost necessary to live to a good old age. What makes a correspondence fascinating is the cumulative effect of slow, gradual, day-to-day development—the long, leisurely unfolding of a character and a life."

These are, it seems to me, not unreasonable requirements, and Theodore Roosevelt met most of them. Certainly he wrote constantly and indefatigably not only on matters of urgent business but by way of keeping in touch with those whom he cherished, and they were many. And certainly nobody ever expressed himself more continuously with zest; you can search in vain among these letters for one that sounds tired and uninterested, and that, I am sure, is not because Mr. Elting Morison, who has done a superb job of editing, deliberately excluded any letters of that character.

As longevity is reckoned now, Roosevelt did not live to "a good old age," but the cumulative effect of his correspondence is almost the same as if he had, because he lived so intensely. There were two or three lifetimes packed within the space of his sixty-one years. Though there is nothing leisurely about the unfolding of his life, the word may be employed to describe the reader's attitude as he follows the tumultuous course which these letters take.

They are not, it is true, notable for literary style. T.R. could be, on occasion, a phrasemaker; we all remember "the strenuous life," "nature-faker," "weasel-words," "muckrakers," and so on, but the level of his prose was pedestrian and undistinguished. It did have clarity and vigor, however, and those are qualities not to be underestimated.

His was a much more complex character than appeared on the surface, and an attentive reading of the letters makes that fact more clearly evident. He was, for example, a formidable egotist, and yet one is struck, in reading the letters to his friends, and to those attached to him by ties of blood, by how keenly he was concerned over their own affairs, whether or not he himself was affected by their course. It is this constant warmth which makes up so much of the engrossing quality of the Roosevelt letters. Reading them, one is always in the midst of life, and is reminded constantly of how much human beings can mean to one another.

Nobody, I am confident, ever wrote better letters to his children than he, because Roosevelt had an unfailing instinct for the kind of detail which would interest a child; I had the feeling, as I read, that had he turned his mind to it, he could have written some superlatively good books for children. That is one of the rarest of literary gifts; one of the reasons for this latent capacity was, perhaps, the fact that he never completely grew up himself; his was a puzzling blend of maturity and immaturity. A particularly engaging feature of these letters, as the children grow older, is the pains to which he goes in explaining what he is doing in the world of affairs. And he never writes down to them; always he writes as one human being to another, but on the level which they can understand. That is another reason why I wish he had tried one thing he never did.

The Biographer's Dilemma

Because I have recently been working in that field, I find my thoughts, as I take up this column again, turning like a magnetic needle in the direction of biography. Henceforward my sympathy for biographers will be greatly heightened, for not until one has attempted the portrait of another human being can one fully realize the difficulties such a task presents.

What I have in mind is not so much the labor of collecting and arranging material or the technical problems offered by any form of writing, as the sense of responsibility engendered by such an undertaking. The biographer's deepest concerns are, or should be, first, to make his subject live, and second, to insure as far as possible that the picture he offers is not a distorted one. If he fails in the first, his book is no more than a series of factual entries; if he writes in bias, though the result may be highly entertaining, he has betrayed both his subject and himself.

If his portrait is to be more than skin-deep, he must distinguish between the public and the private man. That necessity is intensified if he is writing about a public figure, but it is present to some degree in the most ordinary life, for by the public man I mean the face we all present to the world in which we live, however constricted it may be, as opposed to the face we confront in our solitary hours, and of which others catch only an occasional glimpse. It is this private image the biographer must strive to capture, though it is not always possible to do so, for few of us are as revealing of our true selves as was Boswell in his Journals.

In the case of the public figure, the face he presents to the world is often determined by his assessment of what the world expects and must be given if the established image of him—the one he cherishes—is to endure. Sometimes the public image becomes for him his true personality, and for its maintenance some men will sacrifice anything and anybody. In our own time we have seen these instances multiply, partly, I think, because our means of communication have so greatly magnified the opportunities for projecting the public image.

Accordingly, as time goes on, it seems to me that the biographer's work, when applied to the outstanding personalities of the period in which we live, must become increasingly difficult. It will become harder to separate legend from truth. And yet we have been witnessing, for some years past, a steady improvement in the quality of work done in this field. Both in biography and history the gains have been greater than in the art of the novel, and popular interest has turned steadily in their direction.

That it has done so would seem to lend support to a theory advanced by Harold Nicolson when, back in the Twenties, he wrote *The Development of English Biography*. He was of the opinion that the nature of biography in any given period always reflects the state of religious belief at that time. He observed that interest in biography always rose or fell with the public's interest in human personality, in its taste for psychology. This ebb and flow, he thought, is governed by the prevailing level of religious belief. "In periods when the reading public believes in God and in the life after death, their interest centers on what they would call the eternal verities, their interest in human personality declines.

"At such periods biography has been deductive, ethical, didactic, or merely superficial. In periods, however, of speculation, doubt or skepticism, the reading public becomes predominantly interested in human behavior, and biography, in order to meet this interest, becomes inductive, critical, detached and realistic."

There is another aspect of the interest in biography which I have observed for a long time. It is the frequency with which, as people advance in age, they are likely to read biography in preference to fiction, unless their reading of the latter is done simply by way of relaxation, in the form of mysteries, Westerns, and adventure stories. Is this not because, as experience of life widens and deepens, the standards of psychological truth by which we judge the novelist's performance are raised, and that in consequence we grow increasingly impatient with fiction of serious purpose which doesn't rise to the levels of truth about life that we have discovered for ourselves?

Then, too, there is a tendency, perhaps, to measure our own experience against that which we can read in the lives of others. As Ferris Greenslet wrote in his autobiography, *Under the Bridge,* "When we are young we read with excitement and wonder, to find out and forecast; experience is all ahead of us. As it comes, our mood changes; we read for pleasure and participation, sometimes for mere relaxation and change. In the third stage, when experience is x per cent behind us, we read for memory and recognition. To check the books by experience, experience by the books. To add up the profit and loss of the years into the final grand balance sheet."

Gauguin in Life and Fiction

The recent appearance of a new life of Gauguin (*Noble Savage,* by Lawrence and Elisabeth Hanson) will bring to mind for many readers a novel by Somerset Maugham. I refer, of course, to *The Moon and Sixpence,* a tale that belongs on the upper level of Maugham's work. For readers of the new biography who are unacquainted with it, *The Moon and Sixpence* should be of particular interest. Gauguin's life was the obvious source of Maugham's novel; on that foundation he built the story of an English stockbroker, Charles Strickland, who, in middle age, was seized by an overmastering compulsion to paint, and whose life, in its subordination of all decent human impulses to the vision which possessed him, and in its cumulative tragedy, paralleled that of Gauguin.

Although the parallel is close, there are certain wide divergences between Maugham's Strickland and the facts of Gauguin's life. Both men were stockbrokers when they came to the parting of the ways; both sought refuge in the South Seas; both were unrecognized until after death; both were ruthless in the grip of their compulsion; both died in misery. But Maugham allows his character no condoning impulses whatever; his scoundrelism is absolute. Gauguin, at least according to his biographers, continued to love his wife even though he abandoned her, and continued also to hope for a reconciliation. Strickland allowed himself no regrets.

It is difficult to create a character with so little shading and at the same time make him credible, and that Maugham was able to do this is evidence of his craftsmanship. It was accomplished, I think, chiefly by emphasis on the inner drive that impelled Strickland on his course. The force of this is heightened by our awareness that if Strickland spared no one else, neither did he spare himself; if he had no pity for others, he had none for himself.

Both in Gauguin's life and in the use which Maugham made of it we are confronted by a difficult problem in human behavior. We find ourselves questioning whether the human sacrifices entailed by such a compulsion as that by which Gauguin and Strickland were gripped are justified by the artistic achievement which was one of the end results. As one who is inclined to place human values first, and to value the man above the artist, I must state my doubt. I believe great art to be the finest achievement of the human race; yet even at its greatest, it seems to me an adjunct to living, and that our primary obligations as human beings lie in our relations with one another.

What Maugham's story accomplishes is to make us more understanding of what may seem, without sufficient sympathetic insight, absolute selfishness. I know that the older I get the harder I find it to sit in judgment on the behavior of another human being. As Maugham remarks in this story, written, in his customary fashion, in the first person, and thus permitting commentary which might otherwise seem dragged in, "I did not realize how motley are the qualities that go to make up a human being. Now I am well aware that pettiness and grandeur, malice and charity, hatred and love, can find place side by side in the human heart."

While the question I have raised lies at the heart of Maugham's story, as it is the crux of Gauguin's life, *The Moon and Sixpence* also provokes reflection on another matter. Thinking back, no doubt, to the impulses which caused him to embark on this story, Maugham remarks:

"Until long habit has blunted the sensibility, there is something disconcerting to the writer in the instinct which causes him to take an interest in the singularities of human nature so absorbing that his moral sense is powerless against it. He recognizes in himself an artistic satisfaction in the contemplation of evil which a little startles him; but sincerity forces him to confess that the disapproval he feels for certain actions is not nearly so strong as his curiosity in their reasons. The character of a scoundrel, logical and complete, has fascination for his creator which is an outrage to law and order. I expect that Shakespeare devised Iago with a gusto which he never knew when weaving moonbeams with his fancy, he imagined Desdemona. It may be that in his rogues the writer gratifies instincts deep-rooted in him, which the manners and customs of a civilized world have forced back to the mysterious recesses of the unconscious. In giving to the character of his invention flesh and bones he is giving life to that part of himself which finds no other means of expression. His satisfaction is a sense of liberation.

"The writer is more concerned to know than to judge."

What is sauce for the writer is sauce for the reader as well. If it is almost a literary axiom that a novelist rarely succeeds in giving life to a character free of the common frailities, it is equally true that the men and women of fiction whom we remember best are seldom if ever patterns of ideal behavior.

Autobiography vs. Biography

J. Frank Dobie, the literary dean of Texas, recently made two challenging observations. "No autobiography," he wrote, "is as good as the best biography." A few sentences later he remarked, "The finest character revelations in literature have not been by either biographers or autobiographers." I liked Mr. Dobie's article, which had some cogent things to say about the problems by which every autobiographer is faced, but I wish he had attempted to buttress a little more securely the two statements I have quoted.

For the first, he rested his case on the fact that the strongest impression he retains from any "straightout autobiographical narrative" is from Benvenuto Cellini's, but even this, and what he considers the best American autobiography—Benjamin Franklin's—seem to him minor works compared with Boswell's life of Johnson—a judgment with which I have no quarrel. In support of his second contention, which by inference concedes to the novelist or dramatist a power of revelation denied to the autobiographer and the biographer, he argues that the latter two "come to important areas in their subjects that they do not comprehend and, therefore, cannot reveal."

Both these contentions, it seems to me, are open to question. There are, I think, two criteria by which biographies and autobiographies are to be judged for excellence: interest and truth. No man, perhaps, can tell the complete truth about himself, no matter how hard he tries. Boswell came closer to doing so than any man who ever put pen to paper, and if you accept his journals as "straightout autobiographical narrative," which they essentially are, I think it must be granted that remarkable as his life of Johnson is, the journals transcend it in truth, though not in interest. However great the merits of Boswell's biography, it does not lay bare a man's soul as the journals do. He made Johnson extraordinarily alive for us, but he revered him too much to see him with the even more extraordinary objectivity with which he could view himself. This was the more remarkable in a man of Boswell's vanity.

There is one respect, at least, in which the best autobiographies outshine the best biographies, and that is in the recapturing of the subject's boyhood and youth. There, with the objectivity toward one's earlier self that comes with maturity, plus the vividness with which that period is remembered in age, the autobiographer has, and often displays, a great advantage over those who may write about him. It is far easier to say publicly, "I was a fool and a rascal in my twenties," than it is to say, "I have been a fool and a rascal all my life."

What biographer could possibly match Tolstoy's *Childhood, Boyhood and Youth*? Or, in our own day, John Buchan's opening chapters in his autobiography, and Sir Osbert Sitwell's account of his relationship with his extraordinary father? In saying this, I am aware that in a sense I am supporting Mr. Dobie's contention, for the autobiographer, in writing about his young self, is writing, usually, about another person, as Max Beerbohm reminded us in those delightful cartoons about the Old Self and the Young Self.

When we come to examine Mr. Dobie's second statement, we find ourselves on treacherous ground, for the lines are blurred between autobiography, at least, and fiction. Did not Mark Twain, perhaps, write his true autobiography—the one he did not botch—in *Huckleberry Finn* and *The Adventures of Tom Sawyer*—the autobiography, anyway, of the boy who grew up in Hannibal, Missouri?

Mr. Dobie asks what portrait in literature equals that of the "created" character of Hamlet, but goes on to state his conviction that *Hamlet* reveals "the innerness of Shakespeare as no biography based on 10,000 documented facts, if they existed, could reveal it." It is true, as Mr. Dobie remarks, that both the biographer and the autobiographer "come to important areas in their subjects that they do not comprehend, and, therefore cannot reveal," for none of us attains complete self-knowledge or absolute understanding of another person. But is there actually such a thing as a "created" character, and if there is, can it be more completely—that is, truthfully—presented than an actual one?

I doubt very much if any vital figure in fiction was ever made out of whole cloth, any that did not contain recognizable elements of a person or persons known to the author, or qualities peculiar to the author himself. Yet if we grant that improbability, we come up against the statement made by so many novelists, that a character can assume a life of his own, and act beyond the writer's control; in effect, he may act or speak in a manner which the character himself dictates. Can his "creator," then, comprehend and reveal him any more fully than he can comprehend and reveal himself or another actual person? These are teasing questions.

The Ethics of Biography I

A recent editorial in the *Times* (London) *Literary Supplement* raised some interesting questions regarding the ethics of biography. It is obvious that the biographer, like the historian, by the very nature of what he attempts, incurs certain responsibilities of which other writers are free. This is not to say that the novelist, for example, is exempt from ethical considerations; he is not, but they are of a different kind from those which must be weighed by the biographer. What he makes of his characters is his own business, and nobody else's. When he is guilty of mental dishonesty, it is something wholly between himself and his artistic conscience; it involves no one else, beyond the possible disappointment of his readers.

The *Times* editorial was not concerned with these distinctions, merely with the problems of an ethical kind by which the biographer is confronted. As a sort of text for its discussion, the *Times* quoted Lord Acton's remark to the effect that men of action should be judged by the historian at their worst, men of thought at their best. Like much that Lord Acton had to say, it is a statement worth pondering. It may not be as close to a natural law as the more famous "Power tends to corrupt; absolute power corrupts absolutely," but it does have far-reaching implications. The statesman at his worst may invalidate, or at least heavily discount, the best in his performance, but the writer of one great book can be forgiven a mass of mediocrity or worse, and take his stature from the high point of his accomplishment. Wordsworth's name, or Whitman's, shines no less brightly in the history of poetry because of the quantities of drivel that they wrote.

We can study the man of action and analyze his public deeds without reference to his private acts, which may be morally reprehensible, and yet help us not at all to understanding of his public actions. But if the subject of our study is a writer, we find ourselves faced by a very different set of considerations. As the *Times* writer observes, "The life of the writer differs from almost every other kind of life in that there can be no sharp division in it between the public and the private man." How he conducts himself in his private life, whether badly or well, is never irrelevant to what he writes or to our understanding of it. To appraise him justly as an artist, and to comprehend fully why he wrote as he did, the more we know about him in his every aspect, the greater our understanding of his work will be.

It follows, then, that one of the indispensable qualities which the biographer—or the critic, for that matter—must bring to his study of a writer is sympathy. The exercise of that quality, as the *Times* observes, does not necessarily involve moral approval; what it does most to insure is understanding and justice. It is the absence of that quality, more than any other, for example, that brought about a downward estimate of Lytton Strachey as a biographer; he had wit, intelligence, and skill with words, but he was determined to topple his eminent Victorians from their pedestals, not to understand them.

He was, as the *Times* notes, actually more of a Victorian in his approach to his subjects than he was a modern, because he presumed, to a degree much less common today, to sit in judgment. There can be no question regarding the presence in contemporary history and biography of what the *Times* refers to as "a quite new awareness both of the complexity of human nature and of the element of subjective prejudice that is bound up with every attempt to pronounce judgment."

It is easy to understand the attitudes of mind which gave rise to the debunking biography which flourished so freely in the Twenties, and is so infrequent today. When they had their base in conviction and were not merely opportunistic, they represented a revolt against stuffiness and hypocrisy, and accordingly contained something of value. But they also carried within them tendencies which were inimical to fairness and encouraged the distortion of truth. We came to see that these tendencies were hostile to biography on its best level.

Not that our present prevailing attitude, with its insistence on taking into account all the shadings and contradictions in human nature, is without its own pitfalls. The danger is not unlike that which Shaw perceived in the open mind. "When we have done our utmost," he said in the preface to *Androcles and the Lion,* "to arrive at a reasonable conclusion, when we can reason and investigate no more, we still must close our minds for the moment with a snap, and act dogmatically on our conclusions. The man who waits to make an entirely reasonable will dies intestate."

And, of course, valuable as the contributions of modern psychology have been in the creation of this awareness of human complexity, their use by amateur psychologists in the guise of biographers can, as we have had ample opportunity to observe, result in portraits as distorted as those of the most prejudiced debunkers.

The Ethics of Biography II

How much should a biographer tell? How much discretion should he exercise in writing about his subject's private life? How essential to full understanding of the subject's public acts, of his work, his knowledge and mention of his weaknesses as a human being? These are some of the questions recently raised by Stephen Spender.

Mr. Spender began by reminding us of the revolution in biography engendered by the work of Lytton Strachey. As he observes, the lasting effect of that work has not been in the direction of debunking, but in emphasizing what has come to be regarded as almost the biographer's duty—to tell the whole truth. Out of hatred for Victorian values, Strachey wrote with malice, and often with great unfairness, but his skill in the work of demolition released a flood of debunking biographies, often motivated by a superficial knowledge of modern psychology. Happily, these are less frequent now than they were in the Twenties and Thirties, and in spite of his bitchiness, Strachey's influence has been in the main for good.

There is no doubt that he wrote as he did out of adequate provocation. Nineteenth-century biography was prevailingly dishonest. It was written out of an exaggerated sense of propriety. A period that could drape the legs of a piano, that found it necessary to refer to the same human appendages as limbs, could not be expected to view human frailties with equanimity. As Mr. Spender notes, the duty of the Victorian biographer was to conceal as much as to reveal. Even in the more outspoken eighteenth century the biographer avoided unpleasant facts unless they were already common knowledge.

Today the bars are down as much as they are in the choice of language. We have come to believe that the more we know about the man—and particularly the creative man—the better we can understand and evaluate his work. I share this belief, and I think that those writers and their relatives and friends who obstruct the publication of letters act unwisely. All judgments are fallible, whether passed on a man or his work, but surely the more evidence we have at our disposal the less likely we are to be misled.

Nevertheless this quest for the whole truth has its drawbacks. "An argument against publishing material that is damaging to the reputation of the famous," writes Mr. Spender, "is that for many readers the revelation of the imperfect life of a Beethoven or a Shelley detracts from the reader's appreciation of those very achievements in which these men of genius freed themselves from personal weaknesses. Imperfect lives throw doubt on perfect art. Perhaps this would not be so in a world where everyone was a psychologist who knew that *tout comprendre est tout pardonner*."

It is a risk, I think, that we must take. I am not as concerned about the consequences as Mr. Spender seems to be. If I cannot appreciate Byron at his best because he sometimes acted like a cad, the fault is mine, not that of whoever informed me of his misbehavior. It is a common human failing to blame someone else for our shortcomings.

But what Mr. Spender is most concerned about, and rightly, is the invasion of privacy among the living. This is one of the major injustices of our time. It is preposterous, for example, that a President of the United States cannot go fishing without a host of photographers and reporters breathing down his neck. This is grossly unfair and inconsiderate; it is also idiotic.

"The novelty of the present situation," writes Mr. Spender, "is that interest in the artist's biography no longer arises only after he has died. It has caught up with him while he is still alive. It is not even curiosity about what he did yesterday, years ago, or in his youth. It is about what he did today and will do tomorrow. And for this kind of curiosity to be regarded as legitimate he does not have to be an exhibitionist on the scale of a Byron or a Picasso."

Mr. Spender suggests that if today's conditions had been present when Shakespeare lived he would not have ventured to write the sonnets. Were he living now, thinks Mr. Spender, they would have been sold by these friends to American libraries, and research workers would have discovered who the friend and the Dark Lady were. Who knows?

For my own part, I don't much care to whom the sonnets were addressed, or who the Dark Lady was. What matters to me is that they contain some of the best poetry in English. Had I been Shakespeare's contemporary I would have been, no doubt, more curious to know the identity of the people who prompted them. The controversy which has surrounded Dr. Rowse's life of him derives from his confidence that he has solved that problem, but for me the book's great value lies in its vivid evocation of the Elizabethan world. That helps me to know Shakespeare better. That is what biography should do.

Byron the Observer

"The great object," wrote Byron in his Journals, "is sensation—to feel that we exist, even though in pain. It is this 'craving void' which drives us to gaming—to battle—to travel—to intemperate, but keenly felt pursuits of any description, whose principal attraction is the agitation inseparable from their accomplishment." These words offer a rational explanation of Bryon's own life; actually, of course, he would have lived as he did if the thought had never occurred to him. Any man as much a prey to his emotions as Byron was is conditioned to a tempestuous life; add to that a driving energy, a thirst for experience, passionate convictions, and a boundless curiosity about human behavior, and the course he followed was inevitable.

Such men, to whom action is paramount, are not commonly observers. It is one of the fascinations of Byron's complexity that with all his heat, there was this coolness in him also. I do not mean the coolness of selfishness, though Byron, with all the kindness of which he was capable, could be supremely selfish. I mean mental independence and detachment; the first was with him always; the second he surprises us by sometimes showing.

These observations would not have been made had I not come upon a little book edited by Peter Quennell. It is called *Byronic Thoughts: Maxims, Reflections, Portraits, From the Prose and Verse of Lord Byron*. Mr. Quennell's account of how he came to compile it is interesting.

Some time ago, reading the *Maxims* of La Rochefoucauld, he lit upon an observation he knew he had encountered in Byron, in literal translation. He read: "Dans les premières passions, les femmes aiment l'amant, et dans les autres elles aiment l'amour." The clue led him to *Don Juan,* where, in the third canto, he found the lines:

> In her first passion Woman loves her lover,
> In all the others all she loves is Love.

This conjunction caused him to look further into Byron's interest in La Rochefoucauld. He found the Frenchman frequently mentioned in Byron's correspondence. Byron was both stimulated and annoyed by him. "Curse on Rochefoucauld for being always right," he once wrote. "In him a lie were virtue—or, at least, a comfort to his readers." The *Maxims* never ceased to fascinate him, and when he sailed from Genoa on his last voyage, the books he had with him were a Voltaire, a Montaigne, Grimm's letters, Scott's *Life of Swift* and the *Maxims*. This last he read on deck, looking "unusually silent and serious."

It is difficult to avoid the conclusion that La Rochefoucauld's effect upon Byron was considerable. One finds it reflected in Byron's own observations on human life. The core of the Frenchman's attitude toward human behavior was his conviction that selfishness is at its center. "The virtues," he wrote, "join with self-interest as the rivers join with the sea."

The two men had great differences, as Mr. Quennell remarks. Byron, he points out, had no fixed principles, "and retained an emotional regard for beliefs and prejudices that, intellectually, he had long since shed." Unlike the Frenchman, Byron, due to his half-Scottish background—never sufficiently emphasized, I think—had, along with his strong sensual inclinations, a deep sense of sin. Where they met completely, Mr. Quennell points out, was in their "abounding intellectual curiosity, fostered and encouraged by an innate skepticism, constantly ranging to and fro over the varied scenes of human life. Both were passionate observers; and as soon as they had observed some strange personal characteristic, whether it appeared in their own conduct or the behavior of a fellow human being, they felt impelled to analyze it."

"Anything," wrote Byron in one of his letters, "that confirms, or extends one's observations on life and character delights me even when I don't know people—for this reason I would give the world to pass a month with Sheridan, or any lady or gentleman of the old school, and hear them talk every day, and all day, of themselves and acquaintances, and all they have heard and seen in their lives."

Perhaps I have given too much space to the relationship between Byron and La Rochefoucauld, interesting though it is. I had meant to say more about the Byron who is shown to us in Mr. Quennell's anthology. His belief that such a selection from Byron's writings might be useful is supported by this book. We shall always regret, especially in the case of a man about whom opinions have been so divided, that Byron's memoirs were burned after his death by solicitous friends. All the more reason, then, to prize this reflection of him, illustrating, as Mr. Quennell remarks, his talent for observation rather than his imaginative gifts.

Happily, Mr. Quennell has included, in addition to Byron's scattered reflections on human life and conduct, some of his perceptive portraits of the men and women he knew. Though they are not as sharply etched as Carlyle's, they have life and human interest.

The Engaging Mr. Pepys

It is my conviction that most writers would profit by keeping a diary, a notebook, a journal—call it what you will. The practice is of particular value to them unless, like Thomas Wolfe, they are blessed or cursed—for it can be an endowment of dubious value—with the faculty of total recall. Like so many convictions we have failed to act upon, this one of mine leaves me no ground for self-satisfaction. Somewhere in my teens I resolved to keep a diary, and did so for something like two or three weeks. As I remember, most of the entries stated concisely, "Nothing much today." From that same period I recently unearthed a sometimes disconcerting document which must have been ambitiously conceived, for the flyleaf bears at the top the notation, "Book I." Underneath is written, "Notes From My Reading," "Thought Book," "Poems." This project, I see, was started when I was fifteen, and continued for a year or more.

Some of the entries are now, as one might expect, painful reading. A few surprised me because they express opinions to which I can still subscribe, though I hope they might now be better expressed. I shall not bore you, or disconcert myself, by any excerpts; indeed the only reason for referring to these juvenilia is that mention of them may move you to resurrect your own, perhaps to your amusement, and possibly also, as in my own case, to provide some illumination regarding that earlier self, and his connection with what you have since become.

Writers as deeply dissimilar in temperament, attitude, and the nature of their capacities as Emerson and Somerset Maugham drew much from their notebooks, as innumerable other writers have done. But what I am chiefly concerned with today is the diary, for recently I have been reading once more the fascinating, and, I would guess, the most truthful and revealing diary ever published—the one that Samuel Pepys set down in cipher with no expectation, I feel sure, that it would ever be read by anybody but himself.

More than once I have expressed the belief that no man has revealed himself as nakedly as Boswell did in his journals, and in some measure I still think that is true. For all his vanity, he was capable of the deepest and most intense dissatisfaction with himself, but he was a very complex and neurotic man, and the picture he left of himself is not always clearly focused.

Reading Pepys, you feel that you know him through and through. He was not a conscious artist, as Boswell was, nor was he at war with himself. Unlike Boswell, he suffered no great frustrations, lived into a contented old age, and could be happy in the knowledge that he had made the most of his capacities and opportunities. Though not brilliant, he had for many years been a capable and respected public servant, and he had known everybody he wanted to know in the little London of his time.

Boswell's company was evidently enjoyed, not only by Johnson, who loved him, but by other distinguished men of his period, yet as he presents himself in the journals, it is difficult to like him, interesting as he may be. For Pepys one feels an immediate affection. His lack of guile, his gusto, and his communication of his enjoyment, his spontaneity, his transparent honesty about himself, his unmalicious gossip—above all, his obvious delight in life, make him, whatever our mood, a welcome companion. And we see him so clearly against the background of the world in which he moved that we become, for the time being, a part of it ourselves. His pictures of great events, like the coronation of Charles II, the great fire and the plague, we seem to see at close hand.

In its down-to-earth humanity, Pepys' diary outshines that of his contemporary fellow-Londoner, John Evelyn, though less valuable to historians. Evelyn was more widely traveled, a man of broader experience than Pepys, and his diary not only illuminates Restoration England, but the seventeenth century in Europe as well. We do not, however, feel the same intimacy with the narrator. Over in Virginia, Pepys had a near-contemporary, William Byrd, whose diary, also written in secret script, which was not deciphered and published until two centuries after his death, more nearly approaches Pepys' in the quality of self-revelation; his diary attracted attention not only for the light it throws on life in colonial Virginia, but also because of its frank notation of marital intimacies and personal habits.

But Pepys is so completely engaging! You can open him anywhere and be entertained. One thing commonly overlooked about him is that his was a young man's diary. Evelyn, who lived to be eighty, continued his until the time of his death in 1706; Pepys started his in

1660, when he was twenty-seven, and had to abandon it nine years later because of failing eyesight. One wishes he could have continued, even though after his wife's early death (Pepys never remarried) there would have been no more of those touchingly frank accounts of their quarrels and reconciliations, or of his amorous escapades, never too serious, but which so distressed her. Even so, without intending to, he projected himself far beyond the time in which he lived.

The Letters We Write

Some time ago it was announced that Somerset Maugham wished to recall his letters and that he intended to forbid their publication after his death. More recently a similar decision was reported to have been made by Ernest Hemingway. Certainly any man, whether famous or not, should have the right to deny access to his private communications. What is debatable is the wisdom of doing so. In the case of a man whose biography is certain to be written, such a decision seems to me a mistaken one. Letters, like private journals, are invaluable to a biographer. True, they may prove the writer to have been a smaller man than the one presented by his public image, but they can also explain, perhaps to his advantage, why he acted as he did.

All of us ask to be understood, and few things irritate us more than misrepresentation. A biographer deprived of his subject's letters is often working in the dark. You may say a man's conduct is to be judged by his acts, not his words, but his acts frequently need explanation, and everything that throws light upon them is of value. Thomas Wolfe was criticized for breaking with the publisher who had labored tirelessly and effectively to reduce his mountains of manuscript to publishable form, and it is only when one reads Wolfe's letters to Maxwell Perkins that one can understand the motives which prompted him. What seemed like ungrateful behavior proves to have been necessary to Wolfe's belief in himself. Reading that correspondence through, one sees that Wolfe's gratitude and admiration continued until he died.

It is true that in the past unforgivable liberties have been taken with the letters of famous men by those who first edited them. Nobody suffered more in this respect than George Washington, through the bowdlerizing of his letters when they were first made public. This doctoring helped to create the dehumanized conception of his character that has made him so much less approachable than Lincoln. But today's temper does not tolerate such practices. No contemporary editor, having before him the complete text of a diary such as that of Pepys, would consider such an abridgment of it as was made in the mid-Victorian period.

What would we not give for the letters of Shakespeare! They might prove disappointing, in view of the conventions that governed Elizabethan letter writing, for, as Lytton Strachey once pointed out, the prevailing tone of such letters of the period as we have is elaborately formal. To write a letter was as much a literary exercise as to write a sonnet, and letters of such naked force as was displayed by Sir Philip Sidney, writing to his father's secretary, were rare. "Few words," he wrote, "are best. My letters to my father have come to the eyes of some. Neither can I condemn any but you for it. If it be so, you have played the very knave with me; and so I will make you know, if I have good proof of it. But that for so much as is past. For that is to come, I assure you before God, that if ever I know you do so much as read any letter I write to my father without his commandment, or my consent, I will thrust my dagger into you. And trust to it, for I speak it in earnest. In the meantime, farewell."

Shakespeare may never have penned so explosive a message, but had his letters come down to us we might have been spared all the tiresome books about who really wrote the plays, and we might have learned to whom the Sonnets were addressed.

I doubt whether it is possible to form a balanced estimate of any man without some knowledge of his correspondence. Private journals, however uninhibited, can be more misleading than a man's letters. "There is," remarked Somerset Maugham in his *Summing Up,* "a sort of man who pays no attention to his good actions, but is tormented by his bad ones. This is the type that most often writes about himself. He leaves out his redeeming qualities and so appears only weak, unprincipled and vicious." Maugham had in mind Rousseau, who, by stressing certain incidents in his life that we find repugnant, gave them in the *Confessions* a greater importance than they had in his life.

Certainly from that other inveterate self-torturer, James Boswell, we learn more about his frailties from the nakedly revealing *Journals* than we do of such virtues as he had. Even though some of his letters, like those to Zélide, place him in an unprepossessing light, one cannot read his correspondence with Johnson and not see that their friendship was rooted in a deep and firm affection. Boswell's character was far from admirable, and the world's judgment of him as a man has been harsh, but it would be harsher still if his correspondence had been lost to us.

Any public figure, particularly if he is a writer, no matter how little he may have to conceal, runs the risk of misinterpretation if he puts a ban on the publication of his letters. I say particularly if he is a writer because he has already told something of himself in his published work, and those who write about him may draw unjustifiable conclusions from what they think they see revealed there. His letters may correct the picture.

P.S. Hemingway carried through his announced intention, and although his official biographer, Professor Carlos Baker of Princeton, has access to such of Hemingway's letters as are available, he is enjoined from publishing them. At this writing, Maugham is still living, and we may not know until after his death whether he will have enforced a similar censorship.

Parson Weems and the Elusive Washington

No man in our history, not even Lincoln, has had so many distinguished biographers as Washington. They include Chief Justice John Marshall, Jared Sparks, Washington Irving, Edward Everett, Henry Cabot Lodge, and Woodrow Wilson. There have been lives by William Roscoe Thayer, Owen Wister, Paul Leicester Ford, Rupert Hughes, W. E. Woodward, and Douglas Freeman. There are others, but these are the best known names, and we need add only the Rev. Mason L. Weems, commonly referred to as Parson Weems, the author of the first biography. The occasion for this column is the first republication of his book in thirty-five years.

The list I have cited is an imposing one, yet there are those who think, as I do, that the biography which brings Washington fully to life is still to be written, close as Freeman came to it. Perhaps it never will be; perhaps we are asking for a kind of literary alchemy that is impossible. Somehow we seem unable to draw close to this man; something in him escapes and eludes us and a debunking biography like Woodward's defeats itself as much as the official and ponderous work of which the Chief Justice delivered himself.

The long and scholarly introduction which Marcus Cunliffe has written for the new edition of Weems's book is noteworthy not only for what it tells about the history of Washington's biography, but for its discussion of Weems as well. He was an interesting, if repellent figure, this parson-salesman whose life of Washington was to color so much of American folklore. He was apparently a sanctimonious rascal, but he has to be reckoned with.

It is a pity that more is not known about his early life. He was born in Maryland in 1759, the youngest of nineteen children. It is thought that he may have studied medicine in England or Scotland before switching to the ministry. Although he did some preaching from various pulpits, his chief energies went into the promotion and sale of books and pamphlets, including his own. Besides the life of Washington, which appeared first as an 80-page pamphlet a few months after Washington's death in 1799, he wrote lives of Francis Marion, Benjamin Franklin, and William Penn, besides a flock of pamphlets bearing such titles as "God's Revenge Against Murder," "God's Revenge Against Gambling," and "The Drunkard's Looking Glass."

One of the books he promoted was Justice Marshall's life of Washington, which began to appear in 1804. Partly because of the scant attention it paid to Washington's boyhood and youth, partly because of dissatisfaction among subscribers with the format in which it was issued, Weems determined to enlarge the short life he had written. He was a canny rascal, and had learned a lot about the country's reading tastes on his peddling trips. He knew there was a big market for religious work, and he was wide awake to the demand for "improving" juvenile literature, just as he had known that, as he wrote to Matthew Carey, the publisher, "millions are gaping to read something about . . . the Guardian Angel of his Country."

In 1806 Carey brought out for him a fifth printing of the pamphlet life, completely rewritten, and including for the first time two new anecdotes—the one about the cherry tree, and the story of the cabbage seed planted by young George's father in such a way as to spell the boy's name when it sprouted. Two years later, no longer concerned with pushing Marshall's work, Weems expanded his pamphlet into a book of more than 200 pages. He called it *The Life of George Washington; With Curious Anecdotes, Equally Honourable to Himself and Exemplary to His Young Countrymen.* Also he styled himself as "Formerly Rector of Mount-Vernon Parish," an office he had never held and which, indeed, had never existed. That book was to go through 29 printings up to the time of Weems's death in 1825. A century later it had gone through 80, and had been frequently plagiarized. The cherry-tree anecdote found a place in McGuffey's Reader and became known to every American child.

Professor Cunliffe points out that Weems was by no means the only disseminator of his moralizing anecdotes; his and others like them were rife in the Sunday-school literature of the early nineteenth century. Those through which Weems became famous were avoided by many early Washington biographers, like Jared Sparks and Washington Irving, but they were common as weeds in more popular writing, and it was not until late in the nineteenth century that Weems was fully discredited. Professor Cunliffe says what he can in extenuation of Weems's work and its influence, but he is not always convincing. He does point out justly, I think, that for all of Weems's sanctimoniousness, his overblown language and his disregard for truth, his pages often have an exuberance, a colloquial vitality, a sort of primitive vigor that lend them life.

The Old and the Young Self

Max Beerbohm did a series of drawings with captions which were dialogues between the Young Self and the Old Self. In this fashion, always with amusing and sometimes with devastating effect, the budding Shaw, Bennett, or Wells—for Beerbohm's subjects were writers—was confronted by his full-blown personality. Perhaps I should put it the other way, because it is always the Old Self who is confronted by the younger. "Well, well, so this is what you have become," one might in effect say to the other, or, as in the case of Arnold Bennett, with a certain satisfaction, "Well, it all went according to plan."

For the few, the very few, it does. As in Bennett's case, such a consummation requires a singleness of purpose and an obsession with the methodical which most of us do not possess. The encounter on which Beerbohm based his drawings is by no means limited to writers, or to artists in any medium. It comes, sooner or later, to all of us, and more often than not, the encounter is disconcerting, and it can be tragic. It is a happy outcome if the Old Self can be amused by the younger; not so if the Young Self can jeer at what he became.

At this point I find myself thinking of Sinclair Lewis. Like so many writers who were to make their names in other fields, he began by writing poetry. It was, moreover, poetry of a highly romantic kind. Some years later, with *Main Street,* he hit his stride, and held it through several novels. Even in these, the work for which he will be remembered, he was a divided man, loving much that he derided. Perhaps for that reason his later work came to be paler carbon copies of his earlier, to a point which embarrassed those who hoped to see him develop. In his last months, when the shadows were closing in, he returned to the writing of poetry. What, I wonder, did the young Lewis say to the old?

Plutarch, the father of biography, wrote his parallel *Lives,* placing a Greek against a Roman, and thus devising a method of treatment that might profitably have been copied more often. But contrasts are as interesting as likenesses, if not more so, and it seems to me that biography, in the centuries since Plutarch, might also have paid more attention than it customarily has, to the frequent contrast between the Young and the Old Self.

It is impossible to understand or to appraise the Old Self without knowledge of the Young. Those biographers are wise who may seem to devote a disproportionate amount of space to the inheritance and the early years of their subjects. Usually there is to be found the key to all that came after. Only now, in James L. Clifford's *Young Sam Johnson,* have we had an adequate account of Dr. Johnson's early years. Boswell's *Life* made him more real to us than any figure of the eighteenth century, but it did not explain him. He was past middle age when he and Boswell met; Johnson's character and attitudes were fully formed. Thanks to Mr. Clifford's research, we now not only know, but understand him.

There is another angle to the matter we have been discussing. Writers, no matter how wide the separation may become between what they are and what they were, are dependent upon the Young Self. When I say that, I am thinking of novelists particularly, although it applies to poets also, and perhaps more to them than to any other writers, though in a different way. Autobiography, too, owes much to the Young Self; it is no accident that the most pleasurable and the most convincing pages in that form of writing are so often those devoted to the writer's childhood.

In the case of novelists, I have in mind the faculty of recall. It is of inestimable advantage to a novelist if the things he saw as a child, as an adolescent, or in youth, or the emotional experiences through which he passed at those periods, remain clearly and firmly fixed in his mind. Out of such material nine-tenths of first novels are made, and so is a good part of the fiction that is best and longest remembered. The imprints that are made in the early years are the most indelible and the ones that live the longest. They are also the ones that are the easiest to communicate to others. I cannot explain that aspect of them, but I am convinced of its reality.

Much of Tolstoy's *War and Peace* was composed out of remembrance of the Young Self; so, to mention other instances at random, was *David Copperfield* and *Of Human Bondage*. Sometimes the faculty which makes this recapture possible amounts to total recall, as it did in the case of Thomas Wolfe, and then it can become handicap as well as help.

The poet's dependence upon the Young Self is different. It involves the capacity to see as freshly now as he did then. Perhaps that is the reason why so many good poets die young, either bodily or spiritually.

Self-Portraiture

One of the most fascinating books I know and one to which I frequently return is *Five Hundred Self-Portraits*. It contains that many reproductions from painting, drawing, engraving, and sculpture in which the artist either took himself for his subject or made himself a part of it. Ludwig Goldscheider's introduction to the book constitutes a brief history of self-portraiture.

The practice is almost as old as art. The earliest self-portrait of which we have knowledge is that of an Egyptian sculptor, and was made about 2650 B.C. His name was Ni-ankh-Ptah, and he carved it above the representation of himself, squatted in the bottom of a boat, which is part of one of the scenes he depicted in his series of reliefs for the tomb of Ptah-hotep. Two Egyptian painters are believed to have made portraits of themselves, but we do not know their names. In fact, between Ni-ankh-Ptah and the next known artist who tried self-portraiture, there is a lapse of two thousand years.

He was the Greek sculptor Phidias. In 438 B.C. his gold and ivory statue of the goddess Athena, forty feet high, was set up inside the Parthenon. She carried a shield on which there was a sculptured relief showing a battle between Greeks and Amazons, and in the thick of the fight appeared a bald-headed man, high-browed and wrinkled. The figures about him were all idealized types, but his was a naturalistic portrait, and we have Plutarch's word for it that this was Phidias himself.

Beginning with the Middle Ages, self-portraits can be listed at much more frequent intervals. As we come down into later periods, the practice becomes almost universal among artists, so much so that among the painters particularly, those who did not at least once, and more often, several times attempt their own likenesses, are in a small minority. We reach the peak of self-portraiture, both in quality and quantity, when we come to Rembrandt. He mastered this as he mastered every form of art he attempted, and there are more than a hundred existing self-portraits by him, including paintings, drawings, and etchings.

Naturally, the history of self-portraiture in the fine arts invites comparison with autobiography. Here the painter has, it seems to me, an advantage over the writer. One that is always present, no matter what his subject, is that when his work is finished, it is easier for him to view it as a whole, to see it objectively, and to appraise the measure of his success. In self-portraiture, he has additional advantages. For one thing, as Mr. Goldscheider points out, his self-portrait may be often repeated, since, among other things, the chief conditions of painting, light, and shade are always changing, whereas the verbal self-portrait can't, and probably shouldn't be, repeated at all. Memoirs, as he observes, cannot be written over again; they can only be continued.

Moreover, the painter, when he sets out to represent himself, stands on much more tangible ground. He has trained himself to see and to convey what is visible to the eye, and if his attempt is honest, he stands a better chance of achieving truth than the writer, who is always being waylaid by subjective factors. I think the validity of this difference is, on the whole, borne out by the portraits which are collected in this book.

There are exceptions, of course. Not all painters are able to see themselves as objectively as Rembrandt did. When I look at his self-portraits, I think of Boswell. The little Scot had greater vanity, but he had the same capacity to be brutal with himself. Among all the self-portraits by Rembrandt that I have seen, there seems to be none in which he offered an idealized conception of himself.

This was not true, for example, of Botticelli. He had been an invalid from his early youth, and was physically undeveloped and delicate. In his reputed self-portrait, Mr. Goldscheider remarks, he rejected "the hateful reality, and represented himself in the handsome and dignified form that he might assume in what the psychologist calls a 'wishing-dream'; just as Dürer visualized himself as Christ, so Botticelli saw himself as a strapping young Florentine, who might not be ashamed to appear in the company of the handsomest of the Medici."

Dürer, indeed, is one of the most interesting of the self-portraitists. There is on the one hand the remarkably objective and beautifully executed drawing he did of himself at the age of thirteen, and on the other, the later self-portraits in which he adapted his own features to his conception of the face of Christ. And one is amused by Rubens, who obviously delighted in picturing himself as the gay blade he actually was.

John Aubrey I

As every true reader knows, there is a small company of books of which the perfect use is to browse in them. It is best not to read them in consecutive fashion, as most other books demand to be read. They are books in which the nuggets lie scattered and are unexpectedly come upon. Their great charm is that they hold surprise, that you can never guess what the turn of a page may bring you. Boswell's life of Johnson is such a book; so is Burton's *Anatomy of Melancholy;* so are Pepys' diaries, and the essays of Montaigne. In our own time, the four volumes of Sir Osbert Sitwell's autobiography will be such a book for future generations.

To this select company may now be added *Aubrey's Brief Lives.* Although they were written in the seventeenth century and have ever since been a happy hunting ground for biographers and historians, they have only now been made available to the general reader in their original form. Heretofore, Aubrey has been indifferently edited and denied his plain speaking. Born in 1621, he wrote like a man of his time, for which he has paid the penalty of being bowdlerized. But Oliver Lawson Dick, to whom we are indebted for a new edition, has let him talk in his own uninhibited fashion. The result—a book with the juice of life in it.

John Aubrey was born into a family of country gentry. He grew up to be a man of wide acquaintance, of intense love of life, and of wide-ranging curiosity, not only regarding the habits of his fellows, but concerned equally with the adventurous intellectual life of his time. It was a great period in which to live: a time of expanding horizons, when life could easily be lived with zest, even by those whom we call the underprivileged. Mr. Dick, in the excellent *Life and Times of John Aubrey,* with which he prefaces his selections, attributes this atmosphere to the fact that the power of the Church had only recently been broken and had not yet been replaced by the tyranny of the State. A sense of freedom and unlimited opportunity was in the air. Such was the world into which John Aubrey was born—still glowing with the ardors of the Elizabethan age and filled with the vigor which, as Edmund Wilson observes in his Foreword, marked the century to come.

As you read these lives of men and women with whom Aubrey was contemporary or who slightly preceded him in time, you are made aware how much it was an age of opportunity. England had not yet crystallized socially; there was, it is true, a great gap between what could be enjoyed by those who were highly placed and those of "mean birth," but there were no unsurmountable barriers. The way was wide open to strength and ability. One is struck, reading Aubrey, by how many of the great prelates, men of action and intellectual leaders of the time were of humble birth: Cardinal Wolsey was a butcher's son; another started life as a scullion; another was the son of a soap-boiler, and so on.

Aubrey, who was a man of many projects, none of which he carried to completion, wrote more than 400 of these lives, ranging in length from two words to one of 23,000. From these Mr. Dick has selected 134 and arranged them alphabetically. I would say that not one is without interest, although many are concerned with men or women whose names we have never heard, unless we are students of the period. But among them are Shakespeare and Bacon, Spenser and Sidney, Sir Edward Coke, Cardinal Wolsey, Sir Kenelm Digby, Erasmus, William Harvey, George Herbert, Ben Jonson, Baumont and Fletcher, Marvell and Milton—all the famous names are there.

Aubrey was the Boswell of his period; like his eighteenth-century counterpart, he loved the society of his fellows, and conviviality. As Mr. Dick observes, he was usually suffering from a hangover when he set down his observations. Bernard Shaw called him "an old liar," though he thought Aubrey's Lives "a treasure," but Mr. Dick, after careful study, thinks that, though often inaccurate, Aubrey aimed at truth. He was unlike Boswell in that he was reticent about himself, like him in that he would go to any lengths to obtain information in which he was interested. "It was said of him by one of his friends," remarks Edmund Wilson, "that he expected to hear of Aubrey's breaking his neck someday as the result of dashing downstairs to get a story from a departing guest."

He had a flair for pouncing upon a distinguishing physical characteristic or trait of character, an eye for the significant little things that make us remember people we have met. As when he describes Sir John Denham: "His haire was but thin and flaxen, with a moist curle. His gate was slow, and was rather a Stalking (he had long legges). His Eie was a kind of light goose-gray, not big; but it had a strange Piercingness, not as to shining and glory, but (like a Momus) when he conversed with you he look't into your very thoughts."

His best stories are unprintable in a newspaper, but they are preserved in Mr. Dick's book, garnered from the Bodleian Library at Oxford, the British Museum, and other sources.

P.S. One of the things I most admire about Aubrey's verbal portraits is his interest in the human eye. He seldom fails to describe that most revealing feature of the human countenance.

John Aubrey II

Several years ago, when *Aubrey's Brief Lives* was first given American publication by the University of Michigan Press, I wrote a column about that delightful book, but lacked space to say much about John Aubrey, save for his engaging qualities as a writer. He was an equally engaging human being. It is odd that one of the most interesting figures of seventeenth-century England should have had only one previous biography, Anthony Powell's, published in 1949. This indifference is even more arresting than the fact that no work of his was published until more than a century after his death, for that lack was partly his own fault, and partly due to the system of patronage upon which writers of his time—and for nearly a century afterward—were dependent.

Mr. Dick's brief biographical introduction accomplished much in little more than a hundred pages. By a somewhat Boswellian method (for a large part of his picture is painted in Aubrey's own words) he achieved not only a vital portrait of the man himself, but one set vividly against the background in which he moved. Because Aubrey was so much a part of his time, and because Mr. Dick worked with such skill, it is impossible to read *The Life and Times* without a clearer understanding of seventeenth-century England.

The neglect of Aubrey stemmed largely from the reputation for inaccuracy he acquired at the hands of meticulous scholars. Like Herodotus, he was frequently guilty of writing from hearsay, although it must be said in his defense that whenever it was possible for him to check on the statements he made about a subject, he took pains to do so. And like Herodotus again, he had an unfailing gift for making his subject interesting—a quality often absent in writers who are more insistent on documentation.

It was Aubrey's besetting weakness that he was never able to finish any work he began. This was not because he was lazy, but because he was so easily distracted, so eagerly interested in all that went on about him, and in everybody that he met—and there were few notable figures of his time he did not know. Although he was by occupation an antiquary, the range of his interests was remarkably wide, and in some of the fields by which he was attracted, he was far in advance of his time. He can with justice be called the first English archeologist, and a pioneer in educational theory.

He lived in a credulous time, but although Aubrey was as fond as any contemporary of old wives' tales, Mr. Dick observes that he often showed "a scepticism that was most praiseworthy in an age when any statement was accepted just because it was made." This uncritical state of mind (particularly evident in connection with religion) is hard, notes Mr. Dick, "for us to visualize, because it has vanished almost entirely from the modern world except in Eire, where the people are still more likely to accept than to reject even the most obvious falsehood, and where, in consequence, the banshees and the fairies and the leprechauns have kept their last foothold in Europe."

Aubrey was the son of a distinguished and prosperous father. He was, however, ill-equipped with business sense, and lost all the properties he inherited. During the latter part of his life he was almost totally dependent on the kindness of his numerous friends. Some, among them Lord Baltimore and William Penn, offered him land in the American colonies, but though tempted at times, he could never bring himself to take the step. He was less favored in the matter of finding a patron who would defray the expense of publishing his work, but in this he was his own enemy; in the case of his *Monumenta Britannica,* he went so slowly about the work (a command performance on the part of Charles II) that five separate dedications of the book were made, as death removed one hoped-for patron after another.

If writers think they have their troubles now, they should turn to the annals of seventeenth-century publishing. If a writer was lucky enough to secure a patron, he might have to conform to the patron's criticisms. Thomas Tanner, afterward Bishop of St. Asaph, writing to Aubrey about his *Antiquities of Wiltshire,* reminds him that Sir Walter Raleigh burned the manuscript of the latter part of his history of the world because the printer had lost his shirt in publishing the earlier part.

The Unknown Emerson

The other morning, for my own diversion, I compiled a list of the men I regard as the ten greatest Americans. When it was complete, I found it was divided evenly between men of affairs—men predominantly of action—and those who worked in the fields of art and thought. Such a division, of course, cannot be precise, for government is actually an art, and some thinkers and artists have been as dynamic as the men who translated their ideas or their vision of the world into action. Be that as it may, here is my list, in chronological order: Franklin, Washington, Jefferson, Emerson, Lincoln, Francis Parkman, Winslow Homer, William James, Theodore Roosevelt, and Robert Frost.

Having set myself an arbitrary limit of ten, some of the choices were not easy. Somewhere among them, places should perhaps have been found for Thoreau, Whitman, Mark Twain, and Edison. Whether unconsciously or not, I suppose I was trying to make a balanced list; I chose Homer, for example, as the greatest American painter, Parkman as the greatest historian, James as the greatest thinker. Whether Frost should yield place to Whitman as our greatest poet is a debatable point, and I wanted, if possible, to include in my list, at least one contemporary. Four names among the doers cannot, I think, be questioned: Franklin, Washington, Jefferson, and Lincoln. On the fifth I know I shall be challenged, yet I am confident that Theodore Roosevelt's legacy to his country will some day be fully re-established. In naming him rather than his cousin, I confess to a bitter partisanship.

Of these ten men, the one who has had the most direct and formative influence on my beliefs and attitudes is Emerson. I came to the reading of him early—in my teens, as with Whitman—and the imprint he made at that most impressionable age has never been erased.

The popular conception of Emerson, if there is one, emphasizes the rather bloodless and cloud-treading seer, who waited for "the oracle in the pine woods" to speak; the thinker who arrived at his conclusions by flashes of intuition rather than by logical processes. That is a part of him, but there was a side to Emerson which has never been sufficiently emphasized by his biographers. It was recognized and more fully developed than it had been, when Ralph L. Rusk published his excellent biography twelve years ago. Even so, that side of the profile needs still more high-lighting.

What I am getting at is that prior to Mark Twain, Emerson, in his capacity of wide-traveling lecturer, came to know the United States and its average citizens better than any American writer of his time. That is why I have been so much interested in a recent publication of The New York Public Library, "Emerson's American Lecture Engagements," by William Charvat, a Professor of English at Ohio State University. Mr. Charvat's introductory essay is followed by a complete chronological list of Emerson's lectures, which were delivered over the span of almost half a century. It was published first in last winter's issue of the Library's Bulletin, and has now been reprinted as a pamphlet.

Mr. Charvat prepared the list as "a basis for understanding one of the most extraordinary phenomena in the history of American culture. Emerson was the least comprehensible of all major American writers [I would here interpolate, 'at times'] and of all lecturers, yet on the public platform, where he faced auditors of every possible grade of literacy and sophistication, he was not only the most popular of all 'literary' lecturers, but one of the most popular of all lecturers." He was different too in the wide range of the topics he discussed—running from politics to immortality. Most of those who held audiences captive repeated one or two lectures over and over, Emerson spoke on scores of themes.

A few statistics may not be amiss. Between 1833 and 1881 he gave about 1,500 lectures in twenty-two states and in Canada. He ranged from New England to the Pacific Coast. Although Massachusetts and New York heard him most often, he journeyed indefatigably about the country when travel was more often than not an ordeal, by train, by river and canal boat, by sleigh. Never a man of robust health, one marvels that he endured the rigors of these winter travels, undertaken because he had to piece out the meager income from his books and such small investments as he had. His average fee for many years was no more than $25; it was only in his later years that he received as much as $100, and never more than $300.

On these journeys he met and talked with Americans of all types and classes. The West, when he first ventured beyond the Alleghanies, was a far remove, in social and mental climate, from Boston and Concord; he saw the country in the making. He went as far south as Virginia and was once scheduled for a course of lectures in

New Orleans. The project fell through, and as Mr. Rusk points out in his biography, that failure was part of the fateful failure of the American lyceum to bring North and South together in a common forum of ideas. Such an interchange, coming before the Civil War, might have been decisively fruitful.

III

In a Fine Frenzy Rolling?

DURING ITS twenty-one years of publication in the format I devised for it, page two of the New York *Times Book Review* carried a column of poetry reprinted chiefly from new volumes by contemporary poets, and from those magazines which give space to poetry. Now and then, especially if "Speaking of Books" was concerned with the poetry of another period, the selections were made from the poets of that time. The opposite side of the page was occupied by a department called the "Treasure Chest." This consisted of brief excerpts from books I had been reading; as time went on these selections were made with a view to tying them in with the topic discussed that day in "Speaking of Books."

The "Poets' Column" made accessible to contemporary poets the largest potential audience they could reach in the United States—the largest, I think, in the English-speaking world, for at least two and a half million people read the New York *Times* every Sunday. In making the choices for the "Poets' Column" I tried to give equal play to the traditionalists and the modernists; the only test was that the poem must interest me and might interest others. I was sometimes viciously attacked by poets who owed to me a wider hearing than they had ever enjoyed, though most poets, including some of our best, expressed gratitude for the opportunity the "Poets' Column" afforded them.

He is a rash man who would venture an estimate of how many people are writing poetry in this country today, or of how many are habitual readers of it. I am confident, however, that professional and amateur poets together must be numbered in the hundreds of thousands. I would not risk a guess as to how many little poetry magazines there are, although I know they can be numbered by the score. The life of most is brief, but one no sooner dies than another is born. The audience they reach is small indeed; even the oldest and best-known, *Poetry*, has a circulation of less than 6,000. Our magazines of widest circulation rarely publish poetry. A volume of new verse by an established poet does extremely well if it sells as many as 2000 copies; the average sale is well below that figure. Such audiences as were enjoyed by Tennyson or Longfellow a century ago have not been matched by either a T. S. Eliot or a Robert Frost.

Why? I attempted some answers in the pieces that follow. I do not for a moment believe, as is often asserted, that our age is inhospitable to poetry. The magazines and many book publishers may be, but the audience is there, waiting, for poetry in one form or another. It is instinctive in children, though many lose the taste for it as they grow older. But poetry is not confined to words: it can be resident in painting and sculpture and architecture, in a bridge builder's blueprint or an airplane engineer's design—possibly, even in the technique of a surgical operation. Man starves on facts. What is the exploration of space but a kind of poetry? True poetry tries always to recapture the lost innocence of the world; it tries to see things, as with the eyes of a child, for the first time, and when it fails to do so, it is not poetry.

This is something many of the modernists fail to understand. Sophistication is fine and dandy for light verse, and is its motivating force, but it is the natural enemy of poetry. The best poetry welds emotion and thought into an indissoluble unit, but we have today too much poetry that is purely cerebral. In consequence, the hungry sheep look up and are not fed. There has been too much emphasis on wit, an admirable quality in all writing, but one that poetry can dispense with more easily than prose. I shall not beat the tired drum of obscurity: when willful, and dependent on a purely private imagery, it is noxious—but as Coleridge observed, a poem can be the better for not being completely understood. For me, the classic example of that truth is Walter de la Mare's "The Listeners." Who the listeners are and what they are listening for, we do not know, or cannot be sure, yet the poem offers unending delight.

Most of us are agreed by now that man has got himself in a pretty fix by too great reliance on his mental processes, and that the time has arrived when he must shed the shame with which too many intellectuals have detected in themselves evidences of feeling. The spirit of man, which it is one of the functions of poetry to foster and preserve, is not to be served by mind alone. If it is, we might as well draw the curtain now, iron or otherwise, on the future of man.

I know, of course, that our age cannot, for the present, at least, be one of the great ages of lyric poetry. The dew is off the world we live in. Men, for the most part, sing only when they are happy, or, particularly if they are Irish, Jewish, Negro, or Russian, when they are sad. Nowhere in the mass are men happy today, and their sadness, when it is not merely the product of their indifference or their bewilderment, is the sadness of despair. Nothing could be further removed from the temper of our time than the uplifted hearts with which men sang in that marvelous period of full-throated lyricism which was the Elizabethan age, and all the world seemed opening like a flower. Can it ever be so again? Perhaps not, but we still have hearts as well as minds. And I think this: that in a world of mounting tensions and fears, the poet can best serve his time, not by accelerating those forces, but by trying to reduce their pressure.

The Flight of Gulls

The flight of gulls is, I suppose, one of the most beautiful things in nature. Their downward, planing sweep is absolute perfection of motion—a movement, and at the same time a suspension of movement, of which the eye never tires. It satisfies something deep in us, stirs us in a way which we cannot define; it is a thing utterly beyond our capacities, yet to which our response is immediate and complete. The flight of planes, it is true, provokes our admiration; there is a bit of pride there, too, for they were built by us, who have not ourselves the gulls' mastery. But it is not the same thing; we exclaim at the power and certainty of the plane as it sweeps across the sky, but we are not moved in the same way. The gull's flight holds the mysterious element which is poetry.

Watching the gulls as I walked along the East River Drive the other day, I thought it fortunate that New York, from which so much of nature has been thrust out, at least affords such easy opportunity of enjoying the simple but deep pleasure I have been describing. And as I thought about this the flight of the gulls began to stand in my mind as symbolic of some of the lacks that have been so often evident in our contemporary poetry.

In looking at the gulls there is a kind of release from the world that is wholly of our own making; from the man-made problems, the self-centered perplexities that make up so much of our lives, and press upon us in a far more unrelieved way in the city than they do when, in the country, we are in closer touch with the natural world of which we are a part. Man is constantly needing to be reminded of the rest of animate nature. Smile if you like, but something deep in him is answered when he watches the cows slowly crossing the field, coming in from pasture, imperturbable and, if you insist, dumb. A little of his fretfulness, at least, slips away. As when he watches the gulls in flight he is, however imperceptibly, refreshed.

Now what has this to do with the lacks in contemporary poetry? I probably shall not be able to make myself very clear, because what I am trying to set down is not much more than a feeling prompted by the experience with which this column began. But it seems to me that too many poets in recent years have been trying doggedly to live completely in the world of man's own making. They have tried to build their poetry entirely out of the stuff of their own minds, out of that self-centered world by which man is increasingly hemmed in, the more so as he lives in great agglutinations of himself.

There was a natural revolt among the searching, inquiring spirits against "nature poetry." It had become mere prettiness, and the world of nature was too often reflected in the same little conventional reflexes which had been repeated a thousand times over, until the pattern of these responses had become as worn as that of a breakfast food jingle. And the young poets, reacting against this enervation, thumbed their noses at nature and said: Come, we will take refuge in our minds; we will build our poems out of logic and reasoned perception of this life that men live among themselves. And so they cerebrated and cerebrated, and stewed in their own juice.

In *The Name and Nature of Poetry,* which contains some of the wisest things that have been said about poetry since men began to ask themselves what it is, A. E. Housman observed that "poems very seldom consist of poetry and nothing else; and pleasure can be derived also from their other ingredients." These ingredients can be of many kinds, and poets in our own time, no less than those of other centuries, have too often asked us to accept one or more of them in place of the genuine article. In the seventeenth century it might be the tortuous elaboration of intellectualized conceit (to which, in their admiration for what is of genuine worth in the poetry of that period, some moderns have returned); in the eighteenth, it might be epigrammatic wit; and among the Victorians, belief in the morality of the universe.

Among ourselves, it has sometimes been the existence of a sense of social awareness, and good poets have been damned in our time simply because their minds were not tuned to the Marxian harmonies. Or we have been asked to enjoy a poem merely because of its subject matter, as if it made any difference what a poem is about! Even though some materials may lend themselves more readily than others to treatment in poetry, the fact remains that poetry penetrates to those who are able to recognize it, whatever the subject matter it employs. It establishes itself just as effortlessly as that motion of the slanting gull.

It cannot be too often repeated, I think, that, as Housman put it, "poetry is not the thing said but a way of saying it," nor that the intellect is not to be trusted where poetry is concerned, either in its creation or its recognition. Poetry in its essence is felt, not apprehended, and something of what we feel when we watch the gull's flight, or the cows in their calm procession, must enter into both its creation and its reception.

Poetry and Sophistication

"Poetry," Max Eastman has remarked, "is unconditionally upon the side of life." That is, it seems to me, a deeply true and suggestive observation, and one which applies not to poetry alone, but to the best in literature. At first sight, since literature and life are so commonly coupled in our minds, this may seem a little like the elaboration offered by Mr. Coolidge when questioned about the sermon he had just heard. Asked what the preacher's subject was, he said "Sin," and when prodded as to the preacher's views remarked, "He was against it."

Yet, though life is the primary material of literature, not all literature is "upon the side of life." Mr. Eastman tells us that poetry is unlike ennui, or sophistication, and so it is. They are fundamentally incompatible. And literature in general, unless it approaches life with something of the eagerness and ready receptiveness which are the springs of poetry, lacks the power to invigorate and restore.

For the books we love best are the books that reveal a love of life. We react to them as we react to people. When we say that a man is a likable rascal we disapprove of his principles, or his lack of them, but we pay tribute to his zest for living. We forgive a great deal in those who reinforce in us the belief that life is full, adventurous, rewarding, just as we are impatient with those who take away from its savor.

It was not merely the prevalence of willful obscurity which cut down the audience for poetry during recent years. In part, it was also the fact that so much of what was written was sour, apathetic, indifferent in its response to life. It was lacking in intensity of reaction. Mr. Peter Monro Jack, in his review last Sunday of the *Collected Lyrics* of Edna St. Vincent Millay, pointed out quite justly that "the sense of loss haunts every other poem." Yet the insistence of such a mood did not prevent her from being the most popular poet of her period. That she made herself easily understood, that she could always communicate her feeling, is not, I believe, a complete explanation of her popularity, any more than that she spoke, as Mr. Jack reminds us, to youth, of youth's disillusion.

Does it not lie rather in the fact that, to a greater extent than any other lyric poet of her generation, her lines had the quality of poignancy? Looking upon beauty or remembering rapture might make her sad, so that she would write,

> I only know that summer sang in me
> A little while, that sings in me no more.

What mattered was that her perception of the beauty, her memory of the rapture, was not dulled but tinglingly alive.

For what I am saying is not that poetry, or literature in general, must be joyous in its total effect. If we were to insist upon that, we should have to rule out a great part of what we prize most highly in the books which have won for themselves enduring life. Out of the contrast between what was and what is, or between what is and what might have been, have come some of the most profoundly moving and deeply stimulating utterances in both prose and poetry. I mean simply that the literature in which we find the fullest satisfaction is the literature in which we find the fullest reaction to life.

Naturally, those in whom the love of life is strongest suffer the keenest disappointments, feel most intensely the contrasts on which I have just been speaking, and this susceptibility of theirs is imparted to what they write. We like to be in their company because they bring to us the feeling of abundant living. They revive and quicken our own response to life.

Is it not the enormous vitality of a writer like Shakespeare or Tolstoy that makes our reading of him so inexhaustibly rewarding? Life streams out from them. Both were men who knew the summits of joy and the depths of misery; in Shakespeare's case we know the range of his emotional experience only through its reflection in the plays, but it is there for all men to see; Tolstoy has written directly of his, but even if he had not, the quality of his intense reaction to life is implicit in *Anna Karenina* and *War and Peace*.

It is, incidentally, more than a little absurd that *War and Peace* should, of late, have found recommendation to new readers on the grounds of its historic parallel to Hitler's invasion of Russia. That has a passing interest, to be sure, but the true illumination afforded by that greatest of all novels lies not in the repetition of one dictator's great blunder by another, but in its tremendous embrace of life, its running the gamut of human emotion, its unparalleled grasp of the whole fabric of man's living. Books like *War and Peace* need not, and should not, be merely the beneficiaries of timeliness. They have their own lifeblood in them, and they need no restoratives.

The great novels, like the great poems, have a tonic effect. They not only reach out toward life and grasp it; they pass it on as well.

Nature and the Poet I

Introducing a new volume in the Yale Series of Younger Poets (*An Armada of Thirty Whales,* by Daniel G. Hoffman), W. H. Auden asked himself what seemed to him a silly question. "Is there going to be a revival of 'Nature' poetry, and, if so, how will it differ from nature poetry in the past?" It may be a fruitless question, but it is not a silly one, for the very reasons which impelled Mr. Auden to ask it. He was prompted first of all, of course, by the fact that the poet he was introducing takes many of his themes from Nature. But beyond that, there was present in his mind the realization of another fact—that man's relation to Nature has changed, and that it is difficult, if not impossible, for the poet of today to approach Nature with the same mental attitudes which Wordsworth held.

Nature poetry, to be sure, is still written in abundance. Most of it is not very good. It is slavishly traditional, and when Mr. Auden asked himself this question he did not, I am sure, have poetry of that sort in mind. He was thinking, no doubt, of those poets who are trying hard to find a means of expression which seems to them consonant with the world in which they live. That very determination sometimes results in confusion, but when the impulse behind it is thoughtful and true, it is more commanding of respect than the attitude of those who ask no questions and who look toward no new horizons.

Century after century, man has become further and further divorced from Nature. We can easily be deceived by certain phases in his development, by such turns in his attitudes as are characterized by the romantic movement, and the interest in mountains, for example, which developed in the nineteenth century. Actually, he was being drawn into no closer relationship with the natural world about him than he had held before, because, along with his romantic interest, there was growing in intensity his conception of the "conquest of nature."

Little did he think, as the lust for domination grew within him, that his quest for power over natural forces held within it the principle of the boomerang, and that one day he would stand in dread of the very forces over which he had assumed control. Yet that is where he stands today, in the age of atomic fission.

One of the most reassuring aspects of Nature in man's experience had always been the rhythms which he had come to recognize and expect—the simplest of them daylight and dark, the recurrence of spring, the rise and fall of the tides. The effect of these has been, in varying degrees, interfered with, as Mr. Auden observes, by "the way of life which the machine imposes upon us, replacing the rhythmical recurrences of Nature by mathematically identical 'soulless' repetitions." This substitution, he remarks, "has developed in us a horror of all recurrence and a corresponding obsession with novelty."

Nevertheless, Mr. Auden reminds us, however cavalier we may have been in our treatment of Nature, she is "all about us, and, so long as we have bodies, however we may maltreat them, our relation to her has not been severed." As evidence of this, he cites the continuing popularity of hunting, fishing, and mountain climbing, but at the same time questions their beneficence so far as poets are concerned. "In so far as they make the relation to Nature one of contest, the goal of which is human victory, and limit contacts with her to those of the greatest dramatic intensity, they may exacerbate rather than cure that unnatural craving for excess and novel thrills which is the characteristic urban disease. What is really needed is a much more modest, passive and reverent kind of approach."

It is not, certainly, an easy approach for today's poet to make. He is faced, as Mr. Auden points out, not only with the question of contemporary expression, but also with the problem of recovering a way of feeling that both he and his public have largely lost. That sense of the divinity in Nature by which Wordsworth was sustained is difficult for him to hold, much as he may feel the need for it. But is he to adopt the attitude of Mr. Auden's imaginary Accuser, who says, "This is sentimental rubbish. You don't feel that Nature is holy and as a modern man you never can. Genuine art is the mirror of genuine feelings, and the only real feelings you have are of self-pity at your alienation. So be frank, be modern. Express your pity for yourself in the rhythmless language really used by metropolitan man."

The only way to counter this lie, Mr. Auden remarks, "is to realize its half-truth—namely, that our conception of Nature cannot be that of some prescientific magician, nor our modes of expression those of some agricultural community without a written literature." That is only a half-answer to what Mr. Auden recognizes as a lie. The full one must be found by the poet for himself.

Nature and the Poet II

Two weeks ago we were discussing a question W. H. Auden put to himself: "Is there going to be a revival of nature poetry, and, if so, how will it differ from nature poetry in the past?" Since then I have been thinking that his question is one which, like a pebble dropped in the water, sends out widening circles. Mr. Auden, quite naturally, was primarily interested in the change which has taken place in man's relationship with Nature and his attitude toward it; he was wondering how the poet can best face up to the fact of his alienation.

The question is of interest not only as it applies to poetry, but to literature as a whole, and beyond that, to modern man's entire adjustment to his world, of which literature is the expression. For it is idle to pretend that the alienation has not occurred. Modern man, at terrible risk to himself, has entered into competition with Nature, and he is obsessed with the dream of conquest. In this mood it has become increasingly difficult for him to profit by her simple lessons, for him to go into the pine woods and listen, like Emerson, for the oracle to speak. The divinity in which he once clothed her has diminished in his eyes.

As one of her creatures, his life is inevitably deeply colored by the relationship in which he stands with her. In every area of it he is affected by his sense of identity, or lack of it, with the natural world. Even his theories of government, his economic concepts and his personal relationships are involved. As much as the poetry he writes, his novels and his treatises bear witness to his attitude. And as he writes them, he would do well to remember that it is not Nature which changes, but himself, in the nature of his relationship.

Aldous Huxley once wrote an essay in which he ventured the opinion that Wordsworth could not have written the kind of nature poetry he did, had his environment been the tropics instead of the Lake Country of England. Nature, in Wordsworth's experience, had no malignant aspects. He did not see her, as Tennyson rather surprisingly could, "red in tooth and claw." He was untouched by the fierce struggle for survival which would have been so much more apparent in a less smiling environment.

Yet the contrast which Huxley had in mind lies at the heart of Nature. Her aspect is both beneficent and malignant. We cannot afford to ignore either aspect, but we must see them as they actually are, in balance. To shut our eyes to one or the other is to invite deception. In that fine book by John Stewart Collis, *The Triumph of the Tree,* he quotes Chekov: "So long as a man likes the splashing of a fish he is a poet. But when he knows that the splashing is nothing but the chase of the weak by the strong, he is a thinker; but when he does not understand what sense there is in the chase, or what use in the equilibrium which results from destruction, he is becoming silly and dull as he was when a child."

This equilibrium, this sense of the balance in Nature, this awareness of ebb and flow, is something which the writer who aims at a true picture of human conduct must keep before him, as much as if he were trying to describe how nature herself operates. Nor does this need apply only to the writer who tells us stories about human beings in their everyday relations with one another. It applies as well to those concepts of government and economics by which our group lives are dominated.

Take, as the simplest example, the ancient conflict between the conservative and the radical instinct. That conflict, in essence, is simply an extension into human affairs of a principle that obtains in the natural world. As an American Indian once put it, new things must have old things in which to grow. Just as destruction and construction, attack and defense, decline and renewal, are balanced in nature, so are conservatism and radicalism balanced in human affairs. Both are necessary adjuncts of one principle, and if we give to one a greater importance than the other, we put the picture out of perspective. The step forward comes out of the interaction. If either is uninhibited, if one is left free to operate without the counterbalancing effect of the other, the result is either dry rot or anarchy.

Actually, all I am trying to say is, that whether he writes what is termed nature poetry or not, the poet cannot write truly without an awareness of Nature, and of her bearing upon his life; and neither can the novelist or the economist or the historian. Her laws underlie all those which man makes for himself, whether they are laws which he applies to the science of government or to any other of the forms of creative effort in which he has tried to express the quality of his relationship to the world of which he is a part.

Justice for Longfellow I

Every year about 10,000 visitors, coming from all parts of the country, and some from abroad, pass through the graceful doorway of the Wadsworth-Longfellow House in this peaceful, pleasant town. This is the house in which Henry Wadsworth Longfellow, perpetual poet laureate of the American folk, lived through his early years. Unlike his birthplace, now a shambling ruin near the waterfront, the old house on Congress Street is carefully maintained by the Maine Historical Society. Except for the years he spent at Bowdoin, this was his home from the time he was a little child until in 1836, at the age of twenty nine, he left Portland to take up residence in Cambridge, where he was to teach modern languages at Harvard, and to become the best-loved poet we have had, and, be it noted, the first American to be honored by a bust in the Poets' Corner of Westminster Abbey. For Longfellow, in his heyday, was read the world over.

No boy could grow up in Portland with Casco Bay, that loveliest of harbors, in view from his bedroom windows, without loving the sea; and the sea was one of Longfellow's strongest and deepest loves. No other American poet's work, not even Whitman's, draws from it so much. When Longfellow lived in Congress Street the handsome old house looked across fields to the waters of the bay; now business buildings block the view. Deering Oaks, to which the poet paid nostalgic tribute, has been preserved, and forms a charming public park. Save for it, the First Parish Church—just down the street from the Longfellow place—a few other old houses, and the many-islanded bay, the face of Portland is of course greatly changed since the boy looked on the "Spanish sailors with bearded lips." Nevertheless, its charm is still pervasive and quickly felt. I had not walked its streets for many years, but I count it among the most delightful cities I know.

So, too, is Longfellow, already recovering some of the esteem of which he had been shorn in sophisticated circles, one of our pleasantest poets, and eminently deserving of the love he prompted. Like all reactions which have their basis in changing taste, the one of which he was the victim went too far. At his infrequent top level he was a true and fine poet by any standards and in any age; his name you may be certain, will never wither on American soil. He shares this centenary year with Whitman, the greater poet, who never captured, as Longfellow did, the hearts of his countrymen. And Whitman, I think, craved more avidly that acclaim than did his modest and only slightly older contemporary.

The blurbs which appear on our book jackets, and which with amiable disingenuousness often mislead the unwary reader, are not commonly regarded as on a par with the tablets from Sinai, but it would be difficult to question the truth of what is printed on the jacket of the Modern Library edition of *The Poems of Longfellow,* a copy of which I dutifully purchased at the reception desk in the Longfellow House. "To him," I read, "can be attributed a major share of what love for poetry great masses of our people cherish." Some of the poems, the blurb goes truthfully on to say, "are part of our heritage, and we read them over and over again with a nostalgia for our youth and a new appreciation of Longfellow's place among the great lyricists of our national literature."

True as the first half of this tribute is—at least for the oldsters among us—it is the second half which I would emphasize. Longfellow may have been too romantic and too insistent a moralist to hold the attention of the decades just behind us, but as a craftsman of excellent ear, of great versatility, as a translator of sure knowledge and uncommon sympathy and understanding, he merits our unreserved respect and admiration. If a finer rendering can be made of what John Livingston Lowes called "the most flawless of all lyrics," the *Wandrers Nachtlied* of Goethe, than in Longfellow's translation, I should like to see it. Like the original, it is perfection; not a syllable can be changed.

A word should be said, platitudinous though it may be, about Longfellow's virtues as a ballad maker. He caught, as few Americans before or after him, the accent and the feeling that informed those nameless and, no doubt, numerous joint authors of some of the most treasured literature in English and in other tongues. All in all, we have every right to be proud of him, and small cause to be condescending. After all, there are few things more worthy of honor and respect than effectively to have moved the hearts and brightened the days of countless men and women, and to have done so with no cheap and maudlin plucking at the heartstrings. I left the house in which he lived and wrote with renewed affection and regard for a writer who rides securely through the passages of time.

Justice for Longfellow II

Response to a recent column on Longfellow has been so warm that, abetted by a return visit to the city of his birth, I am emboldened to make a few additional remarks. People from as far distant as Holland have expressed satisfaction in the fact that room was found here for a few words in his behalf both as a poet and a scholar.

The reasons for Longfellow's decline I have already touched upon. They are so obvious that they need no elaboration here; I would, nevertheless, like to quote in illustration two stanzas from a poem he wrote in the old house on Congress Street, stanzas which by themselves testify to his worth as a poet. The third and concluding stanza, however, explains why a generation which had turned its back on Victorian attitudes would have none of him. In "The Rainy Day," which he wrote in 1841 (the desk at which he wrote it is proudly exhibited to visitors), Longfellow began:

> The day is cold, and dark, and dreary;
> It rains, and the wind is never weary;
> The vine still clings to the mouldering wall,
> But at every gust the dead leaves fall,
> And the day is dark and dreary
>
> My life is cold, and dark, and dreary,
> It rains, and the wind is never weary;
> My thoughts still cling to the mouldering past,
> But the hopes of youth fall thick in the blast,
> And the days are dark and dreary.

Now Longfellow was to write much better poetry than this, but the poem offers one of many similar instances when he could not leave well enough alone. He tacked on a third stanza, of a kind to make the unattuned modern reader retch. For contemporary taste the poem should end with the lines I have just quoted, but he went on to draw the moral:

> Be still, sad heart! and cease repining;
> Behind the clouds is the sun still shining;
> Thy fate is the common fate of all,
> Into each life some rain must fall,
>   Some days must be dark and dreary.

The added lines themselves, as if in protest, limp.

I have at hand here only two anthologies of American poetry: Selden Rodman's excellent little collection, *100 American Poems* and Oscar Williams' *New Pocket Anthology of American Verse.* Mr. Rodman represented Longfellow by one of his best and lesser known poems, "The Jewish Cemetery at Newport," and said justly of him in his introduction that "it was simply his nature to reflect the literary, the picturesque and the kindly; and he did so in a quiet voice that was invariably melodious and occasionally noble." And Mr. Williams, in a collection not notable for its sense of proportion, at least allots eight pages to Longfellow; they are good selections, but not sufficiently representative in a book that runs to more than 600 pages.

In a previous article, I referred to the lamentable condition of Longfellow's birthplace; the neglect into which it fell was due partly to the fact that he lived there only for the first eight months of his life, whereas the house on Congress Street, built by his Wadsworth grandfather in 1785, has been beautifully preserved; its handsome furnishings, with few exceptions, are those used there by the Wadsworth and Longfellow families before the house was acquired by the Maine Historical Society. The birthplace on Fore Street, which for a time after family reverses caused its sale, was divided into tenements and went from bad to worse, will, I have just learned, soon be torn down. The Thomas Laughlin Company, purchasers of the property, with a concern not shown by the city fathers, has announced its intention of erecting a stone marker with a bronze commemorative plaque. Mr. Laurence Dame, a native Portlander who has long pleaded for some such action, informs me he was moved to indignation when he discovered that Mentone, on the Riviera, proudly displays a bust of Longfellow. He had in mind also the fact that customarily, in European cities, the mere stay in a house for a few weeks, of a famous writer, is commemorated by a tablet. And so, in more ways than one, Longfellow is finding again the silver lining that, in his life, as in his writing, he so assiduously looked for.

Green of Nightfall

This department, I fear, will have to keep its sackcloth and ashes in a more convenient place. In the course of some recent remarks on obscurity and the perverse use of words in contemporary poetry, I seem to have gone off the deep end by quoting in support of my protests a line which reads, "Green of nightfall, alive with the clicking bats." I confessed inability to establish a connection between "green" and "nightfall," and my failure to imagine any sense in which bats might be described as "clicking."

By a score of readers who express general sympathy with my reservations about the content and manner of much of contemporary poetry, I stand rebuked, gently and otherwise, for these particular objections. On the matter of the bats, especially, the weight of evidence is overwhelming. What makes my penitence harder to bear is the fact that I fancied myself here to be on definitely safe ground. For several seasons a bat made his home with me in a house I once had in the country; that is, he took up residence in his dormant daylight state behind a storm door on the upper front porch, where he became so much an accepted member of the household that he was known as Michael.

Though I never heard a clicking sound from Michael or from any other bat of my limited acquaintance, I am assured by my correspondents that the adjective is apt. So many of them identify the sound that I must conclude it is simply one that I never chanced to hear. One correspondent has sent me an article by Ernest P. Walker, assistant director of the United States National Zoological Park, Smithsonian Institution, entitled, "Bats Are My Best Friends," which recently appeared in *The Saturday Evening Post.* Mr. Walker remarks of his favorite companions that "when they are at rest or moving about on me, they give a rapid clicking, like the sound we produce by pulling the tongue from the roof of the mouth. This is clearly audible to humans for three or four feet, and when several are on me and giving their notes, it sounds like frying. They also give the clicking note when flying past me. . . ." And that, I guess, is that.

In the matter of "green of nightfall," the supporting evidence ranges from the impressionistic to the scientific. Mr. Carrol Coates, author of the line I quoted, wrote to point out that his poem was concerned with a southern landscape, adding that "in the southern countryside, during summer, the sun sets *after* nightfall. The scattered light reflects the green of the vegetation against the sky, and its color is green.

An explanation in terms of optics comes from Dr. Adolph Posner. "The scotopic vision," he writes, "or vision in the dark, does not discern any colors but only shades of grey. At dusk when the day ends, vision changes to night vision and the colors gradually become extinguished. The first ones to disappear are those at the red end of the spectrum. The blues and greens remain until the last. At the same time there is a shift in brightness from the yellows to the greens, the yellow being the brightest color in the light adapted eye and the green for the dark adapted eye. When night falls, the green is the last color to disappear. Thus, it is entirely within the province of the poet to refer to this observation in the terse and admirable manner in which it is put in the quotation."

I shall have to be warier in my future choice of horrible examples. While Mr. Coates must be granted full absolution, I find it more difficult to accept Mr. Leslie Fiedler's justification of his line, "the noise of your unhinging knees." He asks me to bear in mind the folk metaphor about creaking joints. "Of course," he writes, "one does not really hear the creaking of joints any more than one really sees 'innocence scatter'd on the grass,' but it is a familiar conceit."

I was aware that Mr. Fiedler was mingling the pathetic and the comic in his poem, which I did not quote in full, and I have no objection to such a blending of effects. What is unfortunate, I think, is the choice of the word "noise," presumably selected, partly at least, for rhyme with a preceding line. It is too explosive, and destroys the very effect at which he was aiming by making ludicrous what was meant to be gently comic—an effect which the word "creak" itself would have preserved.

Mr. Fiedler asks why I find it easy to understand "the quite subtle (and beautiful) conceit of innocence scattered on the grass and impossible to grasp this simpler one. He suggests that it may be because of the deliberate mixture of mood to which I have referred, and suggests that one difficulty some people feel in the face of much contemporary verse arises from their expectation that poetry will be always solemn and intense. I trust that I have explained the basis of my objection; it rests not on the charge of inscrutability or impatience with the mixing of seriousness and humor; merely on what is to me a perverse use of words, a charge which can be leveled against much contemporary poetry with as much justice as can the charge of willful obscurity.

The Bleat Generation

To my possibly tone-deaf ears, the group of San Francisco writers who proclaim themselves the "Beat Generation," have, by the omission of a letter, misnamed themselves. It seems to me the proper word is "bleat." It would appear more appropriate as a title than "Howl," the much publicized poem by Allen Ginsberg, and it would not come far amiss as applied to the stories of Jack Kerouac and other representatives of this so-called "renaissance." Bleating is a monotonous sound, and I think that as a sleep-inducer the writings of this group are more effective than the long-recommended prescription of counting silent sheep as they jump over a stile.

Reading their work, what they have said about themselves, and what has been said about them, has been for me a baffling experience. They say that they are, and we are told that they are, searching for a spiritual base from which to confront the world in which they live. Nobody except a dedicated Marxist can take exception to that objective. A great many of us are engaged in a smiliar search. But the thought that must occur to many readers of the San Francisco group is that they pursue their objective in strange and contradictory ways, of which the strangest and most contradictory, in view of what they profess to seek, is their emphasis upon and preoccupation with sensory experience.

In part, but only in part, this preoccupation would seem to stem from their revolt against the academic poets and critics whom they attack. As one who has protested against the overcerebral approach to poetry, I can sympathize with that revolt, but I cannot see, in the poetry they have produced, an effective answer to what they condemn. This spring [1958] the *Chicago Review* devoted a good part of its issue to the presentation of ten San Francisco poets, and I have been unable to find a memorable poem among them.

The poems are prefaced by a brief statement from Jack Kerouac on "The Origins of Joy in Poetry." "Poetry and prose," he announces, "had for a long time fallen into the false hands of the false. These new pure poets confess forth for the sheer joy of confession. They are children. They are also childlike graybeard Homers singing in the street. They sing, they swing." He goes on to say that the poetry now being written in San Francisco should be called street poetry. It has succeeded in getting poetry out of the classroom and into the street, "where it once was." I should like to know where and when.

God knows, plenty of the poetry that has come out of the colleges in recent years does anything but sing, but if any of the San Francisco product does, I don't know the meaning of song. Much of it, incidentally, is read aloud to the accompaniment of jazz. Is it song when Mr. Ginsberg begins—and later ends—a poem in this fashion?:

> Dawn:
> fatigue
> —white sky
> grey concrete houses
> sun rust red—
> coming home to the furnished room
> —nervewracking lovetalk.
> I don't *want* her

The prose of these San Franciscans seems to me no better. Reading Mr. Kerouac's *On the Road* or *The Subterraneans,* I am reminded of nothing so much as an insistent and garrulous barroom drunk, drooling into your ear. The sentences sometimes run to as much as a page and a half, and are formless. Faulkner at times writes sentences as long, but they are built. These are just so much slaver. Yet there are critics who have written about the "rhythms" of this poetry and prose. Who is mad?

The San Franciscans take pot shots at the Ivy League, and I found it interesting, and perhaps illuminating, to see what spokesmen for another segment of the younger generation have to say about Kerouac & Co. There is a new publication called the *Ivy Magazine,* published in New Haven and edited by a board drawn from students at Brown, Columbia, Cornell, Dartmouth, Harvard, Princeton and Yale. Its current issue contains an article about the "Beat Generation," which begins, quite properly, I think, by denying its existence. Its co-authors, E. S. Casey and R. B. Robertson, III, find the "Silent Generation" more realistic, though they think their elders are overanxious to find a descriptive tag which will fit.

Kerouac, they note, has remarked that "beat" stands for "beatific." However that may be, they are careful to point out that "beat" does not mean weariness; "it's the downbeat of Charlie Parker's sax, its the new generation's diet of drugs, sex, and a gutty rock number." As they see it, an earthy hedonism is the Beat Generation's credo. Moreover, it dissociates itself from society and scorns an interest in politics. These spokesmen for the Ivy Leaguers feel kinship with the "Beat Generation" in that they, too, feel a need to find their identity in a world of collectivity, but separate from them in concern "with the international scene, with the mass cultural media of movies and magazines, and with sports." "The Beatist," they say, "seeks spiritual awareness, yet ends with little more than animal sensuality." The Ivy Leaguer "seeks self-consciousness and world-consciousness at once." Both wish to be "undeceived."

P.S. Since the column above was written, the Beats have ceased to attract notice in New York—except in the phony Bohemia of today's Greenwich Village—and have been succeeded as centers of attention by the Beatles, who, whatever opinion adults may have regarding the quality of their singing, have at least the merit of not taking themselves too seriously.

An Age of Prose?

Now and then somebody refers to our time as an age of prose. Nothing, I think, could be further from the truth. There has never been an age, not even the eighteenth century, when poetry faded from men's minds, and I doubt that there ever will be. For poetry is not merely an attitude, a point of view, a belief; it is an ineradicable need, as deeply essential to us, in one form or another, as the air we breathe. It was one of the first expressions of man's spirit; its life in him has been continuous, and if it should ever die it will be because he has died himself. The less of it we have, the less we are alive. Max Eastman once defined its nature by saying what it was unlike: deadness, ennui, sophistication.

There is no better test of the truth of that observation than by taking note of one's own reactions to poetry when the mind is dull and the spirit low. Our response is faint; we find ourselves unreceptive to images, to rhythms which, in a more heightened mood, excite and delight us. That is the basis for the saying that a poet dies young in all of us; children are unconsciously poets because of the intensity of their living.

A correspondent who finds modern poetry not to his taste recently wrote to ask me if I thought it worth the effort to try to understand the poetry being written today. Granted the fact that too much of modern poetry is not worth in what it returns the demands which the poet makes of his reader, the answer must still be Yes. Because along with the poems that are dead at birth, which are perversely private in their conception and development or which are mere mental gymnastics, there are many that richly repay the concentrated attention and the attitude of receptiveness which we need to bring to them.

Robert Frost once inquired, "What do you write a poem for, anyway, except to see it mix with people's lives?" That, of course, is what poetry does when it is true poetry, deeply felt, honestly thought and skillfully communicated. We have, it is true, poets who do not seem to be writing with Frost's purpose in mind. But if poetry is to be effective in our lives, if it is to answer the need we have for it, its capacity to enhance life must come from the reader as well as the poet.

This dual responsibility has been well stated by Adrienne Cecile Rich before the Maryland Historical Society in an address which I have just been reading in the current issue of *The Maryland Historical Magazine*. Miss Rich's subject was "Some Influences of Poetry Upon the Course of History," and in conclusion she asked how much of a force we might expect poetry to be in this difficult moment in the life of man.

There is, she observed, "a certain burden of proof at this point on the poet, a responsibility to keep silent until he has something to say, and then to say it in a manner that justifies his using poetry rather than prose. Outside certain small cliques, few readers will have patience with dull poetry—and when I say 'dull' I am thinking not only of conventionally trite poetry, but of poetry that sets out to be daringly original and surprising in form, but when once unraveled proves to say nothing which can really arouse or stir the reader."

"Poetry," she continued, "ought to bring a new grasp on reality, to act as a prism-glass on the ordinary light of day, showing it in colors which we had not hitherto guessed. If poets today offer this to their readers, then they deserve to be heard by more than their present limited audience. And being heard will give them a greater impetus to speak, and to speak yet more eloquently. So there is also a responsibility on the part of those who care about poetry as readers, to go on reading what is written today, and tomorrow, in expectation of delight and of an intensified view of the world within and without, past and present."

Miss Rich's conception of poetry's influence on history is, I think, a sound one. History is concerned, she points out, with what in the past has excited men, what has moved them to the point of action; it has, fundamentally, to do with "what perennial or passing desires, purposes and needs have made them willing to go to war or to prison, work at apparently hopeless tasks, struggle with one another or with themselves, suffer physical indignity and mental lacerations, lie awake at night, and face the fear of death and the unknown."

And these, Miss Rich observes, are among the things that have been the concern of poetry as well. "The course of history is a sum of what happens to the emotions and perceptions of separate individuals; whether their vision is constricted or wide-ranging, lazy or full of curiosity, easily satisfied with security and comfort or demanding a spiritual richness and challenge, this vision, writ large, will be reflected in the governments they choose, the institutions they create and destroy, the aspirations which form the keystone to their society. It is important for this vision that poetry mix with people's lives; and so long as it does, it will continue to influence human history."

IV

Irritations: Major and Minor

For better or worse, I have a low boiling point. As time marches on, I find an increasing number of things to be angry about. Happily for me, at least, this is counterbalanced by no diminution of the things I enjoy and admire. Indeed, if exasperations multiply, so do pleasures. It seems to me that today, and especially, perhaps, in the United States, we need to feed our angers as much as we need to nourish our loves. I would like, however, to draw a distinction between hate and anger. The first ends always in destruction; the second can be, although it not always is, constructive. True, to be constructive, it must first destroy the thing at which it is directed, and this must be deserving of destruction. And to accomplish its purpose, the anger must be held; it cannot waver or be dropped. Thus, slavery of any kind cannot be abolished and freedom achieved unless the anger it arouses is persistent. Constantly we have flare-ups of anger at manifold evils in our society and in the arts we practice, but they quickly subside and accomplish nothing. From day to day, reading the papers, listening to the radio, or watching TV, we can see these flare-ups bloom and die. We seem to have lost the capacity to hold our anger. We dissolve it with a wisecrack and a laugh, and so the evils multiply and flourish.

Perhaps this is a pretentious prelude to the irritations, large or small, which are set forth in the pages that follow. Not all of them, perhaps, are deserving of a held anger, but some, I think, are. Among these I would list the "publish or perish" issue in education, my impatience with the literature of despair, and with the fallacy that chaos can be understood and dealt with by reproducing it in the arts. There are other issues demanding a held anger that are discussed in other sections of this book, like the plea I make elsewhere for a more balanced realism in our fiction. A few of the irritations included here are trivial, but I have retained them because it amused me to express them, and for that reason, they may be amusing to others.

Soldiers of Fiction

This department is in sharp disagreement with the review of *From the City, From the Plough* which appeared in the New York *Times Book Review* last Sunday. Mr. Liebling wrote a completely unfavorable review of a British war story so good, in my estimation, that it bothers me to think that for honesty, brevity, impact, and balance in its point of view, we on this side of the water have not produced a book to match it. When it was offered here last spring, *From the City, From the Plough* was turned down by fourteen publishers; lest that put ideas into your head, let me remind you that *All Quiet on the Western Front* was refused by twenty-four.

As much as any book which has a claim to attention in its own right can be, Alexander Baron's novel is the *All Quiet* of World War II. It has the same quiet realism, the same human warmth, the same unstudied simplicity. Mr. Baron's chief concern, like Remarque's, was with the ordinary young citizen torn from his environment and set down in the hell of modern war. Like Remarque, he has told his story without the ideological blinders which disfigure a book like Mr. Mailer's *The Naked and the Dead,* or the involved and pretentious analyzing which weaken Mr. Wolfert's *An Act of Love.* In temper, his book is closer to Mr. Shaw's *The Young Lions,* but it has a greater effectiveness because of its unity and economy.

In Mr. Liebling's eyes, which I think must have moved very rapidly over the pages of Mr. Baron's novel, what deprives this book of the right to serious consideration is the fact that the men who make up the Fifth Battalion of the Wessex Regiment are on the whole a pretty decent lot of guys, including even the officers. The illusion from which Mr. Baron suffers, he would have you believe, is one implanted in English fiction by Laurence Sterne, in the persons of Uncle Toby and Corporal Trim, nourished by Tennyson's "Theirs not to reason why," and somewhat broadened by Kipling's observation about single men in barracks. This is just about the shakiest premise on the basis of which a contemporary novel has been judged, but let that pass. It provides Mr. Liebling with the material for a series of wisecracks about the British character.

The unfairness of his attack gives a somewhat reddish tinge to my immediate foreground. He tells you that "among the 600 N.C.O.'s and 'other ranks' of Mr. Baron's Wessex Regiment . . . there is only one truly unworthy person," but he neglects to tell you that of the 600, Mr. Baron has characterized, and for the most part very sketchily, only a score. This one misfit, Mr. Liebling observes, is, "naturally enough," an Irishman. Is the glory hunting, Nazi-bedazzled Major Maddison, in Mr. Liebling's estimation, an admirable character? Just how many thorough-going S.O.B.'s does he normally expect to encounter among twenty-odd men?

He is very much let down because there happen not to be mentioned any cases of battle psychosis in this battalion, which happened to be made up chiefly of stolid country boys who couldn't acquire a complex, much less a psychosis, if their lives depended on it. He is nettled because the battalion turns up only one deserter, and he didn't really mean it. Mr. Liebling was a war correspondent for *The New Yorker;* what troops, I wonder, did he associate with? And, oh yes, the battalion commander was one of those poor softies who happened to have consideration for his men. "He was a good un," was the Old Man. That lets him out.

Holy mackerel, how long is this kind of nonsense going to go on? What kind of sickness has got at the vitals of the writing men of this country? I don't expect Mr. Liebling to understand Mr. V. S. Prichett's remark about this book: "What strikes one is the truth to nature and particularly in these passages which reveal the extraordinary tolerance of ill-assorted men who are lumped together." Nobody can fully understand that kind of tolerance who has not lived as a soldier in the ranks. But in that comment Mr. Prichett has put his finger on one of the prime realities of this book. Its author served in the ranks, for six long years, in Sicily, Southern Italy, and Western Europe. And his book is the most honest and clear-sighted fictional record of men at war that we have had from World War II.

When the writers of this country stop sneering about the kind of guts that knit together the men of Mr. Baron's Fifth Battalion, the kind of guts that justified Mr. Churchill in making his famous observation about so many and so few, we may get to the point where we can resolve the doubt in George Santayana's mind when he said that we would not know whether the Americans were at bottom a people who stood for material or for spiritual values until they had endured the trials of Job.

This is an angry piece, I know. But it does not arise from a merely momentary irritation. It has its roots in a long-existent conviction that American realism is the realism of a spoiled child.

Robert Frost I

A year ago, following the presentation of the 1958 National Book Awards, I relieved my mind about a number of things: the iniquities attendant upon literary prizes, overlong speeches before captive audiences, and the discomfort which ensues when several hundred people make a simultaneous assault upon a couple of tables bearing assorted glassware and bottled goods. But chiefly, I grew hot over one of the most virulent forms of snobbery we have today—which is literary snobbery. Today I am moved to dispute—and hotly—certain statements made by Professor Lionel Trilling at the eighty-fifth birthday dinner in honor of Robert Frost.

Only last week I was writing about those writers who are indubitably American. Frost is pre-eminently of their company. That this is so, Professor Trilling did not deny, yet I suspect that Frost had difficulty in recognizing himself in the mirror which Professor Trilling held up to him, for it was badly cracked.

Professor Trilling admitted an understandable diffidence to which he gave graceful expression, for the professor has a subtle and trained intelligence, plus a gift for lucid exposition. His difficulty was that although—or perhaps I should say because—he is a native New Yorker, he showed little understanding of the United States. That circumstance has not, however, prevented other sons of this city from grasping more fully the meaning of the American experience. Professor Trilling's failure to do so is, indeed, one widely shared by other American intellectuals.

Before stating the bases for his diffidence, Professor Trilling made that obeisance to "myth" which is obligatory for critics in his camp, and hastily hunted out a symbol or two—critical occupations without which some of our quarterlies could not go to press. It was a trifle unfortunate, I think, in view of Frost's shock of white hair, that the professor should have identified the poet with the Bald Eagle—but let that pass.

Besides the natural diffidence which any speaker would have felt upon this occasion, Professor Trilling named several others. He could not help knowing, he said, that "the manifest America of Robert Frost's poems is not the America that has its place in my own mind"—Frost's manifest America being rural, and his urban. Then, he said, he had for a long time been alienated from Frost's work "by what I saw in it that either itself seemed to denigrate the work of the critical intellect" (an urban faculty, in the professor's estimation) "or that gave its admirers the ground for making the denigration."

Presently Professor Trilling made it clear that *his* Frost "is not the Frost I seem to perceive existing in the minds of so many of his admirers. He is not the Frost that confounds the characteristically modern practice of poetry by his notable democratic simplicity of utterance: on the contrary. He is not the Frost who controverts the bitter modern astonishment at the nature of human life: the opposite is so. He is not the Frost who reassures us by his affirmation of old virtues, simplicities, pieties, and ways of feeling: anything but."

Professor Trilling found his key to the understanding of his Frost in D. H. Lawrence's criticism of American literature; if he had re-read, or read, Emerson instead, he might have lost *his* Frost and discovered the one he turns his back on, for a goodly part of Frost the man and Frost the poet is rooted, deeply rooted, in Emerson, who was his intellectual and spiritual godfather. Lawrence had some perceptive things to say about American writers, but he failed in ultimate understanding of them, and of the American experience.

Professor Trilling confessed that he thinks of Frost as a "terrifying" poet, and that "the universe he conceives is a terrifying universe." Holy mackerel! Frost simply sees the universe as it is and accepts it. He isn't terrified by what he sees, and neither should we be. He takes it in his stride, which is one reason why he is in there pitching at eighty-five; he has a private air-conditioning system denied to most of his younger contemporaries—and, as I said before, he got it from Emerson.

Come out of the Freudian wood, Professor Trilling, and face the facts of life. Don't take Lawrence so seriously; he was a gifted but terribly confused man, as you and most of us at this present moment, are. All this country needs is to recapture its earlier vision. One of the silliest remarks ever made about the American experience came from one of the editors of your favorite magazine, the *Partisan*

Review. Mr. William Phillips solemnly observed that American literature has played hide-and-seek with American experience for lack of "an image, or cluster of images, of the national experience available to literature." No such lack exists, and both of you should reread one of the great American poems. It is by Robert Frost, and it is called "The Gift Outright."

Robert Frost II

The most painstaking and the most interesting interviews with literary figures which we have had in recent years are those that appear regularly in that good quarterly, *The Paris Review*. Some of them have been notable, and I would include among their number Richard Poirier's interview with Robert Frost. I add in passing that these talks are tape recorded, so that what you get is the actual speech of both the interviewer and his victim.

I use the word "victim" advisedly—because, having sat on both ends of that seesaw, I am well acquainted with the pitfalls by which it is beset. Some victims shy at the sight of paper and pencil (the tape recorder seems more impersonal); some are too reticent and others too voluble; some interviewers have excellent short memories, and some not. At best, it's a chancy business, but the method *The Paris Review* has been using provides as full a guarantee of faithful reporting as one can reasonably expect.

There should be more than ordinary interest in the Frost interview because within very recent years a remarkable thing has happened to his reputation. With the exception of Hemingway, he has become the most widely publicized American writer. The fact is the more interesting in view of the circumstances that this did not occur until Frost had passed the age of eighty. Most famous men achieve the spotlight early. You can make an impressive list, beginning, perhaps, with Alexander the Great, and including such names as that of the "upstart crow," Shakespeare, his predecessor Marlowe, numerous great musicians and composers, Byron, Burns, Keats, and Shelley, the younger William Pitt, Alexander Hamilton, Thomas Jefferson, Napoleon. In our own time we have Winston Churchill, Rupert Brooke, Lawrence of Arabia, Bernard Shaw, Stephen Crane, T. S. Eliot, Scott Fitzgerald, and Thomas Wolfe, Sinclair Lewis, and Dylan Thomas. That roster is by no means complete, but it will serve.

Frost has had to wait for the kind of recognition he is now receiving. He was forty before he received recognition as a poet, which is much later than customary. After that his growth in reputation was gradual, but assured. Now, within the span of a few years, his fame has become world-wide. Almost overnight he has acquired the stature of a sage and a national symbol.

This is the man who, not so long ago, was condescended to by critics who could see in him only an authentic, but restrictedly regional quality. It was some belated awareness of the insufficiency of such appraisals that prompted Lionel Trilling to make his ill-fated speech at Frost's eighty-fifth birthday dinner. I do not wish to revive the heat of an old controversy in which I was involved, but there are a few items in the record that I would like to put straight. After the numerous letters pro and con which followed this column's attack upon Mr. Trilling's speech, he paraded his hurt feelings in the summer, 1959, issue of *The Partisan Review,* which reprinted, along with his reaction to the controversy, the text of his address. I did not then reply, but I do so now.

It so happens that *The Paris Review* touches upon that controversy. I was particularly interested to note that when the interviewer asked Frost, "Do you think it was to correct the public assumption that your poetry is represented by the most-anthologized pieces such as 'Birches' that Lionel Trilling in his speech . . . emphasized poems of a darker mood?" Frost replied: "I don't know—I might run my eye over my book after Trilling, and wonder why he hadn't seen it sooner: there's plenty to be dark about, you know. It's full of darkness."

Of course it is, and all I tried to say was that Frost, however terrifying Mr. Trilling may have found some of the poems, was not afraid to go home in the dark, and that it was neither applicable nor necessary to call in D. H. Lawrence to understand him. Frost said that so far as Lawrence's application to him was concerned, he'd be "puzzled, oh, utterly at sea." And when Mr. Poirier asked him, "Did you feel better about his [Trilling's] talk when you read his substantiation of it in *The Partisan Review,*" Frost replied, "I read his *defense* of it. Very clever, very—very interesting. Admired him. He's a very—intellectual man."

Trilling and Frost represent two very different types of mind. The first is completely urban, divorced from the natural phenomena which fascinate Frost and control his thinking; his is what, for want of a better term, I characterize as the country mind or—more fully —man in the state of nature from which, too often and too much, he has been separated. The American Indian lived in complete harmony with his natural environment, and it is this capacity that most of us have lost, so that now we permit the physicists and others who accept that misleading phrase, "the conquest of nature," to frighten the daylights out of us.

Of course Frost is a tragic poet. No thinking man can come to maturity without becoming aware of how bitter is the world into which he was born. What matters is what we do with that knowledge. If we make a courageous acceptance of it, as Frost has done, then we speak to all men, as he is doing now.

P.S. The publication last year of Lawrence Thompson's *Selected Letters of Robert Frost* adds greatly to our understanding of Frost the man, as well as the poet. His was an extraordinarily complex personality, of which his letters give abundant evidence. Like the greatest of men, he could be petty, and the occasional exhibitions of that fault, in some of the letters he wrote, make embarrassing reading for his admirers. One must always remember that he had endured much: a long wait for recognition that came first in a country other than his own; a succession of family tragedies which would have broken a frailer spirit; the misunderstanding, even after recognition, of the true nature of his poetry. He was loath to reveal himself, and kept a mask always at hand; even in his work, one must always read between the lines. He was, in a word, secretive. He had deep-seated fears, though he offered to the world an image of complete self-reliance. Although I had numerous long talks with him, I could not describe myself as an intimate friend, and I was startled once when he said, in a context I cannot recall, "You know, I have been a very ruthless man." So he had been, as all artists are. His integrity of purpose was unshakeable, and whatever his faults and weaknesses, I shall continue to regard him as a great and admirable man, as well as a great poet.

Creative Writing

Certain subjects are worth returning to, and I think today's topic is one. Several years ago I expressed impatience with the term "creative writing" in its accepted application. When used, it signifies the writing of either fiction, drama or poetry. All other forms of literary composition are excluded. The limitation so imposed is both invidious and invalid, and the constant, increasing use of the term to describe college courses in writing, not to speak of the part it plays in literary discussion, is most unfortunate. I have been unable to discover when the term first came into currency. I cannot remember having seen or heard it while I was in college; courses in writing then were simply courses in composition, though much of the work done in them came within the present meaning of the term. I would be most grateful to anyone who can shed any light on its origin.

To create means simply to bring into being, to cause to exist. Where and how and when did "creative writing" acquire the aura which now surrounds it? Though I believe that in great poetry our use of words reaches the highest level of which that form of communication is capable, although I believe that great fiction, beyond entertaining us, can add to our understanding of life, I think there are other forms of writing which demand as much artistry, which are as fully creative in the true sense of the word. As a matter of fact, when we use that adjective, applying it either to a piece of work or a person, we are suggesting a quality that we cannot clearly define. A man may "create" a building, a painting, or a book in the literal sense of the word, yet fail completely to achieve the quality that we try to suggest by the adjective "creative."

Perhaps we are confused by the fact that certain forms of writing—biography and history, for example—can without benefit of art fulfill their primary purpose, which, like that of a news story, is simply to inform, just as the primary purpose of a building is to provide shelter and a desired arrangement of space. But fiction without art, if it is only that of keeping the reader interested in what is to happen next, serves no purpose whatever, so far as the reader is concerned. And a pretty good poem, as someone long ago observed, is like a pretty good egg.

Merely because the event described in a history actually occurred, while the scene pictured in a novel may be imaginary, need not mean that the one is less an act of creation than the other. What matters in either case is that the scene be brought to life, that we read it with the sense of being present, that by the medium of art, we are enabled to see what happened, and to feel its significance. In the same way, merely because the subject of a biography once existed, whereas the character in a novel may be, as he usually is not, completely the product of the author's imagination, need not mean that the one is less an act of creation than the other.

The great essayists, too, may have the quality that we try to suggest by the word "creative." If they spark our minds, if they lead us into fresh paths of thought, have they not performed a creative act? Is Montaigne or Emerson or Thoreau less a "creative" writer than Dickens or Proust or Hemingway? Only if we use the term in the narrow sense in which it is commonly applied. A great writer is creative in the truest sense regardless of the literary form in which he works. So far as literature is concerned, it seems to me that the creative act is simply one of power in the use of words, as in sculpture it is power in the use of forms, and in painting, in the use of color as well. In music, it is power in the use of sounds.

Whenever that power is present, whatever the literary form, whatever the field of art, we have a creative act. That is why I think the present emphasis on particular literary forms in college writing courses is regrettable. We need a return to fundamentals without regard to the form to which they are applied. Our writing courses, it seems to me, are too much concerned with the techniques of fiction, and with critical theories regarding the function and nature of poetry. If these matters are pressed upon a young writer too early, before he has found his own form of expression, they may make him overly self-conscious, and cause him to adopt attitudes foreign to his own temperament and aptitudes.

In spite of recurrent prophecies about the impending doom of the novel, it remains the preferred form for those who aim at "creative writing." Yet much of what is produced is no more creative than the description of goods in a Sears, Roebuck catalogue, or a jumbled telling of last night's dream. The dull documentation of many overlong novels is a contradiction of the magic of which words are capable. If the novel dies, it will not be because it is an outworn form; it will die because of what goes into it.

Publish or Perish I

It's wonderful to have so soon something else to be angry about. Last week, it was the current avant-garde; today, it is the growing pressure on college teachers to publish or be academically damned. The small explosion you are about to hear was touched off by a news story telling how Woodrow Wilson's grandson, Woodrow Wilson Sayre, an assistant professor of philosophy at Tufts University, faces possible dismissal because he has not written enough. "You have been effective in the classroom," he was informed by Dean Charles E. Stearns; but, the dean added, "The promise of scholarly contribution has not materialized."

I had long been under the delusion that to be effective in the classroom was the finest contribution a teacher could make, whether in the primary grades, high school, undergraduate courses, or graduate seminars. If Mr. Sayre can interest Tufts freshmen or seniors in the differences between Anaxagoras and Immanuel Kant, or between Spinoza and William James, and open up a little for his students the life of the mind, Tufts or any other university should be happy to have him on its faculty, even if he were unable to write a single page anyone would care to read. (As it happens, he published only last month an exciting account of an expedition in the Himalayas, *Four Against Everest.*)

It has been hard enough to put up with the demand that every college teacher seeking advancement must have his Ph.D. union card, but this insistence on his writing a lot of contentious pieces, dusted over with footnotes, that only half a dozen other men in his particular field will give more than a glance, seems to me to set a new mark in absurdity. When I was giving thought to an academic career (I did college teaching for two years), I balked at the Ph.D. discipline because I felt I had better things to do with my time than hunt down the conjunctions in Chaucer, whom it gave me much pleasure to read for other purposes. I know that the Ph.D. ordeal has its merits just as any exacting work has, and I know that now and then a Ph.D. thesis is an interesting piece of literature. But I was unwilling to pay the price (three years are a lot in a young man's life); partly, perhaps, because journalism promised more exciting, at least more varied, vistas.

One of my examiners for an A.B. with honors in English was George Lyman Kittredge, the leading Shakespearean scholar of his day, and he, like several other distinguished members of that great Harvard faculty, had no more than his bachelor's degree.

All these men were remarkable teachers as well as scholars. Teaching was their primary function, and they gave it of their best, even though the cost was high in what the work with students took from their writing—and all were good writers.

I know that a university has two functions: training of the young and enlargement of knowledge. There must be unending research if the frontiers of knowledge are to be pushed still farther back, and teachers must be given time for it if they have the equipment and the urge for such work. But what does it matter if young Professor Thinkum cares more about putting bees in the bonnets of the youths who sit under him than he does about reviving the reputation of some writer who is better off under the dust that has deservedly been settling on him for a century or two? Which is the greater task —to open young minds to the marvel of chemistry, or to discover a new ethyl compound? Both are highly useful functions, but it is difficult to say one is more important than the other. If I were obliged to make a choice between the two, I would plump for the first, because if that function is not accomplished, man might as well climb back into the trees, or keep to his cave. We have too many chemicals as it is, and some of them are not doing the world much good, as Miss Rachel Carson recently reminded us.

In fact, we might be a lot better off if some philosophic and economic theories had never been spun. I can't see that Nietzsche did much for the world except help to bring on two devastating wars, and if Marx had never written *Das Kapital* we might well have been saved some of our contemporary headaches. I'll go even farther. Man knows so much he can hardly trust himself with some of that knowledge, for fear of using it on himself. "Know thyself," said the old Greek, but man doesn't know himself yet, and often acts as if he had completely forgotten what little he has learned.

There is no greater profession than teaching, and the best teachers should, in all common sense, be the highest paid workers in the world. One Kittredge on a campus, one Robert Frost, is worth half the contents of the college library. When will college administrators realize that it doesn't matter whether men like Mr. Sayre contribute papers on the fallacies in Hegel or the use of alliteration in Shakespeare, if they can kindle a small flame in the minds of a new generation? This is what counts. Teach the young to use the words we already have—and there are far too many of those.

Publish or Perish II

Because the letters resulting from this column's discussion on April 19 of the "publish or perish" issue in college teaching have been so numerous, so interesting, and sometimes so provocative, they are the subject of today's remarks. At least half the letters thus far received are from men and women working in the academic field.

A large majority supports the views I advanced. For those readers who did not see the April 19 column, I restate them briefly.

They first of all held that if a teacher is effective in the classroom, if he is capable of interesting his students in his subject and of arousing in them an enthusiasm for the life of the mind, it should not matter a hoot, so far as his advancement goes, whether he contributes anything to the enlargement of knowledge in his field. Good teachers are among the most valuable members of any society, and great ones are blessings from God. Any man or woman who has had the good fortune to sit under a great teacher will count him or her one of the major and perhaps decisive influences encountered in life.

I was at pains to say that every university has a twofold purpose: to inform and stimulate the young, and to widen the boundaries of man's knowledge. The teacher who can do both—and there have been many such—is of course the more valuable thereby, but the current insistence that the gifted teacher, who has neither the urge nor the capacity for original contributions in his field, must nevertheless write about it, is pure stupidity. Such insistence on the part of college administrators results in a lot of verbal hogwash, and the academic journals are full of it.

But what I want most to do this morning is to answer several correspondents who consider me an ignoramus because of certain remarks I made about Nietzsche and Marx. I said of the first that I didn't think he had done much for the world except help to bring on two disastrous wars. I stand by that statement. It is perfectly true that certain of his views were magnified and distorted by the German thinking that has twice endangered the Western world—and conceivably may do so again—but the seeds of destruction were implicit in Nietzsche's obsession with the will to power, with the concept of a superior race who must achieve that power. He fed the German neurosis with the nourishment it wanted, and Hitler was his blood descendant. These attackers write as if I had never read a page of philosophy, but I had the good fortune to study under George Herbert Palmer and George Santayana, in a time when American education had fewer weaknesses than it has today.

And Marx, of whom I said that if he had not written we might have been spared some of our contemporary headaches? Of course he had a powerful mind, plus great energy and persistence, but it was also an embittered mind. He couldn't have survived and functioned if it hadn't been for his friend and benefactor, Engels. He saw his children die as a result of the bitter poverty in which he lived for so many years. In the century since *Das Kapital* was published, we have seen some of his most basic assumptions disproved. Was his brand of socialism first attempted, as he had predicted, in a highly industrialized country? Where, in the Soviet Union, are the signs of that "classless society" of which he so confidently dreamed? Where is privilege more strongly enthroned? And what of that "withering away" of the State toward which he looked with equal confidence? The man is a discredited thinker. I grant him this much honor: that he was one of the first to perceive and protest against the injustices created by the industrial revolution, but his panacea was for the birds.

As time goes on, I become more and more convinced that many so-called literate people cannot read. Either they read too fast, or they allow their preconceived ideas to come between them and the print. This failure to take in what is read has come under my observation so often during the conduct of this column that it disturbs and almost frightens me. I do not think I write unclearly, but to judge from some communications I have received, I must write a kind of pidgin English.

Here is a correspondent, for example, who deduces from my expressed impatience with much academic writing that I assume "specialized scholarship is superfluous, and in some way degrading"! The letter from which I quote also arrives at the conclusion that I assume "one can have something to teach without having something to learn." Dear God! Once again I offer the proposal that we give up the words so many of us cannot use or understand, and fall back on the sign language of the American Plains Indian. We might then understand one another a little better.

Finally, there was one letter in which I am once more accused of anti-intellectualism. If that means my rejection of half-baked literary dogmas, pretentious and cryptic analyses, and slavish adherence to the mode of the moment, I accept the accusation happily. But if it means uninterest in or antagonism toward the life of the mind, I say it's spinach and to hell with it.

"Mere Journalism"

Today this is an odds-and-ends column, devoted to sundry matters on each of which I have a few words to say, although none of these topics seems to demand more extended comment. On second thought, one exception: it would be possible to write not only a column, but a full-fledged essay or even a book on the relationship, or as some critics would have it, the lack of one, between journalism and literature. I am provoked to say something now, however briefly, because I am so frequently annoyed by condescending references to "mere journalism"—as if no true writer would soil his hands or his reputation by indulging in such a low form of composition.

What I have to say about it could not be better prefaced than by quoting once more Ezra Pound's aphorism, "Literature is news that stays news." "News" is one of those words I like to think of as wide. There are many useful but narrow words; their application is strictly confined. We speak of "spot news" but we have no precise term for the kind of news that Ezra Pound had in mind, for "literature" itself is too wide a word to denote what sort of tidings were communicated when Shakespeare wrote *King Lear* or Keats the "Ode on a Grecian Urn," Tolstoy his *War and Peace,* or Proust his *Remembrance of Things Past.* Yet some kind of news they unquestionably were, or we would not still be reading them, as we constantly do, with the sense of having discovered in them something timeless yet new.

Actually, it is not this aspect of the distinctions that can be made between journalism and literature that concerns me. What I have in mind is the senseless derogation implied by the phrase "mere journalism." The novel, still, after two centuries, one of the most vital forms of literature, has its roots in "mere journalism"—in such writers as Defoe, Addison, and Steele, all primarily journalists, although even the last two wrote some fiction, if we use that word in its wider sense. Is not any social novelist, from Fielding down, primarily a reporter, even such subtle ones as Proust and Henry James?—although I grant you that either of them would no doubt soon have been fired by any city editor in his senses.

True, much contemporary reporting is crude, shallow, lacking in distinction of any kind; much reporting always was. Ask yourself what gives good reporting its distinction, apart from adherence to truth and freshness of phrase. Is it not the choice of significant detail —and is not that one of the bases of good art? And now for those minor issues.

They had to do with the making and distribution of books—their packaging, for example. This column is proud to claim that it had some part in the reform of the "Jiffy-bag," which can now be opened without depositing a heap of paper garbage in your lap. Most publishers, thank God, in mailing books, now use these improved containers, thereby diminishing the use of profanity (on my part at least), which had previously been reaching a new high. But there are still publishers who encase their books in such a manner that the best safe-blowing techniques are needed to extract the contents.

Next, although sets of books, due to the space limitations under which most of us now live, are less popular than they were, some of us still acquire them. Often they bear labels pasted on the spine. When painters redecorate an apartment, they delight in scuffing off as many of these as possible. Now, once upon a time, publishers of sets bearing these labels provided extra labels. This thoughtful practice seems to have ceased, and so you find yourself faced by a shelf of faceless, untitled volumes.

Then the matter of advertising in books. Older readers will recall the days when it was common practice for publishers to insert several pages at the end of a book in which other titles of theirs were described. If you have some relics of that period in your library, you will sometimes find these pages have a certain historical interest, as all advertising of another era has. The book publishers, mind you, being more considerate people than TV producers and magazine publishers, had the decency to put their advertising at the *end* of the book. Some thought might be given to the revival of this practice. But one thing they should certainly do—and that is to give the date of every edition of a book they publish. Its frequent omission is the subject of a letter I recently had from Thomas O. Mabbott, the authority on Poe, who complains that the absence of dates is often a serious inconvenience to scholars.

One more issue: the illustration of new fiction was once as common as the inclusion of advertising; now it is confined to special editions, or to such a series as the one distributed to members of the Limited Editions Club. Think, considering the kind of people who now often creep between the covers of our novels, what scope a revival of this practice would offer for the talents of a Charles Addams!

"Timely" Books

In an odds-and-ends column for the issue of July 5, I spoke briefly about the differences between journalism and literature, mentioning, among other matters, my impatience with that condescending phrase, "mere journalism." There is, of course, a form of writing that can properly be so described. But even when the phrase is justifiable, it carries with it more than a suggestion that journalism is to literature, let us say, what an ungifted child's drawing is to an etching by Rembrandt, whereas it is easily demonstrable that journalism on a high level is an art which can evince consummate skill. In any case, the general topic is, as I remarked before, one that could bear extensive treatment. Today I propose to pursue the subject a little further.

One of the most striking phenomena of contemporary writing and publishing is the snowballing growth of journalism in the content and style of books. It is, of course, unprecedented only in its volume and its universality of subject. We had journalism long before we had newspapers. If there was none in Homer, there was a great deal in the comedies of Aristophanes. Although the weekly or daily journal was yet to come, there was much of it in the Elizabethan age, and as we all know, the English novel took its rise in the eighteenth century from journals like *The Spectator* and *The Tatler*. Today's manifestations are of a different kind. Religion in the seventeenth and eighteenth centuries was embodied in endless volumes of sermons; today religion is a journalistic topic, as much as political conventions. Whereas the novel was fathered by journalism, it is now being devoured by its parent, and textbooks aside, the greater part of nonfiction is currently journalistic in aim and content.

On the best-seller list on page eight, of the ten fiction titles, five I would describe as essentially journalistic: *Armageddon, Convention, Candy, The Group and The 480*. Of the ten nonfiction titles all but one, Hemingway's. *A Moveable Feast,* seem to me to belong in that category. In the case of two of the fiction titles, the basis on which I call them journalistic may not be sufficiently obvious; I do so because they are both primarily reports on the state of contemporary sexual mores, one of them candidly comic, the other more pretentiously serious. As for the nonfiction, although five in addition to the Hemingway book are ostensibly biography or autobiography, these five all contain distinct journalistic elements.

Furthermore, if one takes note of the new books reviewed or advertised in this issue, half will be found to fit the same pattern, and this, I think, would prove to be true almost any week during recent years. My guess is that the increasing dominance of the journalistic in contemporary writing (apart from the preoccupations of the avant-garde) is most marked in American publishing, although this is an impression I cannot factually substantiate. It is an impression, however, which can be supported by the fact that reporting has long been one of the great American skills. It would be indeed surprising if that inclination and capacity did not make themselves evident in a period when the arts of communication have been developed to an unprecedented pitch.

There is obviously loss here as well as gain, and more, perhaps, of the first than of the second. No generation of men was ever more assiduous than our own in the pursuit and the collection of facts—so much so that we are increasingly overwhelmed by them. True, some of those who pursue and collect them also make an effort to understand their significance, but their digestion lags far behind their their accumulation. The literature of reflection plays an increasingly smaller part in our writing. Just as the more we travel on the magic carpets of our time, the less we see, so the more knowledge we acquire, the less we understand.

The tide in this direction seems irresistible, and it is hard to believe that it will slacken. All the new forms of communication, with which books must compete, tend to work against its reversal. At the present rate of acceleration, perhaps the hour approaches when literature will have become indistinguishable from journalism. This, in spite of the important uses to which journalism can be put, I do not wish to believe, nor do I think I must. If such a transformation were to take place, it would spell the end of man's development as a sentient and rational being. He would have made himself over in the image not of the God with whom he once tried to merge himself, but of those giant computers into which he now feeds his latest accumulation of facts, and upon whose reaction to them he increasingly pins his faith.

He could never hope for another Shakespeare, another Dostoevski or Tolstoy, another Keats, not even another T.S. Eliot. (Was not "The Waste Land," one of the literary milestones of our century, slightly overcast by the lengthening shadow of journalism?) But how can man let this happen? Surely his sense of self-preservation, if nothing else, will save him.

P.S. I have elsewhere singled out *The Ambassador*, by Morris L. West, as a novel with an outer theme drawn from the news of the day, whose real force, however, derives from its concern with the conflict within a man. The "timely" novel falls short of significance only when it is fictional journalism and nothing more.

What to Affirm?

Maybe this piece shouldn't be written just yet; it is prompted by angry reactions; all the same, I would not feel impelled to say what I want to say if what irritates me did not run counter to certain deep convictions. I am fed up with literary writing that bears no relation to life. I have read or heard too often that our young writers are in a terrible plight because there are no values left, because life presents itself to them as meaningless. I am fed up with talk about generations, younger or older; we are all in this together, as the generations have been since the beginning of time. Ours is a difficult period whether you were born in the last century, or at its turn, like the so-called Lost Generation, or two decades later, like the writers with whom Mr. John Aldridge is primarily concerned in *After the Lost Generation.*

There are many perceptive observations in Mr. Aldridge's book, as Robert Gorham Davis indicated in his excellent review last Sunday, and its examination of our postwar novelists was a job worth doing. But there is, it seems to me, a deep confusion at the bottom of Mr. Aldridge's report. Some of that confusion was suggested by Mr. Davis: too much reliance on merely literary evidence, as offered by current fiction, regarding the possibilities of life, even in our bedeviled time; a muddled attitude toward what values are possible, and which can be shared by writer and reader.

It is true, I think, that as Mr. Davis remarked, "What Aldridge, and some of those he speaks for, seem to resist, both in thinking and in literary form, is an adequate reflection of the complexities and diversities of American democratic experience. There is a desire to make 'value' a simple entity which one does or does not have, and not something constantly and variously being manifested by what men choose, create, maintain and fight for." As D.W. Brogan observed several years ago in *The American Character,* the fundamental weakness of American literary realism has been its failure to provide "a picture and standard of the modern world that neither crushed energy and optimism nor was so sugar-coated and irrelevant as to drive the young off in angry derision."

As I have maintained before, part of our literary pessimism stems from the fact that we are a badly spoiled people. Some of it too—more, perhaps, than we have made allowance for—can be laid at the door of American advertising. Future civilizations, if the data of its historians were confined to that token of our ingenuity, might be led to the conclusion that we lived in the best of all possible worlds. Is it unreasonable to suppose that some of our literary snarling can be traced to a natural reaction against the impossibly happy picture of American life which is from day to day conjured up in the text and pictures of which the most widely read American literature is composed?

But are Mr. Aldridge's young novelists as deprived of values as he would have us believe they are? No matter how shaken their certainties, they must know, if they are honest with themselves, that most men try to live so they can respect themselves. They must be aware, no matter how loose their moorings, that there is conflict within them, as there is in every man. Every human being is conscious of the choice between good and evil both in himself and in others. How then can one say that there is no basis for affirmation?

Mr. Aldridge, picturing the plight of the young novelist today, sees him at the mercy of three courses: he can retreat into a private world, he can report the world about him without committing himself to an attitude, or he can choose themes which command attention because of their capacity to shock. The young writer, he maintains, is faced with the unavoidable fact that "the only hope for a successful dramatic effect lies today in the depiction of the grotesque and abnormal; for it is there and there only that the tragic situation of modern life exists."

To say that, it seems to me, is to make a complete misreading of life. Mr. Aldridge protests that "the mediocre and the undaring, the business man who goes unswervingly to business, the family man who lives out his days in domestic mediocrity, are unpresentable in dramatic terms. Their adjustment to life is made at the expense of no conflict. Their happiness has no consequences . . . If the writer sets out to depict them, he finds himself poverty-stricken in events and symbols." To say that is to close one's eyes to life, and to cast out as worthless some of the best fiction that has been written. Drama is present in the most unspectacular of lives, if the novelist, or the dramatist, has eyes to see it. Wasn't there a play called *Death of a Salesman* and a novel called *Babbitt?*

Let me repeat again those wise words of William Faulkner, in accepting the Nobel Prize for Literature: "the young man or woman writing today has forgotten the problems of the human heart in conflict with itself which alone can make good writing, because only that is worth writing about, worth the agony and the sweat. He must," said Faulkner, "leave no room in his workshop for anything but the old verities and truths of the heart, the old universal truths lacking which any story is ephemeral and doomed—love and honor and pity and pride and compassion and sacrifice."

P.S. A word more. Too many of our novelists are throwing in the towel. That is why we have the non-novel. That is why Samuel Beckett's faceless characters wait for Godot instead of hitching up their britches. They grovel in the mud; they will not lift their eyes to the stars. Life is struggle, and the man who will not fight in behalf of human aspiration betrays the long upward climb of his species.

What Is an Intellectual?

Increasingly, I am disturbed by our current fuzziness in the use of words. The number that float in a sea of vagueness constantly increases. First, perhaps, we became aware of what was happening to certain words with a political content or connotation—words like "democracy," "liberal," and "conservative." Their meaning came to depend on who used them. Today, however, I have particularly in mind a word which, it seems to me, has become just as blurred as these. The word is "intellectual," used as a noun denoting a certain type of person. Much of the time it is used in a derogatory sense, and is frequently applied in a way that can lead only to mental confusion. Now and then, I fear, I have so used it myself.

Two weeks ago, in his interesting review of *Stories From The New Yorker,* Arthur Mizener observed that "intellectuals can hardly believe a story in a magazine with *The New Yorker*'s circulation is good. Almost by definition a good story is for them one that has been rejected by a big magazine and has then appeared in a little one." No statement could more aptly illustrate what I have in mind. Its effect is to define an intellectual as a mental snob, as a person with so little discrimination as to assume, let us say, that because a book has wide appeal and a large sale, it must be low-grade literature. We all know that certain people assume such an attitude, but we should also bear in mind that they are not necessarily intellectuals. Certainly they are mental snobs, and either they are mentally dishonest or lacking in intelligence.

By a subtle osmosis, we have come to think of an intellectual as someone who admires and enjoys the work, let us say, of Joyce or

Proust, and who dismisses a novelist like the late John Marquand as merely a slick writer. He is someone who reads the quarterlies, and who might feel embarrassed if one found him turning the pages of *Reader's Digest.* He is someone who ignores the potentials of mass communication and sees only its current evils. He has acquired other characteristics, but all of them, taken together, do not define an intellectual; what they define is a certain type of intellectual.

Many years ago, on my first visit to Paris, I met an eminent French philosopher who surprised me by saying that he was a more or less regular reader of *The Saturday Evening Post.* I asked him why. "Because," he said, "I believe it keeps me in touch with what the great mass of Americans are thinking and feeling." There, it seems to me, you have, in concrete form, one of the basic factors in making of a true intellectual. His interest in *The Post* was one indication of an inquiring, searching mind.

My desk dictionary (*Webster's New World*) defines an intellectual as "a person with intellectual interests or tastes," "a person who does intellectual work," "a member of the intelligentsia." For the purposes of our discussion, none of these except the first is of any possible help. I found the *Shorter Oxford* even less helpful: "an intellectual being; a person having superior powers of intellect."

Probably no more specific definition than the first I quoted is possible. One might vary the wording to read, "a person greatly interested in mental concepts, or the things of the mind," but I am doubtful whether anything would thereby be gained. In any case, what I am primarily concerned with here is our current use of the word. We are using it now as if its application depended chiefly on a person's reading interests, and on his reaction to various kinds of entertainment. This, I contend, is a wholly false interpretation of the word. For example, it would be absurd to contend that a physicist or a mathematician is not an intellectual. His central concern is with mental concepts. Yet, at home as he may be in the mental stratosphere, his reading habits may be, in the light of our current use of the word "intellectual," deplorable. Not all Justices of the Supreme Court have the mental range of the late Justice Holmes, yet if they are really qualified to sit on that bench, whether or not their off-duty reading is confined to whodunits, they are, because their interest and work lie in the realm of the mind, intellectuals.

When we use the word, it seems to me, we need to make clear what type of intellectual we have in mind. It needs to be preceded by an adjective, or else we must find other and sharper generic terms.

And there are further considerations. My desk dictionary, at the end of its definitions of the adjective "intellectual," gives "intelligent" as a synonym. Actually, an intellectual, whether by dictionary definition or by current popular usage, can be beyond those mental concepts with which he is primarily concerned, a very unintelligent person. Those two words are not truly synonymous. Who has not known a non-intellectual, even an illiterate, perhaps, to whom the word "intelligent" could be unhesitatingly applied? Even our literary intellectuals like to write about peasant wisdom. These innocent speakers of profound truths are always cropping up in their novels.

Words are at once powerful and inadequate. Also, they are the most insidious things of man's creation. Our use of them affects our attitudes, and we need constantly to be on guard as to the sense in which we employ them.

Expressing One's Time

There is a canon of contemporary criticism, wearisome in its repetition, often blind in its application, contemptible in its knuckling down to conformity, and in its quality of cant; it insists that a work of art, to be of value, must express its epoch. This dogma is invoked in all the arts: in painting and sculpture, in architecture, in music, and in literature. It sets unreasonable limits to the function of art, it confuses the unthinking and the uninformed, and acceptance of its half-truth is betraying young and talented practitioners in all the media I have mentioned. Because this column is primarily concerned with the written word, I mean to speak chiefly of its literary manifestations, but not entirely, for all the arts tend to move as one in whatever period they operate—especially so, perhaps, in ours. All reflect the mental and emotional attitudes prevalent at the time, and analogies between them are therefore pertinent and useful.

Let me begin by saying that these remarks were suggested by recent reading in two books: Sir Kenneth Clark's *The Nude: A Study in Ideal Form* and William Ernest Hocking's *Strength of Men and Nations: A Message to the U.S.A. vis-à-vis the U.S.S.R.* This may seem a strange conjunction; it will appear less so when I add that Dr. Hocking's deeply perceptive work includes an appendix on "The International Role of Art in Revolutionary Times," and that Sir Kenneth's book, while restricted to a particular subject in painting and sculpture, has wise things to say about the timeless elements in art. The questions raised by these two writers led me to read also several contributions to *Adventures of the Mind:* Paul Tillich's *The Lost Dimension in Religion,* Edith Hamilton's *The Lessons of the Past,* Sir Herbert Read's *Art and Life,* and Clement Greenberg's *The Case for Abstract Art.*

Sir Kenneth Clark points to the Aphrodite of Melos as "the noblest refutation" of the current assumption that a work of art must express its own epoch. Believed now to have been sculptured about 100 B.C., and not, as was first thought, a work of the great age of Phidias, she is, he observes "a baroque composition with classic effect." But he is speaking here merely of technique, just as certain of our younger poets today are turning to old forms, rehabilitating them, and trying to imbue them with contemporary feeling. What I really am concerned with here is the human content of our literature today, and the human content of art in general. Is it, I am asking, as alive as it should be to the relation between art and life, is it doing its best to complete the function of art in our lives?

It is easy enough to understand, given the conditions of our age, *why* so many writers and painters have turned their backs on affirmation and beauty. It is true that sensitive minds must reflect in their work the evils in our time by which they are bedeviled, but may not more be asked of them than simply to reflect what they see? Sir Herbert Read, for example, speaks of the preoccupation of our literature, and other forms of communication, with violence. "Violence," he reminds us, "is not new to literature. The Iliad is full of it. So are the writings of Shakespeare and Cervantes. But those classic writers do not condone violence. They view it as just retribution for sins against the divine order, or as a sacrifice sanctioned by heroism or martyrdom. What is peculiar to the modern literature is violence for the sake of violence."

Under the pressures generated by our technological civilization, he contends, we are losing sight of the final function of art. It is, as Tolstoy argued, not merely "a pleasure, a solace, or an amusement." It is not only "a process co-equally important with science for the life and progress of mankind, but it has the unique function of uniting men in love of each other and of life itself." It is "an education of the sensibilities," and Sir Herbert believes this to be an area in which our education of the young falls short.

Dr. Hocking observes that "The world-turmoil cannot fail to bring with it so wide a loss of order and predictable circumstance that no art can today bear to speak simply in terms of beauty or affirmation. Art must find human experience where it is: in an era of hardness, art must speak for the hard. In sympathy for confusion, modern art must echo confusion. It thus assumes the first half of the artist's task, that of knowing the burden, in order to prepare for the second half—that of lifting the burden. Has 'modern' art simply failed to reach its second half?"

In putting that question, Dr. Hocking, it seems to me, lends support to the contention that art must do more than "express its epoch." That is not a hard thing to do, and many writers and other artists are doing it. What Dr. Hocking calls "the second half" of the artist's burden is the more challenging half, and the one which is falling short of fulfillment. If art does not enrich life, if it does not help to make it the better worth living, if it does not promote understanding and love among men, and foster the love of life itself, we had better give it no more attention, and simply surrender ourselves to such creature comforts as our technological civilization provides. But we shall pay a fearful price for them, and despair will open like a bottomless gulf.

The Insidious Footnote

Today's column is an effort to purge myself, temporarily, of some minor irritations, literary and otherwise. I write about them also because, mistakenly or not, I think we are all interested in one another's dislikes—as much, perhaps, as in our enthusiasms. One of the constant personal problems, one peculiar to no particular time, is the release of aggressions and antipathies. It is my conviction—and I am quite serious about this—that every well-appointed home should have a punching bag. (No, I haven't yet installed one, and perhaps that is one reason why this column, from time to time, blows its top.) The punching bag has obvious advantages over other physical methods of release; it is more economical than breaking crockery, and more comfortable than skinning your knuckles or stubbing your toe. You can swing just as hard as you like, and there is, of course, the further assurance that the punching bag won't hit back.

What am I irritated about? For one thing, footnotes. Over the years, I have become convinced that their excessive use should be prohibited by Federal statute. I say this in spite of the fact that many footnotes I have read were more interesting than the text to which they were appended.

Nevertheless, I resent being requested by the writer of a book to transfer my attention to a note at the bottom of the page which often might better have been incorporated in the body of the text. Their use can be an insidious habit to which even some excellent writers become greatly addicted. I have always, for example, found the work of Van Wyck Brooks rewarding reading, but he has long been a zealous footnoter, carrying the practice to such extremes as to have been amusingly parodied by Frank Sullivan in a *New Yorker* piece written nearly twenty years ago, and called "A Garland of Ibids for Van Wyck Brooks."

Occasionally the use of footnotes—as I am sure is not true in the case of Mr. Brooks—is no more than an affectation—an effort to appear scholarly and discriminating which, in its end effect, is merely annoying to the reader. But skillfully and sparingly employed they are useful, and on occasion, even necessary adjuncts to certain kinds of writing. Incidentally, a sensible, and for the unpracticed writer, a helpful explanation of their proper use may be found in *The Modern Researcher,* by Jacques Barzun and Henry F. Graff.

So much for footnotes. Recently, Mark Van Doren, in his introduction to a selection from Carl Sandburg's poems remarked that like all the other American poets who came into prominence during the same period, he "brought something back to poetry that had been sadly missing in the early years of this century. It was humor, the indispensable ingredient of art as it is of life." It is, I fear, even more sadly missing now. In its place, we have something always referred to as "wit." This is not wit as we commonly think of it, but the capacity to link unlike things, and sometimes this mating of incongruities is enough to set one's teeth on edge. In any case, I prefer my wit in prose, its natural habitat. From poetry I want something else.

Leslie Fiedler, in his *Love and Death in the American Novel* spins out his 600-page analysis of what has been wrong with American fiction without the aid of a single footnote, but on other grounds has heightened my need for a punching bag, if only to express my impatience with the Freudian interpretation of literature when it is carried to the point where Hemingway's love of fishing, or what Mr. Fiedler characterizes as his "emphasis on the ritual murder of fish," is described as concealing "that it is not so much the sport as the occasion for immersion which is essential to the holy marriage of males." Whoops, and Mr. Fiedler is away on a rhetorical splurge: "Water is the symbol of the barrier between the Great Good Place and the busy world of women; and everywhere in our fiction, the masculine paradise is laved by great rivers or the vast ocean, washed by the ripples of Lake Glimmerglass or the spume of Glens Falls, even—in Poe—drowned, swallowed up in a liquid white avalanche."

Not for him any of the simple and basic explanations: that all men like occasionally to consort by themselves, that rivers and the sea played a great part in the making of Americans, that a good trout stream is not necessarily an "occasion for immersion." Much as I agree with that part of Mr. Fiedler's thesis which deals with the American novelist's long-term failure to deal adequately with adult love or to create more than a very few credible women—a criticism which has been made over and over again in this column—I am irked by his Freudian flights of fancy.

A few more snarling footnotes: the contortionist postures of clothes models, aptitude and intelligence tests, cockeyed typographical arrangements, zany advertising. O Lord, how long?

Communication Is Not a One-Way Street

It may seem strange, and perhaps deserving of explanation, for a man who at the most charitable estimate must be described as in late middle age, to shift, in a way, his position on some intellectual attitudes for which he has made his stand through many years, and for which, in some quarters, he is unfavorably known. That is precisely what I propose to do in today's column. Fundamentally, the position is unchanged, and that is why I have used the phrase, "in a way." In detail, however, in specific application of the principles and beliefs which have guided me in writing about books and writers, I hereby confess myself to have been often at fault. I am aware, in fuller measure than ever before, that I have frequently overstated my case, that I have at times unjustly attacked, and that out of sincere concern for the ultimate objective I have sometimes scanted the present performance.

This begins to sound suspiciously like one of those confessions with which the Soviets have made us sickeningly familiar, but I have not been brain-washed—at least, not in the sense in which we ordinarily use that term. I would say that I have simply learned a little more, both about myself and the people and books with whom and with which I have been concerned. Centrally, my position as to what makes good or great writing, both in prose and poetry, remains what it was.

First of all, I believe that the craving for communication lies at the core of art, whether literary or otherwise. Not infrequently, a worker in the arts tells us that he writes or paints only to please himself, nor is his sincerity always to be questioned; but I believe that whether he is consciously aware of it or not, he is always subject to the common wish to have others think as he thinks, to feel what he has felt, to believe as he does, to dream what he has dreamed. For to these feelings, thoughts, beliefs, and dreams, we want, being human, some response. It is for such reasons, aside from the hope of financial gain or the pursuit of reputation, and for the easement which results from spitting it all out, that we write at all.

A strong case might be made, I think, for the contention that those of us most fully possessed of self-knowledge and who are in the fullest harmony with life, have no need to write, in the creative sense. Living is enough, and in such an uncomplicated response, perhaps, is to be found the ideal state of man. Nevertheless, as Proust pointed out, the world owes its neurotics (that most unsatisfactory word) an enormous debt. For without their self-torture, their confusions, their search for understanding and for truth, man would be an ever poorer creature than he is, and far less mindful of his untapped potentialities.

Let us assume, then, that the need for communication lies, as I said, at the core of art. It does not follow that, figuratively speaking, the communication must be in words of one syllable, or even in words that we all know and understand. Communication is not a one-way street, and the writer or the painter may justly ask that we meet him halfway. We demand effort of him; he has an equal right to demand it of us. But both can demand too much; we cannot blame the artist for failing to do what he did not attempt (though we often do), nor can he blame us (though he sometimes does) for not making an effort at comprehension which is unwarranted in view of the unimportance of what he has to offer.

It is for these reasons, I think, that so much nonsense has been said or written from both sides on such matters as what we so loosely call "modern" poetry or "modern" painting. Those who are guilty of this nonsense fail to remember that communication is a two-way street. Insofar as poetry is concerned, the climate is perceptibly changing; there is steadily increasing recognition of the need to meet halfway, particularly on the part of the poets; in this respect, the reading public lags behind.

In this column I have sometimes attacked poets who were lagging on their side, and I have attacked critical writing which was similarly unmindful of the reader's rights. I have attacked novels which seemed to me to take no account of man's duality, a conception without which a great novel cannot be written. Sometimes these novels were by writers of fine inherent gifts, but I bore down hard on them because I felt they were oblivious to or ignorant of, one of the essentials of the art they were practicing.

I say that I have shifted my position because more and more I see that some poets are not as willfully difficult as I thought them; it was I who had not gone halfway. More and more I see that while I believe myself justified in asking that novelists who write about our world should strive to find an affirmative base from which to approach it, they are often unable, for one reason or another, to do so; I was sometimes petulant because they had not found such a base, forgetting that perhaps they had been trying as hard as myself to find a serviceable set of values in describing and assessing the world about them.

V

For the Sake of Argument

LIKE SOME OF THE COLUMNS in the previous chapter, certain of the questions raised in this section were written largely for the purpose of stirring up the animals. Not necessarily to raise the reader's hackles, but perhaps to nudge him into the exercise of that faculty so often avoided by us all—the simulation, at least, of thought. For the unwary writer, there is a danger in this appealing practice. As every public commentator, whether on politics, morals, customs, or the arts, soon learns, there is no surer way of getting and holding the reader's attention than by attacking an idea or a notion cherished by the majority—and even more surely, by attacking some individual. All the world may love a lover, but assuredly it loves a fight. Leaning too heavily on this gambit can easily become a vice. Its most eminent and most successful practitioners in our time were H. L. Mencken and George Bernard Shaw. Most of the pieces that follow do little more than ask questions and sometimes do not stay for an answer. *Why, how, when,* and *where* are the four most important adverbs in English, and of them all, *why* is my favorite.

The Writer and the Bomb

This department had no sooner unburdened itself of a thought or two regarding the difficulty, for writers in this country, of defining and illustrating "the American way of life" for the benefit of totalitarian-minded readers abroad, than a new and unmeasurable quantity was injected into the problem with the announcement of the release of atomic energy. It was hard enough only a few days ago to conceive of an overall pattern which would fit that shadowy and threadbare phrase. It is an integration that must be made, and one that our writers can help in making; but a factor as yet imponderable, bearing within it the seeds of incalculable change, has now burst upon an already bewildered world.

What will be the psychological effect upon all thinking and imaginative people, and particularly upon the generation which will create the post-war literature, of the enormous Fact now lodged in every inquiring and speculative mind? Until, if ever, we have bulwarked ourselves against irresponsible use of the destructive power now at man's command, we must all live under the terrific shadow cast by the latest triumph of man's ingenuity. Every year, every month, week and day that this new force remains an unpredictable agent in human affairs, is a bit of borrowed time.

Will it produce a generation of absolute fatalists, who will choose to live by the principle, "eat, drink, and be merry"? Or will it create an iron determination to make the only bearable equation—one in which man's foresight, common sense, and morality at last equal his ingenuity and technical skill?

These are at the moment, perhaps, idle and unanswerable questions. It would take a very arrogant and cocksure mentality to put forth anything like a cut-and-dried prediction. In this column and elsewhere, I have had the temerity to venture the guess that our young post-war writers would not repeat in comparable degree the attitudes embodied in the creative writing of the years immediately following World War I; that they are in a stronger position mentally and emotionally to withstand such disappointments as may come to them, than was the generation which preceded them. But I had not included in my calculations the entrance of any factor of the magnitude of this by which we are now confronted.

Yet, one of my reasons for believing that the literature of the years just ahead would not match the adolescent cynicism and self-centeredness of the Twenties was the attainment of maturity in youth which seems likely to be one of the most valuable by-products of this war, in so far as its effects upon the United States are concerned. Should not that same maturity, developed by the extraordinary responsibilities carried by very young men in this war, help them to realize the necessity of the effort to make the world reasonably safe against the terrible threats which are implicit in this greatest of the conquests of science?

More than ever, it seems to me, a burden of responsibility lies upon the writers of the world. Literature, of all the arts, cannot fiddle while the atom is broken down and its unchartable possibilities for good or ill are released for such use as men may make of them. Writers, as never before, are met by a group of obligations toward their readers. Now more than ever it is important that their work should build toward the creation of reciprocal understanding and goodwill among mankind; that it should illuminate the possibilities and rewards that can be won from life; that it should do all within its power (and that is much) to make the tremendous efforts which will be necessary if the gains of the centuries are to be held.

This is not to suggest that every novel written from this day forth, and every poem, every play, should append a moral or carry a lesson. We know too well, from past experience, what happens to art when conscious didactic purpose is the generating force behind the artist's work. But what is not merely desirable but necessary, it seems to me, is that the critical content of our creative writing should be constructive in purpose. The last thing that the world at this moment needs is the emergence of a new Dean Swift. Our writers, if they are to play any sort of part in the world ahead, cannot content themselves with pointing up the idiocy and the degradation of which man is capable. They are needed, and desperately, to show him what he *can* and *must* be, if his heritage on this planet is not to be lost forever.

To perform such a service will demand that "firmly anchored ethical standard [to repeat the phrase quoted here last week from John Dos Passos] that American writing has been struggling towards for half a century." It will demand to continue with the same quotation, "that unshakable moral attitude toward the world we live in and toward its temporary standards that is the basic essential of any powerful work of the imagination." It means that the writer who cannot find an affirmative base from which to portray the world about him is wasting not only his time but our own. And there may be, in the familiar words of Mr. Marquand, so little time.

P.S. This column was published in August of 1945. Twenty years have passed, but I find little to add. Although we have learned to live with the threat of the bomb, its presence continues to dominate our thinking. It has made us timorous of action in foreign affairs, it has blunted our sense of principle. Writers, naturally, have shared the common fear. I think this acute apprehensiveness has contributed to the growth of crazy humor, to the dehumanization of art in all its forms, to the emphasis on sex, which, after self-preservation, is the strongest human drive. The state of fear does not foster rational thinking. It stimulates irrational behavior, and all this is reflected in our writing. If there were but one precept to ask the young writer to consider, I think it should be, Try to keep a cool head; try to keep a sense of proportion. And to do that demands courage, the one virtue our species has retained in undiminished form. That, and his curiosity, got man where he is. Without them, he might as well surrender to the ants, whose human counterpart we have in the totalitarian states. Writers today, it seems to me, have the greatest opportunity they have ever enjoyed, to justify their curious craft. More surely than statesmen, they can save us from self-destruction.

Major and Minor Writers

What do we mean—or rather, what should we mean—when we talk about major and minor novelists? Last Sunday, in his interesting article about the work of Christopher Isherwood, Mr. Alfred Kazin laid down a rule of measurement which, it seems to me, is open to question.

"It is a great distinction," he wrote, "to be a minor novelist today; it is much more difficult than to imitate the great novelists. We have many excellent minor poets; we have almost no novelists—only great armies of people who have taken advantage of the deceptive looseness of the novel to write political tracts, memories of battle, romances, biographies and apocalyptic visions. To be a real minor novelist is to do the undisguisable work of fiction—which is to create a real human scene whose meanings follow from what has been freshly demonstrated—without the imperative world-meaning, the search for basic control, which has marked the crisis of modern thought. The great novelists of our day—the Kafkas, the Joyces, the Prousts, the Thomas Manns—have known how to transpose narrative into new keys for the understanding, but only by beating out whole new forms for the novel."

By way of further distinction, Mr. Kazin finds that the minor novelist can carry on his work without making it the vehicle of his "total intellectual and religious life," whereas the great novelist finds it necessary to make that integration. And, "the minor novelist is not a pioneer, but a well-bred artist. He stands for enjoyment, as the major novelists stand for a new conception of man and history."

The words "major" and "minor" are slippery and unsatisfactory tools. As commonly employed, I find them somehow irritating because they are used categorically, when actually they are purely comparative terms, and have for their true meaning, "greater than" or "lesser than." Language, when you come to think of it, is extraordinarily poor in marking the gradations of literary or any other values. How many writers there are of whom the word "minor" is used who have contributed something individual and precious in their work.

However that may be, I think Mr. Kazin's distinctions demand a little examination. He seems to take it for granted that the great novelist is necessarily a great, or shall we say, original thinker. That, it seems to me, is a quite unreasonable assumption. I see no reason whatever why a novelist, in order to be considered "major," should stand for "a new conception of man and history." By close approximation to common consent, Tolstoy's *War and Peace* is generally regarded as the greatest novel yet written. It is true that Tolstoy there concerns himself with a theory of history, but it is not for that reason that *War and Peace* has won such unparalleled critical acclaim. It has had that acclaim because it is the most inclusive and deeply veracious picture of human life that we have in fiction. It would still be that if Tolstoy had not been in the least concerned with his theory of history.

By Mr. Kazin's yardstick, Henry Fielding is not a thinker at all, yet he remains indubitably one of the great novelists in English literature. And to step for a moment outside the novel, Shakespeare, accepting pretty completely the attitudes of his period, could not, while we think of him as a supreme artist, be regarded as an original thinker. Would Mr. Kazin characterize Jane Austen as a "minor" novelist? There is not the slightest connection between her work and the intellectual life of her period, yet it lives because it had its roots in the acute perception of human nature. What about Henry James, now enjoying a great revival of interest among the intelligentsia? What was he interested in beyond the devious courses of human conduct and the teasing problem of how to pin them on paper?

Nor can I see that the four writers whom Mr. Kazin has singled out as the great novelists of our day—Joyce, Proust, Kafka and Thomas Mann—have provided us with "a new conception of man and history." If the world remembers them, it will be for the same reason that we remember other novelists long since dead—because they wrote of men and women in terms that we find as valid now as when their books were written. Joyce has a heavy load to carry into posterity, Proust will find his readers only among those who can endure his hothouse world, Kafka was still looking for the answers when he died. Mann achieved a personal integration through his work, but where is the "new conception"?

Mr. Kazin says the minor novelist stands for enjoyment. So does any novelist worth his salt; otherwise, why should we trouble to read him? He says the minor novelist is not a pioneer, but neither are some of the greatest novelists in the history of literature.

It is understandable why Mr. Kazin should make these extraordinary demands upon the writer of fiction. Our time is a confused and rudderless one, and we look for help in all directions.

The Sense of Expectancy I

What do we mean when we talk about an American literature? What makes it our own? What gives it native character? As this department was remarking a few Sundays ago, there comes a time when the words which we use to express mental concepts turn sour or flat upon the tongue. Often it is because we have fallen into the habit of using them in parrot fashion, without stopping to ask ourselves just what it is we wish to convey. We mumble something about "the American way of life," and find it hard to be explicit if we are pressed.

Everybody is aware that there are no more dangerous generalizations than those which are made about national temperament and character. Yet they are sometimes helpful, and frequently valid. We speak of British tenacity, and who, after the Battle of Britain, could ever again doubt its truth? So, too, it is a commonplace to talk about grace and clarity and logic as characteristic of French literature. And might we not say that English literature is distinguished by intense love of place, filled with echoes of John of Gaunt's "This blessed plot, this earth, this realm, this England"? Is not Russian literature, at least in its great period, deeply colored by its burning sense of man's duality—man-God, man-beast?

What, then, of ourselves? Have we as yet achieved a genuine native quality, a something which is unmistakably our own; and if so, what is it? We shall not have answered the question, surely, if we point merely to the use of American material, or the development of an American idiom. As Saint-Exupéry reminds us elsewhere on this page, "a nation is certainly not the sum of the regions, customs, farms, and the rest that man's intelligence is able at any moment to add up. It is a Being." The use of native material does not of itself create the spirit of a national literature. The material must be assimilated, understood, interpreted; and if it is to be of interest beyond our own boundaries, it must be linked to the common experience of mankind.

It is more than a century ago that the confident voice of Emerson rang out in *The American Scholar* and told American writers that they had "listened too long to the courtly muses of Europe." He ended that memorable address upon a note of calm but resolute expectancy. Nothing that he wrote has greater force, greater truth, for us today. Whitman, in this his ardent disciple, was to repeat the challenge, and we have been conscious of their exhortations ever since. Too conscious, perhaps, like the adolescent who is impatient for the razor on his cheek. When was it we began to talk about the Great American Novel? A long time ago, surely. Never was there a people so impatient to be grown, so intensely interested in its own growing pains! We never tire of measuring ourselves, and how we love being measured!

I begin to think that we shall always be that way, and I rather hope we shall. If there is anything which this nation has to give to the world beyond the refinements of electric refrigeration and Beautyrest mattresses, it is surely that sense of expectancy which has possessed us as a people from the beginning, and which, up to this time, we have never completely lost. There are individual human beings like that, for whom the door to the future is always open. It is a trait which has its disadvantages, and sometimes they are heavy. It makes for easy trusting and overconfidence, but it is the nearest thing we know to perpetual youth.

The sense of expectancy—it lies at the core of all that Emerson wrote, and makes him, in his thought, the most truly representative American writer, even now. In him you have, thus far, the most intense expression of the American genius. It is this same sense which informs the magnificent final sentences of Thoreau's *Walden*: "The life in us is like the water in the river. It may rise this year higher than man has ever known it, and flood the parched uplands; even this may be the eventful year, which will drown out all our muskrats. . . . I do not say that John or Jonathan will realize all this; but such is the character of that morrow which mere lapse of time can never make to dawn. The light which puts out our eyes is darkness to us. Only that day dawns to which we are awake. There is more day to dawn. The sun is but a morning star."

It is this sense of expectancy which permeates so much of our poetry, even as it lay at the heart of every westward thrust of the pioneers. You will find it here and there in the best of our novels; and much as we may sneer at the success-story formula of popular magazine fiction, rest assured that it contains something which meets a deeply ingrained demand that has its roots in the national temperament. It is the writers in whom the sense of expectancy is alive that the wide American public takes to its heart, because in them it finds its own hopes and aspirations reflected. When Americans deny the future, they deny themselves.

The Sense of Expectancy II

Last week this department ventured the opinion that if there is a definitely recognizable native quality in American literature it may be the sense of expectancy which is so deeply a part of the national temperament. We seem to keep that sense even when we are most sharply critical of ourselves. Thus the novels that Sinclair Lewis wrote in his most effective period, though they are the product of irritation and dissatisfaction with certain aspects of American life, nevertheless end on a note of expectancy.

Do you remember the last page of *Main Street*? Carol Kennicott has realized the ineffectiveness of her rebellion against Main Street standards, but when Doc Kennicott asks her, "Don't you ever get tired of fretting and stewing and experimenting?" she answers, "I haven't even started," and leading him to the nursery door, points to their sleeping child and exclaims, "Think what that baby will see and meddle with before she dies in the year 2000!" Reflectively she goes on: "I've never excused my failures by sneering at my aspirations, by pretending to have gone beyond them. I do not admit that Main Street is as beautiful as it should be!"

And so Babbitt, confiding in his son, regretfully aware that "practically, I've never done a single thing I've wanted to in my whole life," finds comfort in the thought that "maybe you'll carry things on further. I don't know. But I do get a kind of sneaking pleasure out of the fact that you knew what you wanted to do and did it." And Martin Arrowsmith, when we leave him, is saying, "I feel as if I were really beginning to work now. This new quinine stuff may prove pretty good. We'll plug along on it for two or three years, and maybe we'll get something permanent—and probably we'll fail!"

In *Mark Twain's America,* Bernard De Voto made an eloquently argued case for his contention that "there is more of America in Mark Twain's books than in any others." Writing of Huckleberry Finn's journey down the Mississippi, he says: "In a sense, Huck speaks to the national shrewdness, facing adequately what he meets, succeeding by means of native intelligence whose roots are ours—and ours only. In a sense, he exists for a delight or wonder inseparable from the American race. This passage down the flooded river, through pageantry and spectacle, amid an infinite variety of life, something of surprise or gratification surely to be met with each new incident—it is the heritage of a nation not unjustly symbolized by the river's flow. Huck sleeping under the stars or wakefully drifting through an immensity dotted only by far lights or scurrying to a cave while the forest bends under a cloudburst satisfies blind gropings of the mind. The margin widens to obscurity. Beyond awareness, a need for freedom, an insatiable hunger for its use, finds in him a kind of satisfaction. . . ."

What is this, again, but the sense of expectancy in its purest form? It is the keynote that Stephen Vincent Benét struck in the opening line of *Western Star*—"Americans are always moving on."

The late Constance Lindsay Skinner was profoundly right in her feeling that the life of America was best symbolized in its rivers. In projecting The Rivers of America Series she reminded us that "we began to be Americans on the rivers. By the rivers the explorers and fur traders entered America. The pioneers, who followed them, built their homes and raised their grain and stock generally at, or near, the mouths of rivers. As their numbers increased they spread up the valleys, keeping close to the streams, since water is an indispensable element of the sustenance of the soil and all animal life. The rivers were the only highways of communication and commerce between solitary hamlets. Settlements expanded from the rivers. To repeat, the first foreigners on these shores began their transition from Europeans to Americans as River Folk."

First the rivers and then the railroads. Both have played a larger part in making us what we are than has been the case with any other people. It is not strange that they have colored our imaginations so deeply. The rivers beckoned; so did the rails. The American sentiment about trains is something peculiar to ourselves; they have always been for us something much more than merely a mechanical means of getting from one place to another, and such a phrase as "on the wrong side of the railroad tracks" has connotations which are definitely and distinctly American.

Miss Skinner, emphasizing the fact that this nation came to birth upon the rivers, wondered if that fact had colored our temperament. "Are we," she asked, "a restless people because motion flowed by us continuously in our youth? Are we optimistic, eager, imaginative, daring and even recklessly experimental because of the beckoning of the tides 'bright with flashing light' which ran swiftly past our known shores into domains beyond our vision?" Perhaps, but certainly both the river and the railroad are symbols of expectancy. Both carry our eyes, and then our hearts and wills, beyond the bend.

P.S. This column was written in 1943, at a time when our railroads were still a prized asset, and before air travel and the super highway had so deeply encroached upon their function.

A Strange Convention

250 years ago, or to be precise, late in February, 1711, Joseph Addison sat down to write a piece for the first issue of a paper to be known as *The Spectator*. "I have observed," he began, "that a Reader seldom peruses a Book with Pleasure, 'till he knows whether the Writer of it be a black or a fair Man, of a mild or cholerick Disposition, Married or a Bachelor, with other Particulars of the like nature, that conduce very much to the right understanding of an Author." He then proceeded to tell his readers something about himself.

So far as I know, this was the first statement in print to uphold the convention that the private lives of authors are of more than ordinary interest. Why they should be so considered is one of the things I have puzzled about for years, and up to this time I have encountered no completely satisfactory answer. Since Addison's time, the convention has not only persisted, but has enormously grown. A framed copy of his words would not be out of place above the desk of every publisher's publicity director, but there seems to be no need for such a reminder.

The New Yorker, a magazine in which, had he lived two centuries later, Addison would have been greatly interested, has effectively disposed of some conventions, but not of this one. It gave the deathblow, in this country anyway, to the double-barreled caption for a humorous drawing. It established a new convention: that an exchange of remarks was not necessary to drive home the point of a funny picture. One person in the drawing speaks, or none. You may still find specimens of the question and reply formula in Punch, but the British, it is occasionally observed, are more tenacious of the past than ourselves.

The New Yorker broke another lance in its series of profiles. It proceeded blithely on the assumption that its readers might conceivably be interested in the personal idiosyncrasies of the people it wrote about, even if they did not happen to be writers. And so the Profiles were filled to the brim with crotchets. Before their pattern was evolved, it hardly seemed worth mentioning what anybody except the author of a current best seller ate for breakfast, and whether he used pajamas, or was accustomed to sleep in the raw. *The New Yorker* gave intimate details about all kinds of people, including some, indeed, concerning whom it was difficult to guess why anybody should be interested at all. But this iconoclasm did nothing to diminish the assumption that to a degree unparalleled except by Presidents and movie stars, the writer's life must be an open book to his readers.

The convention, too, bred subconventions. It became almost impossible to conceive of a writer who had not tried at least a dozen occupations before publishing his first book. Some of these occupations were practically demanded of him, if he were to qualify for public attention. Somewhere along the line, after leaving high school, he must have served a term as a dishwasher. If he had, from time to time, hopped freights, that was a help. Particularly during the Thirties, it was essential to have had a crack at an occupation that put you in rapport with the underdog.

Now, essentially, the curiosity that is fed by such details as these is entirely natural. Certainly we are all interested in the likes and dislikes of our friends; whether they prefer dogs or cats, or abhor all animals and babies; whether the sea or the mountains appeals to them, or whether they find themselves homesick for pavement and acutely uncomfortable in the presence of the birds, bees, and flowers.

But why, I ask you, isn't public interest in these matters presumed to include—*The New Yorker* nothwithstanding—the vagaries of distinguished surgeons and engineers, the peculiarities of research scientists and of those individuals who once were known as captains of industry? Why is it presumed to be a matter of such public concern that Percival Peculiar, whose first novel is having its brief day in the sun, is devoted to a pair of poodles which he is reluctant to let out of his sight?

Seriously, I suppose the fact that we identify ourselves more readily with the writers we happen to be reading than we do with the builder of the bridge we happen to be looking at, or with the man who has devised a new technique in thoracic surgery, has something to do with it. If we don't identify ourselves with the author himself, and with the experiences which have been his, we are likely to do so with one of his characters.

There is an intimate relationship between writer and reader which provides one of the best reasons why, no matter what extensions are made in the field of communication between human beings, there will always be a peculiarily close relationship between a man seated in a chair and the book which he has before him. There are no distracting factors to come between, as there are in radio and television. We don't hear his voice; we don't see him. There is only what he says. And we can either throw him in the wastebasket, or consort with him tomorrow night, or next year.

The Child in Literature

There is an aspect of the nineteenth century that has rarely been touched upon. Both from a literary and a psychological point of view it is one of the most interesting manifestations of that period. Not until then did childhood come to play a considerable part in imaginative writing. I am not talking about verses and stories written *for* children; these too developed slowly, but Caxton printed Aesop's fables for children as early as 1484. What interests me is this: that so much time elapsed before the life of childhood, remembered by adults, was seen to provide good material for writers.

There is little need to remind you of what has happened within the last century; we have innumerable stories about children, written for adults to read, we have plays about them, we have autobiographical novels which with difficulty get past the adolescent years, we have autobiographies of which the most vivid and interesting parts are those devoted to the years of childhood.

It may be worth noting that children figured prominently in painting long before they did in literature; much could be written about that, but I shall merely make note of the fact, and pass on. Children figure almost not at all in the Greek and Latin classics; if they appear at all, it is only momentarily.

And what of children in the Old Testament? For the most part, they are slaughtered. There are few among them whom we remember as individuals. There was the little maid in the household of Naaman, who wished that he might see her lord the prophet that dwelt in Samaria who would cure him of leprosy, but that is all she says, and she appears no more. There was the Shumanite's son who went out into the hot sun to help the reapers glean, and cried out, "My head, my head!" There was little Samuel who went to serve in the temple, but the most memorable thing said about him is that every year his mother came to bring him a little coat she had made for him.

Perhaps the most vivid incident of the Old Testament, in which children play a part, is the story of what happened to the prophet Elisha when he went on a journey: "There came forth little children out of the city, and mocked him, and said unto him, 'Go up, thou bald head; go up, thou bald head.' And he turned back, and looked on them, and cursed them in the name of the Lord. And there came forth two she bears out of the wood, and tare forty and two children of them." We are not told what Elisha thought of this savage punishment; the chronicler merely continues, "And he went from thence to Mount Carmel, and from thence he returned to Samaria."

There is not much of life that Shakespeare did not touch, yet children figure but little in his plays; when they do, although we are always uncertain of their age, they seem overly precocious, and gifted with a command of language which would astound us if we encountered it among our own offspring, or the children of our friends. Certainly this is true of little Mamillius in *The Winter's Tale,* and of the page Moth in *Love's Labor's Lost,* who has, I believe, more lines to speak than any other child in Shakespeare. If there are any others, besides Lady Macduff's young son, I cannot recall them.

The seventeenth and eighteenth centuries in general had small concern for children in literature, unless you see fit to include Swift's "Modest Proposal" in that category. They have no part in the poetry and plays of those centuries, and are seldom encountered in the novels of Richardson, Fielding, and Smollett. A change does, however, become apparent in the autobiographical writing of the eighteenth century, and there the memory of childhood does begin to enter literature—earliest of all, perhaps, in a paper Steele wrote for the *Tatler,* in which he recalled the emotions he experienced at the death of his father. And everyone remembers, of course, the opening pages of Franklin's *Autobiography*.

With the nineteenth century, the interest in childhood experience become marked and general. One thinks at once of Charles Lamb, of Scott, George Eliot, Dickens and Thackeray, Hawthorne and Tolstoy, to mention but a few outstanding names. And with that mounting interest came books of a kind never before written—books like Lewis Carroll's *Alice in Wonderland,* and *The Wind in the Willows* of Kenneth Grahame, who was to say that he wrote about children because they were "the only really living people." It would be difficult to say of such books whom they interest more—children or ourselves.

How is one to explain so great a change? Was it merely that once the thing had been done, there was a spreading desire to try to recapture that vanished world for oneself? Or was it the expression of a deeper need for self-understanding which was born as life became more complicated? Was it merely a forerunner of contemporary man's increasing inclination to introspection? Whatever the cause, the effect on literature in general has been enriching, and at times enchanting.

P.S. For several of the observations made in the foregoing column, I should acknowledge my indebtedness to one of the great teachers it was my good fortune to have. Charles Townsend Copeland of Harvard, who taught generations of students the craft of writing, left among his papers an unpublished essay on children in literature which provided the impetus—and some of the information—for what I have written. In spite of the proliferation of synthetic books for children—one of the curses of contemporary publishing—the development that Copeland traced—and for the first time, I think, has persisted and grown. One of the most interesting novels of this century, Christina Stead's *The Man Who Loved Children,* has added a new dimension to that development. Nothing comparable to it had hitherto been written in English.

The Sweet Uses of Publicity

Much water has gone under the bridge since sedate listings were the norm of publishers' advertising. We have to look sharp these days to make sure whether it is a brassiere or a book we are being urged to buy. I, for one, grow quite bewildered whenever I turn an eye —or is it an ear?—to the hucksters' crying of their literary wares, and I often wonder whether I've wandered into the wrong department. Here is a copywriter who signals for my attention by asking: "Do you get up in the morning almost as tired as you were the night before? Do you often have to drag yourself through your day's work?" Just as my eye is prepared to find the name of a new patent medicine, it falls somewhere on the word "book," and I discover that I am being invited to buy a volume on how to relax.

Or, finding myself confronted by a line of large and bold-faced type reading "What a woman!" and under it a half-page picture of an equally bold-faced damsel, I am about to look for the name of the theater where this new super-colossal drama is to open when I discover that this lady is expected to take her place as "one of the unforgettable women of fiction."

Such experiences have become so frequent as to be no longer novel, but the other day I saw an ad which made me realize that we are indeed on or over the threshold of momentous change. On the cover of *Publishers' Weekly* was a picture of a highly photogenic young woman, and under it the words, "Her novel is the book the entire trade has been waiting for." Nothing strange or new about that; her picture had appeared there before when *Forever Amber* was about to be published. My realization that I was standing on my head came when I turned the page.

There, on the double-spread advertising Miss Kathleen Winsor's new novel, the picture was repeated in smaller size, and under it were these significant words: "The recurrent theme of all our advertising will be this striking new photograph of the author." It was that word "theme" that shook me to my gizzard. The recurrent theme of all advertising would not be what Miss Winsor's novel was about, or even merely that this was the new work by the author of *Forever Amber*. It would be simply the pleasing contours of Miss Winsor's physiognomy.

Surely the handwriting on the wall is plain. The sober prophets who have been proclaiming that we were about to enter a new literary era were speaking more truly than they knew—but for very different reasons than those which they had offered. Here was in the making the literary revolution to end all literary revolutions. The whole basis of literary appreciation for the reader, all the sage advice that has been spoken or written about literary apprenticeship—these are being swept relentlessly into the discard. Henceforth the bedeviled publisher need ask but one question of the aspiring author: "How well do you photograph?"—provided, of course, that there is any visible reason for asking the question at all.

This impending upheaval must necessarily deal a deathblow to the schools of creative writing which have been springing up all over the country. It should bring comfort and reassurance to those sour-visaged and sour-minded pessimists who protest from time to time, "But you can't teach anybody to write." And while the schools will go under, their loss should be the beauty parlors' gain.

There are, it seems to me, quite unexplored avenues along which this new development may take us. If you insist on being logical about the significance of this revolution in book advertising, you must take the position, I suppose, that the use of the author's picture as a recurrent theme is merely a means of halting the wayward reader and causing him to read the accompanying text. Well, then, isn't there more than one way of skinning this particular cat? What's wrong with a publisher discovering an author with a face that would stop a clock, and using that as a recurrent theme? After all, pretty faces are a dime a dozen these days, and they have been displayed to the point of surfeit both on the screen and in the ads. Why not strike a fresh and startling note?

Rightly or wrongly, the craving for novelty is generally held to be one of the touchstones for the understanding of American character. I am willing to wager a complete set of the Elsie Dinsmore books against a single copy of *Star Money* to prove that a face which is the ultimate in ugliness, if used as a recurrent theme, will halt more readers in their tracks than will the repetition of fare, however pleasant, for which our appetite has become a little jaded. Whether that suggestion is adopted or not, it should be apparent to the least concerned reader that a new day is at hand, and that what it will bring us no man knows.

P.S. Perhaps not everything I forecast in this column fifteen years ago has come to pass, but surely the emphasis on publicity, and publicity not too far removed from the kind by which I was then amused, has snowballed to new dimensions. *Personality, personality, personality*—the word has become a shibboleth. You cannot turn the pages of a popular magazine but some *personality* stares you in the face, and you are invited to explore the psyche behind it. And the book world? There is Ian Fleming, in the person of his hero James Bond, pointing his gun at you. How in in the world did Shakespeare get where he did without the sweet uses of publicity?

Who's in Orbit Now?

For some time now, and ever more frequently, I have been asking myself why, in the face of the astounding advances being made in the exploration of outer space, I find myself one of a minority (how large or small it is I do not know) who feel indifference and even hostility toward these latest evidences of that magnificent curiosity and daring which have made man the dominant species on the planet he inhabits. Have I lost interest in new horizons? That would be a sad plight in which to find oneself after a lifetime of fascination by what lies beyond the bend in the river, by what lies over the crest of the hill. I cannot concede that to be the answer; all my adult life, and even earlier, exploration of one kind or another has stirred in me the deepest responses of which I am capable.

Why, then, am I repelled? Why am I not more attracted by the often ingenious and imaginative forays of science fiction, some of it written by men of superior gifts? Why am I not more stirred by the probable prospect of landing a man, whether Russian or American, on the surface of the moon? I think I know the answer to these questions. I believe it to be the fact that man is still so far from having made an adequate adjustment to his native environment that his capacity to maintain his dominant position, his ability even to survive, have become questionable. Let him bend his best efforts, his utmost scientific capacity, to setting his own house in order.

I should like to see *The Balance of Nature,* by Lorus and Margery Milne, required reading in every American high school. It is essential for opening minds to grasp the concept of the interrelationship of all forms of life, of man's part in that relationship, and how he has abused it to the point of imperiling his own future. Good as this book is, and though other writers have stressed the importance of the balance nature strives to maintain, we need many more studies of this kind, written in terms, like the Milne book, which the average reader can readily understand.

The need is essential in order to combat the fallacies which lie behind that most misleading slogan of our age—"the conquest of nature." Francis Bacon, who fathered the methods of modern science, put in a few words, as most fundamental truths can be put, one which modern man needs desperately to heed. He said, "The only way to master nature is to obey her." Man has been diligent and profoundly intelligent in discovering what some, at least, of nature's laws are. We do not know, and may never know them all, but what is far more disturbing is that we have tried to transcend some of those that we do know. There is plenty of testimony to that effect in the Milne book and in the work of other ecologists.

Instead of beating out our brains in devising means of sustaining human life in other, outer environments where, in the opinion of some scientists like Pierre Teilhard de Chardin, such a possibility is extremely doubtful, why not apply them to mastering the problems presented by the growth of human population, to solving the manner of our handling our relationships with the other forms of life which inhabit this planet? Constantly, the ecologists tell us, we tamper with the delicate balances of the natural world.

Just as man has devised, and keeps on devising, ever more potent weapons for use in warfare against his own kind, so too, he has ever more powerful means of interferring with the laws that operate in the world about him. We have read much in recent years about the untapped natural resources of the sea, and their value for the future that man may have. But we still do not know enough about what nuclear tests are doing to oceanic life. No agreement has been reached on how much radioactivity can safely be set free in the ocean.

Late in the day of our wholesale destruction of the forests and other natural resources, long after we had needlessly polluted so many of our rivers and smaller streams, the conservation movement gained sufficient strength to make some headway against the destructive forces. A considerable literature of conservation came into being, and grew to be an effective agent in protecting our future. We need a larger similar literature in the field of ecology—a popular literature which will drive home the issues at stake. As the Milnes point out, "The balance of nature has so many facets, each in such a fluid state that the latest news tends to come in newspapers and magazines, often in columns written by reporters on the basis of press releases. After a time, progress reports appear in scientific journals. Later still," they add, "summary accounts appear in books." Of all these, we need an increasing number.

The more man becomes herded in great agglomerations, in which, through technological advances, he becomes more and more divorced from the natural world, as simpler, more rural civilizations were not, the more even his agriculture becomes mechanized and scientifically administered, he loses touch with the other forms of life to which he is bound by ties stronger than he has become able to realize. His arrogance must make way for a new humility.

The Poet-Physicists

When Einstein died the other day, the New York *Times* editorially observed that the great mathematical physicists are the epic poets of our time. "The universe as we conceive it," the editorial remarked, "is their intellectual creation." These were justifiable statements, but I should like to set down some reservations about them. Certainly no writer of our time has grappled with the great abstractions of time and space as the physicists have, but neither have the scientists fully assumed the role of the epic poet. In its time, at least, the epic poem has been within the grasp of the average intelligent man; the great physicists of the modern age have been comprehensible only to other physicists. Their conceptions have had to be filtered through, and imperfectly at best, to the layman.

The universe as the average intelligent man conceives it is not the conception which Einstein had of it. The big scientific conceptions have become progressively more difficult to understand. What might be called the first of them—the fact that the earth is not flat, but round—was the easiest of all; the assumption required no more than ordinary powers of observation and deduction. Somewhat more difficult, but still within the average man's grasp, was the conception of a universe of which man and his earth were not, as he had so long assumed, the center. In some ways, at least, the evolutionary theory was still harder for the average man to accept, if not to understand.

But it is when we get down to the findings of our own century that the real difficulties begin. It takes very much more than a high school course in physics, for example, to understand and accept that matter and energy are different manifestations of the same thing. The layman understands that, somehow, this conception led to the release of atomic energy, and that this in turn led to something still more concrete—the atomic and the hydrogen bomb. But the intervening steps are beyond his comprehension.

Nevertheless there is no doubt that it is the scientist rather than the poet (and I am using the term poet now in its widest sense) who has captured the imaginations of men today. The dynamo, the internal combustion engine, the vacuum tube, the test tube, the cyclotron, the computer, are the genii of the contemporary world, and we stand agape at the wonders, pleasing or dreadful, which they bring forth. The men who are their masters have taken over the big conceptions; the poets no longer apply themselves to the spiritual immensities with which Dante and Milton were concerned; they content themselves with such scraps as the scientists have left them.

Or so it seems. But are they really so bereft? Mankind is still as answerable to divine justice as it was when Dante wrote; the relations between man and his Creator are still as important as Milton made them in *Paradise Lost*. Science has pulled colossal rabbits out of its hat, and will no doubt pull others, but can it help us find our way to their best use? May there not still be work, and work of a major kind, for the poets to do?

They have this advantage, the writers who deal imaginatively and creatively with man in relation to the world around him: they relate the big conceptions to ourselves as individuals in a way that science does not. Science, on its imaginative flights, is not concerned with John Smith as John Smith. John has become an impersonal unit in an impersonal whole; he is merely an animate being that falls within the radius of the bomb's destructibility, or a statistical unit in the graph of the social scientist. But to the poet he is still John Smith, and because the poet presents him to us as such, we are better able to identify ourselves with him, and to conceive that what is true of him may be true of us, and that what happens to him may happen to ourselves.

I do not mean this in application to the merely physical facts. We do not need the poet to tell us of what the bomb is materially capable, or what material conditions the rise of population may produce. The poet is concerned with how we confront the facts, with the impact upon us of the great conceptions, whether they are scientific or spiritual. As W. MacNeile Dixon wrote in *The Human Situation,* it is "in the exploration of human nature rather than of the material world that we are likely to come to some understanding of our most pressing problems." Its secrets are the deeper ones.

Dixon reminds us of the poets' "inextinguishable sympathy with humanity," and finds in it the source of their understanding. They owe this "not to science or philosophy, but to their profounder appreciation of the strange situation in which we find ourselves, to their sense of the pitiful estate of man who, with all the forces of nature proclaiming an alien creed, still holds to his intuitions, who knows and knows well that he cannot support himself otherwise than by clinging—as a sailor clings to his raft in angry seas—to his passion for justice, his trust in the affections of the heart, his love of the lovely, his lonely struggle for the best, however clumsy and mistaken he may be in his present estimates of what is indeed best."

Fiction and Tranquillity

Suppose we put aside for the time being the perennial question as to whether the novel is dead or dying, or merely taking a siesta, and examine a little more closely Sir Harold Nicolson's belief that it is a literary form which can flourish only in a time of tranquillity.

He did not, to be sure, put it quite that baldly. He specified a certain type of tranquillity. It is the kind, he said, "when the bulk of the community accept without question the contemporary social and ethical convention, and when civilization is not threatened by any grave external or internal upheaval."

It was then, he thought, that "a minority of gifted men and women, bored by the prevailing uniformity, create the novel, either as an escape into a more exciting and adventurous world or as a vehicle for social, religious or moral propaganda. The appeal of the novel, both to its author and to his public, becomes an appeal from the familiar to the unusual, from monotony to excitement, from the average to the exceptional."

Certainly the time in which we live does not possess the kind of tranquillity which Sir Harold specified, or, so far as I am aware, tranquillity of any kind whatsoever. I say that in spite of the fact that I do not know, and doubt whether anyone else does, whether the bulk of the community, either in England, the United States, or anywhere else in the world except, possibly, among the Aleuts, the Igorots, or the inhabitants of Tierra del Fuego, accept without question the contemporary social and ethical convention. All I know is that some do, some don't. It depends a lot upon in which circles you move, and while primitive societies are, each in its way, pretty rigid and uniform in structure and beliefs, even on Main Street the variations are plentiful. In Sir Harold's London or my New York they are bewildering.

Whether or not we accept the conventional social and ethical attitudes, certainly all of us, even possibly the Aleuts, the Igorots and the people of Tierra del Fuego, feel ourselves threatened by grave upheaval, either external or internal, or both. And suppose, even, that the bulk of us does question the prevailing attitudes. Are we, on such grounds, justified in concluding that we are in no shape to write and read novels? Let's make a little excursion into the not so distant past.

The nineteenth century is commonly regarded as the period in which the novel reached its highest level of achievement. It produced those novelists to whom the term "giant" is customarily affixed: Stendhal, Balzac, Dickens, Thackeray, Dostoevski, Turgenev, and Tolstoy. Again by common consent, or something pretty close to it, the Russians I have named are generally regarded as having brought the novel to its fullest flower. Did they live in an atmosphere of tranquillity? All through the time in which they wrote the structure of society was rumbling and occasionally erupting under their feet.

Does the work of either Dostoevski or Tolstoy reflect a tranquil mind? Men more tortured within themselves seldom have lived.

Was the period in which Stendhal wrote a time of calm? He was a Frenchman, and accordingly less exercised than his contemporaries across the Channel, but it does not seem to me that you can describe as a time of tranquillity those years of upheaval in which the shadow of Napoleon was lengthening across the world. England, at least, was in a state of jitters not too far removed in its intensity from the spasms of fear to which our contemporary world is subjected.

And do not let us be too ready to think of the Victorian age as one wrapped in eiderdown. Maybe life was tranquill in an English vicarage; was it so in the world that young Charles Dickens knew, visiting his father in the debtor's prison? Was it a tranquil world for those who endured the chief horrors of the Victorian age, the child laborers and the slaveys? Britain had its own Buchenwalds in that time; less dramatic, perhaps, but none the less frightful and none the less degrading to the human spirit.

The ancients, Sir Harold remarked, did not write novels because "they were so busy with art, philosophy, politics, administration and war that they never achieved the special type of tranquillity in which the art of fiction becomes creative and relevant." What else, I wonder, except making money and consorting with the other sex—two activities which Sir Harold unaccountably omitted—has mankind ever been busy with?

No, if the novel is dying or dead, its demise will have to be attributed to other reasons than these. This is a world that has never been free of menacing phantoms of one kind or another, and I doubt very much that their presence will ever be banished. If all the four freedoms are ever attained, it will be, I think, on another planet than this. Freedom of speech and freedom of worship—these are within the grasp of reasonable men—but freedom from want and freedom from fear are not, in my lexicon, included in the book of nature. Not now, and not ever. The sooner our writers reconcile themselves to that unprepossessing fact, the freer they will be.

Getting to Know the Animals

When Caroline Kennedy demanded of Col. John Glenn, "Where's the monkey?" she gave voice to one of the keenest interests of childhood. Rare is the child—indeed, I have yet to see one—who does not exhibit more interest in animals than in the older specimens, at least, of his own species. Animals have dominated the literature for small children, just as they dominate the world of toys. They do so because we are certain of the child's response to them. As he grows older, the interest persists, but in varying degrees; it may decline and it may even increase to a degree which overshadows interest in other human beings.

I speak of these matters because I have been wondering whether any significance attaches to the recent popularity among adults of certain books about animals. Is this mere chance, or may it be accounted for in other ways? The question must be pursued cautiously for what should be obvious reasons. Everybody knows that the taste for certain kinds of reading fluctuates from period to period; the Elizabethans were as fascinated by how-to books as we are, and produced them in similar profusion, but during intervening centuries the phenomenon was less marked. At the beginning of the present century the historical romance (as opposed to the more serious historical novel) enjoyed wider popularity than it does today. And so the pendulum swings.

Certainly interest in books about animals is nothing new. Bestiaries were a frequent form of medieval literature, and Aesop's fables were earlier still. Though his stories are traditionally credited to a Phrygian slave of the sixth century B.C., some of them have been found inscribed on Egyptian papyri several centuries before that time. Men have written about animals since they began to write, just as they have been drawing them since the days of the cave men. Nevertheless, the literature about animals has varied in extent and character from one time to another.

The eighteenth century, for example, seems to have been little concerned about them, save in a practical way. Interest in wild animals, certainly, was less than it came to be in the nineteenth century, or than it is today. Its growth was due, probably, to the increasing popularity of big-game hunting. The eighteenth-century English sportsman was content for the most part to chase the fox, and those bulky volumes by retired British colonels, recounting their hunting exploits in India and elsewhere, were still to be written.

A big change took place when we began to write about animals as individuals, in the way that Joy Adamson has written about Elsa the lioness, or Gavin Maxwell about his otters. This is not, of course, strictly a contemporary attitude. Though Kipling, in the *Jungle Books*, was not writing about animals he had known, his creatures were to a certain extent individualized, as, in greater degree, were the animals in Kenneth Grahame's *The Wind in the Willows.* Jack London, in *The Call of the Wild,* and Ernest Thompson Seton, in some of his stories, made a similar approach.

This attitude—interest in animals as individuals—seems to be characteristic of recent books about them. *Born Free, Living Free, Ring of Bright Water* and *The Incredible Journey* all share it. I suspect this to be one of the reasons for their popularity. Joy Adamson's books, of course, had the perennial appeal of novelty. Nobody before her had written with such convincing detail about an attachment between a wild animal and human beings. Something of the same interest applies to *Ring of Bright Water;* the average reader has never seen an otter, and certainly has not lived with one. I have one reservation about Mr. Maxwell's book. Interesting as it is, one puts it down with the feeling that its author cares more about animals than he does about human beings. That preference is true, I believe, of a good many people.

Aside from these considerations, the fact remains that during the last few years books about animals have reached a new level of popularity. Best-seller lists were first published in 1895. Though they are by no means infallible indicators of popular taste—for we must take into account not only the reliability of booksellers' reports, but the books asked for in public libraries as well—they do provide a rough estimate of reading preferences, even though they tend to create them. In more than half a century there were not as many books about animals so listed as in the last three years.

Does that fact point to a form of escape? Is it a reflection of man's recurrent disgust with man, which, incidentally, reached its intensest expression in a period far less distraught than our own, when Dean Swift represented horses as superior to men? Is it a relief to read about animals rather than the kind of people who populate much of current fiction? I shall not attempt to answer the questions I have raised. I am only wondering.

P.S. The phenomenon noted above has continued to grow. Since this column was written, Sterling North's *Rascal,* the story of a boy and his pet racoon, became one of the most popular books of its period, and several others of similar characters have found a host of readers. Naturally, in an era obsessed by sex, we have been offered books about the sexual habits and behavior of animals other than man. I have arrived at no explanation of the phenomenon other than those suggested by the questions asked in the column's concluding paragraph.

Are Maps Literature?

JASPER NATIONAL PARK, CANADA.

Are maps literature? For my own part I am satisfied they are; I can read them with profit and enjoyment when other printed fare, even the best, seems at the time flat and unrewarding. Possibly my enjoyment is heightened by the fact that I once helped to make one, when I first came to this Northwest country, even though batting my way through the tough and tangled underbrush of Puget Sound was the hardest physical work I have ever done. Now, sitting here in a cabin beside the Athabasca as it races north to merge eventually with the Arctic Sea, I can conceive of no better reading than the map before me, as I follow upon it the river courses of the Province of Alberta, of British Columbia and the Northwest Territories.

When I was a boy it was my dream to follow the Mackenzie down to its mouth, but I was not as determined as Joseph Conrad, who, as a youngster, put his finger on a map of Africa, and pointing to the Congo, said: "Some day I will go there." Now I can console myself with the knowledge I did not have when I pored over the map of northern Canada—the Mackenzie flows through interminable stretches of all but barren tundra.

The urge to travel down that particular river no longer teases me, but the desire to go still farther north is strong. How the points of the compass vary in appeal! For some it is the South that pulls and for others the East; my own eyes have always looked to the West and North. A.E. Housman was no wanderer, but he spoke truth for me when he wrote:

> Comrade, look not on the West;
> 'Twill have the heart out of your breast.

Fortunately, I was sparing of adjectives when I spoke last week of western Montana; and while I take nothing back of what I said about Glacier National Park, I must confess that even its beauties dwindle as one comes from them into the heart of the Canadian Rockies. Few places live up to the rhapsodies which have been written about them; the harbor of Rio does, and the massed might of Manhattan as you come up the bay in the early morning; so do the snow-capped bastions of Mount Robson and Mount Edith Cavell; and so did Lake Louise, most touted of scenic beauties on this continent (for the Grand Canyon is more than a view), when I arrived there after days of almost constant rain.

But what am I about? The question was, Are maps literature? And didn't I say last Sunday that presently I would be writing about the literary aspects of the Northwest? Well, "presently" is one of those elastic words. It begins to look now as if I wouldn't get on to Seattle after all, and since no city can truly be called the literary capital of the Northwest, perhaps no great harm will be done. Besides, I have a hunch that there is more literary ferment steaming about the University of Montana at Missoula than anywhere else in the states of Wyoming, Montana, Idaho, Washington and Oregon. And Missoula, incidentally, is one of the most delightful towns it has ever been my fortune to wander into. In beauty of setting, in friendliness, cleanliness and intelligent awareness, evidenced by its willingness to grow slowly and steadily (not to mention its resources for the fisherman), Missoula seems to me a model Western city.

Oh, yes—are maps literature? Of course they are, even in their lowest form, which is the automobile road map. Some of these wear the air of their betters; the Montana State Highways Commission does a particularly good job with its specimens of the genus. (Why, by the way, can't the railroads and the oil companies get together and take note of each other's existence?) Reading the maps issued by either, one would suppose that transportation existed in only one form. The official road map of the Province of Alberta (Government issued) does take note, I see, of air routes. Incidentally, if your imagination is suffering from Koreatis and other contemporary ailments, get yourself a map of the Canadian Airways. If that doesn't put ideas in your head, you are less susceptible to such stimuli than I.

These last remarks, I am aware, are enough to brand me as an intractable escapist. That's all right with me; if I can't see things in better perspective after this journey—whether they are literary, social, political, or merely personal—my trek will have been in vain; only I know that it has not been so. I haven't felt so fully alive since I was twenty-one, when I looked out of my tent on Puget Sound and watched the ships of the Blue Funnel Line heading for the Straits of Juan de Fuca, the Pacific and Australia.

All that aside, I do earnestly recommend maps as literature. Place-names alone are fascinating; so are the river courses, and the relation to them of the mountain ranges. They give rein, as only the best writers can, to your imagination, and again like these, they yield in proportion to what you bring to them.

P.S. Just a correction or two. The University of Washington has proved to be more a center of literary ferment and accomplishment than the University of Montana, where the most publicized product has been the muddled Freudian judgments on American literature of Professor Leslie A. Fiedler. At least the late Theodore Roethke, teaching at the University of Washington, sparked the emergence of a group of interesting young poets of the Northwest. In the matter of place-names, I recommend that somebody devote a little time to those of Texas. They have the most extraordinary variety and range of any State in the Union.

VI

Some Backward Glances

All but one of the columns in this section are thumbnail appraisals of individual writers who are no longer living. Most of them are concerned with literary figures of our own time. Not all of them were writers of the first rank. Some of them were held in higher esteem when they lived than they are today, and others now are given greater regard than was accorded them while they lived. All have been subject to the slightly mysterious, yet always to be accounted for ebb and flow of literary reputations that no writer, however great, can hope to escape. I suppose this recurrent alteration in status is more characteristic of workers in the arts than of men of action. With them too, the pendulum swings, but not as universally. The fame of Alexander the Great has persisted ever since he died wishing for more worlds to conquer. The work of the poets and the taletellers, of the dealers in ideas, is more sensitive to the prevailing winds of a given period. We pay lip service to classics that have endured for centuries. Who knows what the twenty-first century will make of James Joyce or T. S. Eliot, or for that matter, what the twenty-second—if man still occupies the foreground in either—will make of Shakespeare?

Homage to O. Henry

Purely by chance, because I found them in a room where I was a guest, I have recently been reading several volumes of O. Henry's short stories. In last Sunday's issue I referred to him briefly, pointing out the fact that he was the first writer of consequence to take for his field the many-faceted life of New York, and that when people were talking about Ward McAllister's absurd Four Hundred, O. Henry was writing about the "Four Million." He was a pathbreaker who should not be forgotten, and today I'd like to talk about him at some length.

In cool estimation, after not having read him for many years, I think that he suffered an undeserved eclipse of reputation, at least so far as the critics are concerned, and in the view of these readers who anxiously strive to adopt the literary attitudes that are currently fashionable at any particular time. He should be vigorously resurrected as the most understanding writer about New York that we have had, as a delightful humorist, and above all, as a mature and tolerant observer of the human comedy.

At his best, he was an accomplished craftsman who has been unfairly blackballed because of a few technical weaknesses. At his worst, I admit he could be pretty dreadful, but in extenuation of that fact one should remember that he worked at incredibly high pressure, like such greater writers as Dickens and Dostoevski, and that like them, he was spurred on by constant financial need.

This denigration of an excellent and original writer must be laid at the door of those misguided, arrogant, and contemptuous critics to whom a writer's popularity with the ordinary reader is as the traditional red rag to a bull. If he scores with the hungry millions of sheep that are not fed, he is *ipso facto* suspect, as Herman Wouk, let us say, and Betty Smith are today (though neither of these writers can match O. Henry at his best), or as John Marquand was not so long ago, and in some obdurate quarters, still is. Such critics as these will not face the mote in Henry James's eye, or the balderdash in Melville, and in saying this I do not mean to deny that these were writers of big caliber.

These critics have inflated the posthumous reputation of Scott Fitzgerald beyond the bounds of common sense; he was unquestionablv a gifted writer who, in *The Great Gatsby,* wrote one almost flawless book, and who, had he lived into full maturity and self-knowledge, might have done still finer work. I mention him here because there are things in O. Henry which remind me of him, and lead me to suspect that Fitzgerald had read him with profit. They shared in the short story a love of fantasy; O. Henry would greatly have admired "The Diamond as Big as the Ritz," and he might well have written such a story as "The Offshore Pirate." Both of them loved this city before it had become a ghastly simulacrum of itself, but O. Henry, as a wiser and more observant man, was closer to its heartbeat than Fitzgerald ever came, except for a few fine descriptive passages in "Gatsby."

Like Fitzgerald, but with an even defter touch, O. Henry could strike off a phrase that lingers in the memory, as when he wrote of the "thistledown moods" of a girl. If you read him at length, as I have just been doing, he is an exasperating writer, because of the flashes of brilliance repeatedly being obscured, like clouds racing across a harvest moon. He was guilty sometimes of other sins than the trick endings that were his undoing with our critical sobersides; now and then he forsook sentiment for sentimentality; occasionally his natural humor was a trifle forced, and there were times when he got a little drunk on his mastery of words.

At his best, he is delightful, and one marvels at the mental vitality that enabled him to write 250 stories in the space of six years. He was a born storyteller who, if he had never put pen to paper, would have held a willing audience spellbound over a round of drinks. Nor was this all. He could have been a brilliant essayist who bore his acute knowledge of men and women lightly, and who had a humorously speculative mind that reminds me of Clarence Day in his incomparable *This Simian World.*

I don't believe we have had a writer who was as completely at his ease in writing about all the queer characters who make up America; he was at home and convincing on every social level, as so few of our writers have been. He was just as aware as Ring Lardner of human pretensions, but he had a tolerance far exceeding Lardner's, and although his own life gave him much more occasion for bitterness—as in his three years' unjust imprisonment for embezzlement—he never descended into Lardner's limbo of despair. He was a remarkable man, and deserving of our respect.

He has been cursed for the blight he is supposed to have brought upon the American short story, but a lot of our young practitioners in that form might profitably sit at his feet. In reaction against the trick formulas to which he was prone, we went to school to Chekhov; mood and atmosphere, at least until symbols and myth took over, became the requisites of our short-story writing, and in unexpert hands nothing on God's earth can be more boring. Writers for the little magazines, please take note and ask yourselves, Why do men tell stories to one another?

GWTW

Twenty years ago this week, on June 30, 1936, the Macmillan Company brought out a book which was to make publishing history and to establish itself as the most popular novel of the twentieth century. Before the year was out it had sold more than a million copies, but that was only a beginning. By the first of the present year the total authorized sales in all languages had amounted to 8,000,000 copies, and the book had appeared in thirty languages and forty countries. Printings in the English language had run to 5,000,000, and more than 4,000,000 copies had been sold in the United States. The book was, of course, Margaret Mitchell's Civil War novel, *Gone With the Wind.* Even now, after two decades, it maintains a fast-selling pace. During the past year, in various editions published in this country alone, 35,000 copies were sold. Needless to say, these are phenomenal figures, and no book of the present century has even approached them. The only American novel which has had comparable distribution is a forgotten book which a Congregational clergyman, Charles Monroe Sheldon, published sixty years ago. It was a religious novel, called *In His Steps.* Due to a flaw in the copyright, it was widely pirated, and accurate figures of its sale are not to be had, but they are believed to amount to about 8,000,000 copies.

As everybody knows, *Gone With the Wind* became not only the most popular novel of the century, but also the most popular motion picture yet made. More than $4,000,000 was spent on its production, and it has grossed more than $40,000,000. It has been seen by an estimated total of 100,000,000 people in nearly every country of the world. At one theater in London it ran for four and a half years. Never in the history of the motion picture industry has so much public interest been displayed in the question as to which actors were to play the leading parts. Such a mark did this movie set that in spite of our unflagging interest in the Civil War, that subject, so far as the films are concerned, has been rarely attempted since.

Margaret Mitchell was thirty-six-years-old when her book was published. She had been at work on it for ten years. The daughter of an Atlanta lawyer, she came of a family that had been settled in the Atlanta area before the city's founding. She grew up on tales of the Civil War and its aftermath. Her father was an authority on Georgia and Southern history, a president of the Atlanta Historical Society. She had been immersed in her subject from childhood, and as a reporter and feature writer on the staff of the Atlanta *Journal* she had written a series of sketches of Georgian generals in the Civil War. In 1926, because of an ankle injury, she resigned from the paper and started work on what was to become *Gone With the Wind.*

The book, then, was no accident. She brought to it depth of feeling, intimate and prolonged acquaintance with her subject, and, what really turned the trick, an innate and remarkable storytelling gift. She had, too, in spite of the stock quality of some of her characters, an acute understanding of human nature and a sound psychological sense. She was shrewd, too, in her departure from old conventions governing the writing of romances about the South. She chose for her heroine, not the pattern of the Southern lady, who, in the person of Melanie, she placed in contrast to Scarlett O'Hara, but a ruthless, rebellious, on-the-make young woman whom she made one of the most sharply portrayed characters in American fiction.

It may have been no accident either that this heroine of hers, coming along at a time when Americans the country over were being buffeted by circumstance, was presented as one who took circumstance in her stride and consistently refused defeat. Whatever her faults, and they were many and glaring, Scarlett had resolution and courage, an ability and a determination to see things through. She was not an unwelcome apparition when she stepped out on the national stage. That backbone of hers, plus Margaret Mitchell's narrative skill, accounts in large measure, I think, not only for the book's popularity at home, but also for its reception throughout the rest of a bedeviled world.

I do not mean to place *Gone With the Wind* among the greatest achievements in the art of fiction, so far as that art can illuminate and interpret man's passage through life. It is not a profound or original book, but it is an exceptionally vivid and consistently interesting one. The picture of the besieged city has not merely the quality of historical accuracy, but the visual impact of truth. I think the degree of art and of human understanding also, which went into the creation of this book has been generally underestimated, and that *Gone With the Wind,* for various reasons, will have as long a life as any book that has been written in our time.

Lewis and Marquand

In Mark Schorer's life of Sinclair Lewis he mentions an interview with John Marquand which apeared in *Time* magazine in 1949. The interviewer had referred to certain similarities between the two men as satirists, and Marquand was reported as saying, "I would hesitate to rank myself with Lewis; I don't think I have nearly the same stature. But I am working in his vineyard." In 1949 Lewis' best work was long behind him, and Marquand was thinking, of course, of the books which had made Lewis famous. His own novels were to show a similar, if less marked decline. Nevertheless, it was an unduly modest statement and, as such, characteristic of Marquand.

There is no doubt, of course, that *Main Street, Babbitt,* and *Elmer Gantry,* the books in which Lewis' satire was uppermost, had a greater impact on the country than anything Marquand wrote, even though Boston was rocked by *The Late George Apley* and even though it reached a wide and appreciative audience elsewhere. Lewis' other major novels were not primarily satiric; *Arrowsmith* was fundamentally a hymn of praise for the dedicated scientist, even if a few minor characters were satirically treated, and *Dodsworth* was perhaps the first serious effort in fiction to present a big business man as something more than a predator. The portrait of Fran Dodsworth was not so much satire as a release for the resentment Lewis felt toward his first wife—a resentment he was to feel toward the second also.

I do not remember or have at hand the interview with Marquand, but I imagine the similarities observed by the interviewer were much the same as those I pointed out in a column written last year on the occasion of Marquand's death. The chief likeness, obviously, is that he and Lewis loved much of what they pilloried. Marquand at heart admired and felt at one with his inhibited New Englanders, just as Lewis, not too secretly, felt about the Babbitts he mimicked and ridiculed. In this they were both far apart from such a satirist as Swift, in whom man's disgust with man reached a withering intensity unparalleled in any writer before or after him. *A Voyage to the Country of the Houyhnhnms,* you may remember, reduces man to the level he himself assigns to the beasts; the horses, in that bitter fantasy, are the superior creatures. They are the philosophers, man the ignoble animal.

Wherein did Lewis and Marquand differ? Lewis wrote in white-hot anger, no doubt partly directed at the division within himself. He wanted to free himself from the background he derided, but never could, and ended by defending it. It was his good fortune as a writer that the timing of his attacks matched the readiness of the country to applaud them. It was ready for demolition of the myth that all was sweetness and light in the American small town or village; it was ready for an unflattering image of the small-town booster. Mencken helped prepare the ground not only there, but for an assault on the evangelical clergy as well. In its most intense form, satire assumes a savage irony, as it did in Swift, but Lewis is rarely ironical. His work was too much the product of his emotions, too little of his mind.

Marquand's irony was not savage; it was pervasive, but it was cool and gentle. It is his unflagging use of it that differentiates him from Lewis as a satirist. Lewis' humor is boisterous and overcharged; Marquand's is wry. Lewis had the greater force, Marquand the greater subtlety. Sometimes I think his best novel was one in which his own background and his private allegiances were little involved—*Melville Goodwin, U.S.A.* He had, however, enough Army experience to help him understand the military mind and the Army as a way of life. The book was published ten years ago; I think its impact would be greater were it appearing now, when public consciousness of the role being played by the military in our national life has much increased. Even though Marquand's novel does not deal with the menace implicit in the military's rise to power—which had only begun when he wrote it—its pertinence is greater for us now than then.

Melville Goodwin himself is one of the most fully realized characters in American fiction, presented with all his limitations and all his strength. Typical though he may be of the molding imposed by West Point, he exists also as an individual in his own right. Much the same may be said of his wife Muriel, and she and Dottie Peale, who came so near to putting an end to General Goodwin's career, are the two most finished and credible portraits in Marquand's gallery of women. Most of his women lack substance; Muriel and Dottie do not.

No novelists of our century more fully exemplify Pope's axiom of the bent twig than do Lewis and Marquand, so much were most of their books the product of their conditioning. In both are reflected over and over again the irritations and frustrations of their youth. Marquand reached the fuller maturity, for as Alfred Kazin acutely observed in *On Native Grounds,* Lewis' men are boys at heart. Many women insist that all men are precisely that, but I think most of us have known some in whom the boy is deeply and safely buried. Melville Goodwin, I might add, was not one of them.

And Lewis Again

Like many others, I have been thinking much of Sinclair Lewis. I did not know him well, but like everybody who knew him at all, I cannot think of him as a person with indifference. His personality had an impact as vivid as his best writing, and as I think about him

I am aware for the first time of how all human beings may be thought of as partaking chiefly, in their nature, of one of the four ancient elements—earth, air, fire, and water. All of us, it now seems to me, are predominantly to be identified with one or the other. And certainly Lewis' element was fire. His flame was fitful, as is the nature of fire, but flame it was. So fiercely did it burn so much of the time that one wonders he was not sooner consumed.

It is natural, then, that thinking of him as a person, one should think first of his warmth—of the great generosity of spirit, the close mingling of tenderness and sharp irritability, the headlong impulse. These were powerful components in his nature, and they found their way into his writing as well. Equally, one thinks of how unmistakably, both in his life and in his work, he was American. So many of our national characteristics were magnified in him—our restlessness, our energy, our impatience, our quick friendliness, our idealism. He was bone of our bone.

Was he a great writer? It is a hard question, because he was at once so powerful and so limited. Certainly he was great in some respects. I once spoke of him as the greatest photographer in American fiction; perhaps he was the greatest in any. But his strength contained his weakness as well. Photography can go just so far and no farther, and Lewis seldom stepped outside the bounds of his method.

The books by which he will be remembered were written within a ten-year period, beginning mith *Main Street* in 1920 and ending with *Dodsworth* in 1929. His early work was of indifferent quality, like his later. Yet so great was his vitality that from one book to the next, in his declining period, one kept hoping for something comparable with the major books. That hope still lives, worn thin though it is, as one awaits his last novel, soon to be published. It is the story, I believe, of Dodsworth's later years.

Writing twenty-two years ago, when *Dodsworth* was published, E. M. Forster accurately forecast the nature of the work that would follow. "Photography," he maintained, "is a pursuit for the young. So long as a writer has the freshness of youth on him he can work the snapshot method, but when it passes he has nothing to fall back upon. It is here that he differs from the artist (and it is here that I differ with Mr. Forster, for the photographer can be an artist, too, as Lewis was, within the limits of his medium).

"The artist," Forster continued, "has the power of retaining and digesting experiences, which, years later, he may bring forth in a different form; to the end of his life he is accompanied by a secret store." But it is not the artist in the writer that accounts for this ability; it is the possession of a reflective temperament, which Lewis did not have. To go back to the elements with which I started, had there been in his composition more air (the element that makes for poetry, even more than fire), or more water, which in its flow makes for philosophy, he would have been a greater writer, and one whose future course could not have been so easily predicted. Fire burns itself out; air and water are, like earth, more constant elements.

What seems to me to be confusion in Forster's distinction becomes more apparent in the words which followed those I have quoted. "The artist," he wrote, "may not be good. He may be very bad. He generally is. And it is not to celebrate him and to decry the photographer that I draw this distinction between them. But it does explain, I think, why quick, spontaneous writers . . . are apt, when they lose their spontaneity, to have nothing left, and to be condemned by critics as superficial. They are not superficial, they are merely not artistic; they are members of a different profession, the photographic, and the historian of the future will cease to worry over this, will pick up the earlier and brighter volumes in which their genius is enshrined, and will find there not only that genius, but a record of our age."

"Quick" and "spontaneous"—those are the betraying words. Forster uses them as though they were antithetical to the artist, which they are not. Quick and spontaneous Lewis assuredly was, but his telling strokes did not suffer from that fact. However quick and spontaneous their execution, they were the product of selection —the use of the right, the significant detail, and if that is not one of the primary constituents of art, I do not know what art is. And his seizure of the right and significant detail was not accident, for it was accomplished, in his best work, time and again.

In our disappointment over the later years of Lewis' writing career, in our wish that his great gifts might have been supplemented by others which he did not have, the thing to keep in mind is contained in those words of Goethe which I quoted a few weeks ago, in which he said that if a man's writings were "right at the step where they originated, they remain always right, however the writer may develop or alter himself in after times."

Thoreau Then and Now

One hundred years ago today Henry David Thoreau died at the age of forty-four. Such fame as he had in his lifetime was modest and limited. To most of his fellow countrymen his name was unknown, and Europe had never heard of him. "The country," said Emerson in his address at the funeral services, "knows not yet, or in the least part, how great a son it has lost." Today his reputation is world-wide. Save for Herman Melville, no other American writer of his period has had so great an increase in fame.

His first book, *A Week on the Concord and Merrimack Rivers,* was published in 1849, when he was thirty-two, at his own expense. Besides the account of the river trip he had made with his brother some years before, he put into it most of what he had written up to that time—essays, lectures, poems. Much in the book was excellent, but its heterogeneous character was a handicap, and like all his books, it lacked the sense of structure, which with him, as with Emerson, rarely extended beyond the sentence and the paragraph, in both of which, at his best, he was masterly. Of the 1,000 copies printed, less than 300 were sold, and he wryly entered in his journal, "I have now a library of nearly 900 volumes, over 700 of which I wrote myself."

Walden, on which his fame chiefly rests, appeared five years later, in 1854. The almost equally famous essay on "Civil Disobedience," which was to serve as text for Gandhi in his war of passive resistance, was originally a lecture and first appeared, oddly enough, in a transcendentalist symposium called *Aesthetic Papers.* Three books, in addition to his Journals, were not published until after his death. They are *Cape Cod, The Maine Woods* and *A Yankee in Canada.* He also accumulated a vast amount of material for a book on the North American Indian tribes. One regrets that he did not live to pursue this project, for he understood the Indian and felt a kinship with him.

Why was Thoreau's fame so slow in growth, and why has it so greatly increased in our own time? The chronological facts I have cited supply only a partial answer to the first question, and are relevant only in his lifetime. The world has honored many writers who were as temperamentally difficult as Thoreau, but in his case I think that temperament played a part in the delayed recognition. I emphasize this because I can think of no writer in whose work the man himself is so insistently present, sometimes in an overbearing, arrogant way. He was a prickly man, and a very self-centered one. That is one reason, though by no means the only one, why he was the arch nonconformist in American culture.

Emerson, who knew him as well as anyone, and from whom, for all their differences, he unquestionably derives, said of him as a person: "There was somewhat military in his nature, not to be subdued, always manly and able, but rarely tender, as if he did not feel himself except in opposition. He wanted a fallacy to expose, a blunder to pillory, I may say required a little sense of victory, a roll of the drum, to call his powers into full exercise. It cost him nothing to say No; indeed he found it easier than to say Yes. It seemed as if his first instinct on hearing a proposition was to controvert it, so impatient was he of our daily thought. This habit, of course, is a little chilling to the social affections. 'I love Henry,' said one of his friends, 'but I cannot like him; and as for taking his arm, I should as soon think of taking the arm of an elm-tree.'"

Why, then, have the repellent qualities in Thoreau—qualities present in every extremely individualistic personality—been little hindrance to the mounting esteem in which he is held? Because, I think, we admire toughness, and Thoreau was tough. Because although conformity envelops us, we like the man who can say No. We like, too, the realism we find in him. Unlike his transcendentalist friends he kept his feet, most of the time, on the ground.

But Thoreau's virtues transcend contemporary taste. In the attempt to explain the course of his reputation I have dwelt on some of his faults. They were many, both as man and writer, but one must honor a man whose life was lived in the pursuit of values, a life dedicated to determining in what true wealth consists. He wanted to heighten the sense of life in men. He hated the materialism of the society in which he lived, and in which we still live. He is full of paradoxes himself, and it interests me that although we accept and praise him as a modern, if he were still alive no man would be more outspoken against the most powerful current of the time—the aggrandizement of the state, for he said: "I heartily accept the motto, 'That government is best which governs least.'"

I have said nothing about his remarkable union with nature, or his concern over man's increasing divorce from it, or the sinewy strength of his style at its best. He will be read, I think, as long as any other American writer.

The Rise of Ring Lardner

Ring Lardner's posthumous rise in the estimation of the critical fraternity (I plead guilty to abuse of that last word, for critics are far from constituting a fraternity) makes an ironical footnote in American literary history. The irony derives from the fact that Lardner, although he was aware of his worth as a writer, refused, up to the time of his death in 1933, to regard himself with that solemn self-satisfaction so characteristic of those contemporary critics who put on their ceremonial robes whenever they discuss a writer's work. This ability to take a hard look at himself—as hard as he took of so many other people—is one of the facets of his complex personality emphasized by his son Ring, Jr., in a revealing article about his father published in *Midland: The Magazine of the Middle West.*

As the son observes, Lardner's stories made people laugh rather than think, although there is plenty to think about in the best of them. As Ring, Jr. notes, the critics who now find him worthy of serious consideration, are uncomfortable in their fresh-found perspicacity. They strive "to unearth a deeper purpose [than the entertainment he aimed at] beneath his most casual efforts, and especially a tragic symbolism behind his purest strain of nonsense." As one who wrote with enthusiasm about Lardner's work as early as 1926, I wait impatiently for that authoritarian analysis of the turbid and darkly Freudian depths in his fiction which may some day be offered us by such a dedicated prober as Leslie Fiedler, whose interpretation of *Huckleberry Finn* would have made Mark Twain bite his cigar in two.

Let me interject that these strictures do not apply to the excellent introduction Maxwell Geismar wrote for his *Ring Lardner Reader,* for Geismar's is a sensitive and sensible appraisal of Lardner's talent. To the insights it provides, Ring Lardner, Jr., has added others which are helpful in arriving at a just estimate of one of the best short-story writers we have produced. Especially incisive is his observation to the effect that his father's work "was a continuous indictment of people who took themselves too seriously." No writer is as deadly as Lardner in depicting bores, a refreshing gift in a period when so many writers seem wholly unaware that their characters are boring.

True, he who bores me may not bore you, and the writer I find exciting may leave you cold; for that reason it is best not to generalize too freely. I find myself in an apparent minority, for example, when I confess that Salinger's devotion to the Glass family evokes no warm response in me; I find the Glasses tedious. This was not true of *Catcher in the Rye,* which if it does not speak for an entire generation of teenagers, reflects enough of them to justify the vogue it has enjoyed. I have been meaning to reread Tarkington's *Seventeen,* which may suffer from the fact that Tarkington was the adult indulgently observing the teenager, whereas Salinger allowed his youngster to speak for himself. Yet I have a suspicion that Tarkington's Willie Baxter was the more amusing, and, perhaps, truer to the norm than Holden Caulfield.

There is another area in which Lardner's skill is outstanding—the one which was first and most widely recognized—his uncanny ear for the speech of semi-literates. In this domain he has had no match. In one of his rare book reviews he noted that "We say somethin' and nothin', but we say anything and everything," and that "kinda, sorta and fella" were much closer to the spoken tongue than "kinder, sorter, and feller."

One of the frustrations he suffered from—and in silence—says his son, was "to be grouped indiscriminately with writers on a different level entirely, such as Damon Runyon. It wasn't that he resented the graduation of another sportswriter to magazine fiction, or that he couldn't see some humor in the man's work when Runyon didn't strive too hard for it. What was difficult to take was the insensitivity to his own meticulous rendering of American speech patterns and the nuances of oral language among the uneducated. Lardner's characters were drawn from the living world around him. Runyon's inhabited a fairyland of his own devising, in which tough guys with golden hearts spoke a synthetic language that consisted largely of incongruously mixing high flown words with slang."

Evidence of Lardner's close observation is provided by his reply to a copy editor on *The Saturday Evening Post* who tried to correct the first episode of *You Know Me Al* on the grounds that the more common words were misspelled while much harder ones were written correctly. Lardner proved to him that this was exactly what ballplayers did when they undertook prose composition. They thought they knew the easy words; they asked about or looked up the hard ones.

The critics have insisted that Lardner disliked baseball life and felt only scorn for the players. Not at all, says his son; he liked the life and was fond of the men he traveled with. If he did, the fact lightens a little for us the deep shadows of his tragic last years.

Bright College Years

One of my many prejudices has long been held against James Russell Lowell, for his ecstatic but ill-founded tribute to the month of June. I suppose the line beginning, "What is so rare," is better known to Americans than almost any other in our poetry. "Then, if ever," he continued, "come perfect days." He should have been shot for that gross corruption of the truth. June, with the possible exception of March, is the most unreliable month on the calendar. Let me put in a plug for my birth-month of September (even admitting the line-storms and hurricanes), or better still, for the golden month of October. But June! You can never count on her, except for the prevailing fair weather at Harvard commencements.

I speak with authority. Last week (at this writing), in company with 203 contemporaries, plus wives and widows, I attended a fiftieth class reunion. It did me good, like a reunion should. And why not? In spite of three wars, the internal combustion engine, and the Great Depression, more than 300 of the original 664 youngsters who congregated at Cambridge in the fall of 1909 were still reasonably alive. Two hundred and four of them were still sufficiently interested to spend four days together recalling the past and speculating on the future. For three of those days, Lowell notwithstanding, the sun did not shine. Commencement Day dawned fine and clear, and was threatened only when Gov. Endicott Peabody, preceding U Thant, the chief Commencement speaker, put in a plea for the Democratic party. There was a brief shower, during which many of the 12,000 there assembled, fled, though some returned to listen to Mr. Thant's optimistic views regarding the future of a bedeviled world.

Sitting there, or walking about part of the time, for it becomes increasingly hard for me to listen to speeches (as a nation, we talk too much), I began somehow to think about the literary scene of fifty years ago. First I thought of some of its material aspects. When the class of 1913 entered Harvard—and throughout its college life—our textbooks, hard-bound, were in the price range of the better paperbacks today. I see, looking at one still on my shelves, that I paid $1.50 for William James's *Psychology*, and am reminded that tuition was then one-tenth of what it is today. You could eat three meals a day (frequent roast beef included) at Memorial Hall for $5.25 a week. Although the cocktail hour had not yet been invented, the cocktail had, and could be bought at the best bars (there were no public ones in Cambridge) at two for a quarter.

Most of us (the class of 1913) were avid readers of Kipling and H. G. Wells; they, for the average undergraduate with literary inclinations, were the living gods, and no Americans of the time seemed to match their stature, although I recall that Gilbert Seldes, one of my co-editors of *The Harvard Monthly* (unhappily now defunct), contributed a long and appreciative appraisal of Henry James, far in advance of the James revival. Melville had been long forgotten, and I fear that many of us were too ready to accept Professor Wendell's condescending attitude toward American literature. We were, in his estimation, still colonials, although Mark Twain had been famous for many years.

The American literary scene, when my class entered Harvard, was not exciting. It was still full of Victorian holdovers—a poetry that contented itself with ineffectual echoes of Tennyson (it is not my intention to denigrate him) and with novels which, with rare exceptions, were not facing the facts of American life. Those facts were pleasanter then than now, because I think we are confronted with ourselves today as we have never been before: a nation burdened with guilt—not only because of the Negro (for whose plight both North and South are equally culpable), but also because of the American Indian, to whom, colored also, we owe much more (never acknowledged) than to the more articulate minority. Let's face the hard facts, disillusioning though they are: the Negro's vote counts; the Indian's doesn't. We have trampled on them both, and may God forgive us.

It is certainly true that man throughout history has been cruelly guilty of exploiting his fellows. Yet his accomplishments have been astonishing. His ingenuity passes belief. He reaches for the stars and makes a mess of his own little planet. Willingly, I would not contribute a nickel toward placing a man on the moon, and the reason for that attitude is—we have still a job to do here. Let's forget the childish idea of competition. Our planet, the only one we will ever inhabit—and don't kid yourself about that, in spite of all this space nonsense—is a pretty good place on which to live. How would you like Venus's 800 degrees, by our Fahrenheit?

Mann and the Mountain

There can be no doubt that at the time of his death, and for some years before it, Thomas Mann was easily the world's most eminent living man of letters. Through almost the entire first half of this century, he was the most distinguished writer of German birth; in France his world pre-eminence was challenged only, and that not too seriously, by André Gide; in England, after Hardy died in 1928, the only eligibles for similar distinction were, in order of seniority, Shaw, and the lesser known figures of Conrad, Wells, Bennett, Galsworthy, and Eliot. In Russia, after Tolstoy's death in 1910, the only writer to achieve world fame was Gorki. In the United States, Dreiser, Lewis, Faulkner, Hemingway, and the rest, whatever their virtues, could not match the solidity and sustained character of Mann's performance.

These are facts I think we must accept, in spite of the further fact than many people, myself among them, while recognizing Mann's great abilities, do not number him among the writers they most admire. In saying this, I am aware that I am perhaps describing the limits of my own interests and taste, and defining, possibly, the nature of my own prejudices. There is, I think, no cause for shame in this; our individual interests, tastes, and prejudices are, it seems to me, among the inalienable rights of men. Much as I admire certain facets of Mann's work, it is not, in its total effect, my dish of tea. Possibly I have no right to say this, in view of the fact that much of his work I have not read; but I think that when one does not attempt to explore fully the writings of a man whose output one has generously sampled, it is usually because one does not feel irresistibly attracted. When you are aware of this disinclination, you may be pretty sure that however much the writer in question may mean to others, he is not for you.

For these reasons, it seems to me best that I do not attempt any balanced appraisal of what Thomas Mann accomplished; for that I would need close acquaintance with his work as a whole, as well as a stronger feeling of sympathy with the objectives that dictated his performance as an artist. But I do feel free to speak of what there was in him that I enjoyed, and of the reservations I hold.

Among them are, of course, the three works on which his fame, in this country at least, chiefly rested: *Buddenbrooks, The Magic Mountain,* and the tetralogy, *Joseph and His Brothers.* They are all of them formidable books, and, for the most part, written in what may be described as formidable prose; at times I have found it exasperating prose. This is not the fault of his translators; the fault lies first of all, in my estimation, in the nature of the German tongue, which lends itself admirably to poetry, but when applied to prose, becomes awkward and unwieldy. German poetry can be rendered in English with remarkable exactness, losing less in the process than any other language with which I am acquainted. German prose, on the other hand, frequently benefits by skilled translation into English.

But the cause for exasperation cannot be assigned solely to the structure of the German language; some of it must be ascribed to certain characteristic qualities of the German mentality and temperament. Some of those qualities command our admiration; extraordinary diligence and thoroughness, for example; but against these we must balance the lack of a light touch, the absence of subtlety, and the capacity of so many German writers for boring the hell out of readers. All that makes the best French prose a delight, or that made Paris an entrancing city, is absent from German prose and from Berlin; in saying that, I know of course that I am doing scant justice to cities out of the Prussian orbit. Thomas Mann suffered from these failings.

On the credit side, however, one must grant that he observed the temper of the time in which he lived with no little depth of understanding; that is the inner core of *The Magic Mountain,* and there are traces of it even in his remarkable amplification of the Joseph story, which is, I think, a peculiarly German act of creation; no Frenchman, hardly an Englishman, and certainly no American, would have dreamed of attempting what Mann did in that vastly learned and frequently engaging *tour de force.*

He pondered deeply over the disquieting symptoms of his time, and yet he was, I think, as most artists are, politically naïve. There is no question that he had a liberal mind in the best sense of that word, yet he allowed his name to be used in ways which were against the tenets of good sense. He gave much thought to the position of the artist in modern society, and reversed his point of view concerning it. Originally he believed that politics do not concern the artist; he abandoned this belief out of his conviction that the artist must participate in politics in order to preserve the kind of society in which it is possible for him to function. The question is, I believe, debatable. He was a complex and very interesting man, and something of what he did will endure.

The Impudent Sage

The impudent, and one-time omnipotent, sage of Baltimore will be seventy-five tomorrow. In consonance with that solemn occasion, it may be fitting to refer to him by his full baptismal name, Henry Louis Mencken, even though he ranks among the few (R.L.S., T.R., G.B.S., F.P.A. and F.D.R.) who are as well known by their initials as by their given and family names. It would be a happier day for the Republic if he were to be twenty-five again; and I say this, not merely in the vein of anniversary compliment, but in all seriousness. There was a time, I confess, when I thought of him as a vigorous but essentially destructive force, but the years have altered that youthful judgment, and I regard him now as an irritant and tonic which we needed then, and need again today.

It was my good fortune to meet most of the leading literary figures of the Twenties, when Mencken was at his apogee, but to my present regret, I have never laid eyes on the Bad Boy of American Letters. My one conversation with him was brief, and over the telephone. But like almost everybody else, I read him, as far back as the *Smart Set* days, down through the hectic years in which he poured his vitality into the columns of the Baltimore *Sun* and the pages of *The American Mercury*.

To the college generation immediately following my own. Mencken was high priest, tutor, and demigod, and his utterances were law. He flashed across the literary skies of the Twenties like a comet with a long and fiery tail, though those whom he ceaselessly attacked were more prone to see him as the serpent in the Garden of Eden. His impact on American life and letters was pervasive and powerful. Then, in the Thirties and after, his grip on the sympathies and imaginations of the young steadily slackened, partly because he himself was out of sympathy with the New Deal, and also because many of the battles he had fought had been largely won. Mencken had become suspect, and slowly he lapsed into comparative and, after a nearly fatal illness, almost complete silence. During that period of decline in his reputation as a social critic, he buttressed his already considerable contribution to the study of the American language. He stands now as its foremost scholar and interpreter.

Solid though his achievement has been in the recesses of his study, Mencken was made for the arena, and the designation he has cherished most is that of newspaper man. He was one of the best that we, whose journalism is more vital than that of any other nation, have produced. Like every other newspaper man worth his salt, he has been interested in almost everything, and he has shared, more vehemently than most, their innate distrust of the academic. That is one reason why he is needed now: to wage battle against the solemn pundits who have been busily divorcing literature from life, and who have substituted for the English of tradition or the American variation we have developed from it a horrendous jargon of their own concoction on which some day, it is my fervent hope, they will strangle and choke.

Nor would his usefulness end there. He would swoop down like a hawk on the muddy pretensions of the symbol-crazy novelists, on the tenuous refinements of the worshiping plodders in the footsteps of James the Old Pretender. Although his sense of beauty was keen, he never had much to say about poetry; but although that most essential of the arts is now regaining its senses, it would be invigorating to have him tear into the straggling rear-guard of the already outmoded avant-garde.

Sampling him again in the excellent selection from his work made by Alistair Cooke, *The Vintage Mencken,* one is struck by several outstanding qualities. First, and the most essential in any writer, he could make words do his bidding; he was their master, and he could make each one count. Second, as Mr. Cooke observes in his very perceptive introduction, he was, even in his heyday, "vastly underrated as a humorist." Like every good humorist, he must be taken with a grain of salt, particularly since, like all typically American humor, his, too, rests chiefly upon exaggeration.

Again, like all true humorists, he rests on a solid base of sound common sense, for actually the essence of humor (though not of wit) is a sensible and balanced adaptation to life. That, of course, is why fanatics of any kind, whether Prohibitionists, Fundamentalists, or Do-Gooders of any description, are never amusing. If you read him carefully, and with an open mind, you will see that behind even the most outrageous overstatements of which Mencken is capable, there lurks the shadow of good sense, sharpened by a consistently realistic approach to all matters of human behavior. Even his most fragrant cynicisms are tinctured with human understanding. Though he utters more quarter and half truths than full ones, little that he says can be discarded as complete nonsense, whether he is talking about the relationship between the sexes, democracy, or the essence of true faith.

To end on a literary note: nobody, I think, has ever described as succinctly as he the reasons for the death of the genteel tradition: "a dearth of intellectual audacity and of esthetic passion."

Albert Camus and Man's Long Dialogue

As man and writer, the outstanding fact about Albert Camus, who has been awarded the Nobel Prize for literature, is his deep and active involvement in the world of his time. This concern with the intellectual and moral climate in which he lives is more pronounced in his work than in that of any contemporary writer of world reputation. In a period more conscious of itself, more continuously occupied with describing itself, than any other in the world's past, this may account in some measure for the committee's choice.

Europe, with good reason, questions the future more searchingly, and more apprehensively, perhaps, than any other part of the world. She looks back over a long and brilliant past and forward into a future of problematical length and indistinguishable character. And Camus, more insistently than any of her writers, has been asking himself questions about her future and that of mankind.

Although he has written novels, plays, essays and a vast amount of polemical journalism, he is essentially a philosopher and a moralist. He is not a formal philosopher, in the sense of one who has evolved a system. But he has above all else a questioning mind, which, from Socrates down, has been the distinguishing mark of the breed.

The Nobel Prizes do not include an award for philosophy, but this is the fourth time that the prize for literature has gone to a writer whose work is notable chiefly for its philosophical content. Rudolf Eucken, Henri Bergson, and Bertrand Russell were thus honored, and although the forms in which Camus has expressed himself have been more varied than theirs it is as a thinker rather than as an artist that he has commanded attention.

The bent of his mind was evident when he finished his formal schooling. Born in Algeria of a Spanish mother and an Alsatian father, he took his degree at the University of Algiers in philosophy, with a thesis on Plotinus and St. Augustine. For several years afterward he was absorbed in the world of the theater; as a dramatist he is little known in this country. We know him for his novels, *The Stranger, The Plague,* and *The Fall,* his philosophical essays, his dedicated work as a journalist during the French Resistance and his controversies with Jean-Paul Sartre.

It is easy enough to understand the commanding position Camus has assumed in the intellectual life of France, to see why so many of her younger generation have looked to him for guidance. He began by sharing their despair, their conviction of the emptiness of life. They were convinced, as anyone must be who reads him with an open mind, of his complete intellectual honesty—subtle though he can be; they were impressed by his unwillingness to accept easy affirmations, and they respected his evident effort to find a solid base from which to confront the disordered world which we all share.

Camus is only forty-four; he is still seeking that base, as any reflective reader of *The Fall* must be aware. Certain things he has been able eloquently to affirm: the importance of the individual and of the individual's sense of responsibility. He can unreservedly condemn, as Sartre cannot, the justifications that the Communists put forth in defense of indefensible acts. He sees clearly that man is confronted now by the most important choice in his history; either he goes forward or he destroys himself.

Although Camus' most recent work, *The Fall*, is fictional in form, it is actually a philosophical monologue, which must be read between the lines, because of its ironic, oblique approach. It is the work of a man who still seeks the ultimate answer to life. And yet, in spite of this indeterminate quality, I think it is a book that any human being, unless he is impregnably insulated by self-deception, can read with profit. Camus makes you examine and question your best motives, a thing all of us must do if we are to live honestly.

What I like best about it, and what I must admire in all of Camus that I have read, is his freedom from arrogance. That is the great virtue of the skeptical mind; it does not presume to know. It does not ignorantly assume, it does not presumptuously deny. It inquires, it seeks to know. Camus has this quality in fuller degree, perhaps, than any contemporary writer. He said once, several years ago, one of the saddest things that can be said about the world of today: "Man's long dialogue has come to an end." He meant, of course, that it has somehow become difficult for men to reason with one another, thus bringing us face to face with the fact that the man you cannot reason with is a man to be feared, and that this century might fittingly be called the century of fear.

The award is a good one, yet I cannot forbear regret that another skeptic, another writer of great integrity, whose time grows short, was again passed by. I refer to Robert Frost.

The Sun Also Sets

He met a fitting, if unfortunate, end; it would have been anticlimatic had Hemingway died in his bed. Death had grazed him often in the kind of life he lived; indeed, so great was death's fascination for him, that he seemed at times to seek it. He was, in any case, one of those people who are accident-prone. He suffered many, and certainly one would wish to believe that when death claimed him, it was by virtue of the last accident in a long series.

When a writer of such distinct and dramatic personality comes to the final curtain, one thinks first of the man himself—and then of what he wrote. That is the order in which I wish to speak of him. It has been truly said that he was the Byron of our time—not only another handsome, gifted youth who found himself famous almost overnight but closely akin in temperament too, unlike as they were in many ways, both as men and writers. Both were fundamentally men of action who were at the same time endowed—or burdened, if you like—with a sensitivity which made them writers also. Scarred as Hemingway's powerful body was by one mischance or another, the skin was thin, physically and spiritually. There is a wistfulness about the eyes and mouth in some of the pictures taken in his last years, (notably in one by Karsh of Ottawa) that strikes to one's heart.

Dedicated artist though he was—a man fiercely devoted to his craft—and a more disciplined one than Byron, he was capable at times of the same contempt for writing as a way of life, and so he had to prove himself in other ways. It is a virus that attacks all writers who are constitutionally both doer and poet. Hemingway was both. Like Byron again, he craved sensation. He would have applauded, if he read it, Byron's remark in his Journals: "The great object is sensation—to feel that we exist, even in pain. It is this 'craving void' which drives us to gaming—to battle—to travel—to intemperate, but keenly felt pursuits of any description, whose principal attraction is the agitation inseparable from their accomplishment." Both Hemingway and Byron were passionate observers; both could identify themselves wholly with a cause, as Byron did over Greek independence, and Hemingway in his hatred of fascism. Finally, again like Byron, he will be remembered as much for the legend he wove about himself, as for the best of what he wrote.

Though we never met, I had some correspondence with him in recent years which was sufficiently revealing, I think, to warrant mention here. Partly, this came out of a mutual love for the Rocky Mountain country, and aside from the manner of his death, I think it fitting that he died and will be buried in Idaho, his final choice of a home. We had something of an argument as to whether the Big Horns have foothills, but let that pass. Writing to him eight years ago, I expressed the hope that he would some day do a novel about the Far West. In answer he said that his wife had been urging him to do so ever since he took her out to Wyoming, adding, "But I thought *The Big Sky* was so good I wouldn't have to do it."

When I wrote to tell him how much I liked *The Old Man and the Sea,* he replied: "I love the hills and the sea about the same. When I'm either place I can't stand to leave. . . . I don't know how it is with you, but every time I come back from being at sea everybody seems sort of phony. It is the same way up in the hills."

There is more I might tell about this exchange of letters, but I must leave myself room for a few remarks about his stature as a writer. He was the greatest descriptive writer of our time, and in this his economy of words, and his choice of them was as superb as Kipling's, and sometimes better. He gave a new dignity and strength to the American short story. Beside his best work in that field, the contemporary fuss over Scott Fitzgerald seems faintly ridiculous. Fitzgerald, for all his gifts, never approached, in that form, the mastery that Hemingway achieved. Hemingway was a master of mood, of atmosphere, and these are, perhaps, the basic qualities of the great short story.

It is, indeed, his possession of that gift that gives distinction to the best of his novels. That is the aura that clings to *The Sun Also Rises,* however inconsequential most of its people are; it is what makes the poignancy of *A Farewell to Arms,* what broods over *For Whom the Bell Tolls,* and lends an overpowering unity to *The Old Man and the Sea.* It is present now and then even in his inferior works, like *Across the River and Into the Trees.* And that is why I referred to him earlier as a poet. There have been great novelists who were untouched by poetry—Balzac was one, Dreiser another.

There are debits in the accounting, of course, but I shall not dwell on them here. He was not a thinker. He did not, on the evidence of his novels, understand women or their relations with men; he did not understand the social, political, and economic currents of his time. He never achieved emotional maturity or a balanced view of human life. But he was a great writer nevertheless, and an artist to the bone. He will have a lasting place, not only in American literature, but in that of the world. As a writer of determined convictions, he might delete half the adjectives in this piece about him, but I shall let them stand.

The Supreme Poet of Love

Two hundred years ago today, in the hamlet of Alloway in Ayrshire, Robert Burns was born. Other poets share his world-wide fame, but none has ever held a quite comparable place in the hearts and minds of his own countrymen or evoked a quite similar affection among those of another race. None has written songs which are so much the possession of the world, and few poets, even those of greater stature, have spoken to all men as did this Scottish peasant. His was the rarest gift among writers: the capacity to reach both the most subtle and the most untutored minds. In his own time Coleridge acknowledged his genius, Yeats in ours. And beside their reactions you must place those of the plowboys and the serving-maids who were ready, when his work was first published, to use their little savings for the purchase of a copy.

The biographers have found him more provocative material than the critics. There is much that the literary historians can say about him—his part in the romantic movement, his anticipation, in some respects, of what Wordsworth brought into English poetry, but the poems and songs themselves, however much they elicit appreciation, somehow resist and defy analysis. They are like certain manifestations of nature, to be accepted without question or critical consideration.

The man himself, unlike his poetry, is not easy to understand. Much in him can be explained, but there is always something that eludes us. His rebelliousness of spirit can be accounted for, in large measure at least, by the experience of his childhood and youth—stark poverty and the uncompromising righteousness of his most honorable and well-intentioned father. If it had not been for the elder Burns' typical Scottish determination to secure for his sons a better education, however meager, than his own, Robert, his eldest, might never have accomplished what he did. The father was, too, a man of deep intuitions; he recognized early that Robert was a remarkable child, yet he feared for him, and on his deathbed, expressed that concern—rightly felt, considering the dark final years of Robert's life.

He died at thirty-seven; Byron was to die at thirty-six. I mention them together because along with the deep dissimilarities of background, there were equally deep likenesses. Both were men of tempestuous temperament, preyed upon by fluctuations of mood; both had an enormous energy for life, of which, in a way, their poetry was a byproduct. Both were dissolute, yet here, too, the differences were great. Women played a large part in both their lives, but Byron, I think, was revenging himself through women because of his unhappy relations with his mother. Burns, however contradictory and inexcusable his behavior sometimes seems to be, really loved. Their transparent sincerity helps to make his love poems among the greatest we have.

His early death was not so much the result of dissipation—he was a man with a low tolerance for strong drink—as it was the gradual succumbing, through years of strain, of a body—his heart in particular—which had been irreparably injured by physical work beyond his strength as a boy. One of the contradictions in him was that although he was a countryman to the bone, and came gladly back to Ayrshire after his two years of adulation in Edinburgh, he was not a successful farmer. Yet this was not due to a lack of practicality, for he successfully performed his exacting duties as an exciseman.

Apparently it was from his mother (who, unlike her husband, never considered him an unusual child and rather favored his younger brother Gilbert) that Burns derived his love and his gift for song. And the fascinating, and again contradictory fact about his capacity to write songs that have won the world's heart is that he was never able to sing himself. As a child he seemed almost tone-deaf. As he grew older, and when with boon companions, a little liquor took its effect, music entered his speech, but he was never a singer. How strange a lack in the man who wrote "Flow Gently, Sweet Afton," and "Ye Banks and Braes of Bonny Doon!"

It seems to me—and perhaps this is because of my own Scottish blood—that enough credit has never been given Burns for the revolution in poetry that is generally attributed to Wordsworth. Before the *Lyrical Ballads,* Burns was writing poetry of the kind that Wordsworth felt needed to be written: he was writing about the everyday life of ordinary men, and using their speech to do so. Technically, he borrowed from his predecessors, but in attitude he was blazing a path as surely as any poet has ever done.

This is one of the men, particularly among writers, whom I would like to have seen in life. Many of us would give a great deal to have seen Shakespeare in the flesh and I suppose all of us have in our minds certain figures for whom the existent pictures are not enough. Scott said of Burns that he had never seen such another eye in a human head. I would have liked to see those eyes flash fire, as they so often did.

D. H. Lawrence and the U.S.A.

Today the Old Self of this column, in the manner of Max Beerbohm's famous series of drawings, is confronted, somewhat to his confusion and dismay, by the Young Self. Five years ago, dissenting from the view of Robert Frost presented by Lionel Trilling at a dinner in celebration of Frost's eighty-fifth birthday, I made some references to D. H. Lawrence's opinions about the great American writers and the American experience. Mr. Trilling had used some of those opinions in support of his conception of the nature of Frost's work. My present confusion and dismay is not due to any change of attitude toward Mr. Trilling's view of Frost, for I still think that to picture him as "a terrifying poet" is a distortion of the truth. What confounds me is the obtuseness with which I spoke of Lawrence.

I said then that although Lawrence had some perceptive things to say about American writers, "he failed in ultimate understanding of them, and of the American experience." This was, I must now admit, far from the truth. After a lapse of many years, I have just finished rereading Lawrence's *Studies in Classic American Literature.* The book first appeared in 1923. Either my early reading of it was cursory, or my literary sensibilities have greatly altered, for on the basis of this later reading, I must say that I regard it as one of the most illuminating books in its field.

Indeed, when I have said that, I have not said enough. I would go so far as to maintain that it is a book no intelligent, open-minded American can read without a better understanding of his country and of several writers who produced some of its greatest books. It is, moreover, a work of disturbing and possibly prophetic truth so far as the ultimate future of the American people is concerned. There are few contemporary critics who would dispute Lawrence's title to genius, however imperfect some of his work was, and however exaggerated were some of his attitudes. Even his wildest flights take off from the earth. All his opinions rest on a substratum of truth, for he was a man capable of profound insights, both into literature and life.

This book appeared at a time when even the disillusionments which accompanied World War I and its immediate aftermath were insufficient to destroy the fabric of "the American dream." Among other things, you may recall, there would soon be a chicken in every pot and two cars in every garage. (We may almost have realized these two American promises, but more of us now than then are asking, So what?)

When Lawrence finished the book, which had been several years in the making, he was living in New Mexico; he had begun it before coming to the United States. "Look at me," he wrote in his Foreword, "trying to be midwife to the unborn homunculus!"—meaning of course, the nation and its literature which were to come. Were he alive today, he would, I think, be even more deeply confirmed in his fears about our development as a people. What his opinion would be about the current state of American literature I will not venture to guess. But he would still find us intent on the value of plumbing and fixed in our determination to save the world—still bemused about ourselves and the values by which we live.

The writers he discussed at some length were Franklin, the Frenchman, de Crèvecoeur, who became enamored of our rural frontier, Cooper, Poe, Hawthorne, Richard Henry Dana, Melville, and Whitman. There are passing references to Emerson and Thoreau. Oddly, he never mentioned Mark Twain. About all the writers whose books he considered in some detail, he has penetrating things to say. These dissections are so acute that whether one accepts them *in toto* or not, the impact of his views is such that one can never see any of these men in quite the same way again. To me these estimates seem predominantly just; in each case the admiration he feels is tempered by his perception of underlying weaknesses.

I take exception to his treatment of Franklin, even though some of his barbs are well placed. He is more than a trifle condescending to Ben, whom I think of as the first American "man of the world." Lawrence seems to ignore the fact that Franklin comported himself as an intellectual equal in eighteenth-century England and France. Not even Lawrence escapes the customary English tone of patronage where colonials, or former colonials, are concerned.

Yet it must be granted that Lawrence drove deep into the American consciousness and unconscious as well. How contradictory for so many of us to believe, as we have, that the Puritans came here in search of that freedom of worship which they themselves denied to others! By 1700, as Lawrence observes, there was more freedom of worship in England than here. I believe him correct in his contention that our first settlers came for other reasons—to escape from themselves, from the European past, from authority of any kind; something deep in us created the lawless West. "Somewhere deep in every American heart," says Lawrence, "lies a rebellion against the old parenthood of Europe. Yet no American feels he has completely escaped its mastery."

Read and ponder his chapter on "The Spirit of Place." Read and ponder also his repeated observations on the duality in all of us.

Some of these are profoundly true in their application to literature and to life.

Ellen Glasgow I

The death of Ellen Glasgow marks the passing of one of the finest artists in American fiction. Aside from her merits as a novelist she commanded one of the best prose styles of our time; she never wrote a shoddy line. She had humor, she had wit, and though she saw life as essentially a tragic spectacle she had a courage which made the dominant note of her fiction. It was her passionate conviction that the novel, if it aims to rise above the level of mere entertainment, should illuminate the life it depicts, and this was one of the achievements of her own work.

The literary historians will say of her first of all that she rescued the fiction of the South from sentimentality; that, with her, realism crossed the Potomac. She began her literary career in vigorous rebellion against the rosewater romance in which the fiction of her region was bathed, and she held firmly to her purpose in all that she wrote. But like other literary rebels before her, she lived to frown on the fruits of her rebellion. Of writers like Faulkner and Caldwell she had this to say in *A Certain Measure.*

"I have refused to be carried away by the present grotesque revival in Southern fiction, which is a remote logical result of our earlier hallucination, the sentimental fallacy. The sense of horror is not only human, it is useful, and entirely legitimate, literary motif. None of us, I imagine, is completely immune from its power. And heaven forbid that I should set out as a champion of that forlorn hope—human behavior. One may admit that the Southern States have more than an equal share of degeneracy and deterioration; but the multitude of half-wits, and whole idiots, and nymphomaniacs, and paranoiacs, and rakehells in general, that populate the modern literary South could flourish nowhere but in the weird pages of melodrama. There is no harm in the fashion, one surmises, until it poses as realism. It may be magnificent, indeed, but it is not realism, and it is not peculiarly Southern."

Being more clear-eyed, and of a tougher and sharper mental fiber than was common among those of whom she was chiefly to write, she saw her Virginian ladies and gentlemen living in a maze of illusions, divorced from the world of actuality. She was determined to employ a realistic approach in her picture of the society which they composed, but she was equally determined that her realism would not be the bare factual transcript of experience. She early realized that a merely documentary realism—what she refers to in *A Certain Measure* as "the notebook style," by whomever it has been used to the exclusion of the interior life of human beings, has produced only a surface reading of life. "Behavior alone," as she once wisely observed, "is only the outer envelope of personality," and it is one of the strengths of her fiction that she pierced beneath that covering.

Her best novels, to my mind, were *The Romantic Comedians, Barren Ground,* and *The Sheltered Life.* Also, these three together exhibited all her gifts. *The Romantic Comedians* has the lightest touch; in it her irony and wit have the freest play. In *Barren Ground,* where she was intent upon establishing and maintaining a tragic mood, she rigidly excluded the humor which was natural to her, lest she weaken the unified effect for which she was working.

That book and *The Sheltered Life* are, it seems to me, technically her purest achievements, the one for its unbroken unity, the other for its skillful counterpoint. In *Barren Ground* an unforgettable record of indomitable spirit comes to us solely through the transmitted experience of the single person through whose sensibilities the entire narrative takes its course. It is, I think, the most deeply felt of all Miss Glasgow's novels. Her friends knew that, like Dorinda Oakley of *Barren Ground,* she had learned to live without joy.

In *The Sheltered Life* she employed, for the unfolding of her story, a very different method. As she herself wrote of the book, "Age and youth look on the same scenes, the same events and occasions, the same tragedy in the end. Between these conflicting points of view the story flows on, as a stream flows in a narrow valley. Nothing happens that is not seen, on one side, through the steady gaze of the old man seeing life as it is, and, on the other side, by the young girl, seeing life as she would wish it to be." It is the unobtrusive art of that counterpoint, the perfect balance of the two viewpoints, balanced as they are in life itself, which secure for *The Sheltered Life* its echoing truth.

I don't suppose that any woman novelist since Jane Austen has displayed a keener understanding of the male ego than Ellen Glasgow. Her old men were among the best of her creations, but she showed as great perception in writing of her own sex. She had an untiring interest in the technique of the novel, but she never forgot that its cornerstone is its concern with character.

Ellen Glasgow II

It is now ten years since Ellen Glasgow's death. In common with greater and lesser writers she has already been subject to the ordinary vicissitudes of literary reputation. One observes, for example, Mr. Alfred Kazin, in his current collection of essays, *The Inmost Leaf,* conspicuously retreating from his earlier estimate of her work. In his *On Native Grounds,* published in 1942, he had no hesitation in applying the word "great" to certain of her novels, or in finding her talent "much stronger and more interesting" than Willa Cather's. Today he writes that her novels, "though they figure respectably on the shelves, possess too little real force and nowadays serve mostly those tiresome spokesmen for gentility, like J. Donald Adams, who are always warning us against modern literature."

Though I have some difficulty in recognizing myself in this description, I have none in reaching the conclusion that Mr. Kazin's perceptions came closer to the truth in what he wrote thirteen years ago than do his present observations; they were youthful, yet free from that frequent fault of youthful intellectual judgments—condescension. It is Mr. Kazin's right, as it is that of any other critic, to reverse his judgment, but one expects to find some reasonable explanation for the reversal.

Ellen Glasgow was one of those writers who have a long and steady development. She did not, like so many of our contemporaries, burst upon the literary scene with a brilliant first novel, and then fizzle out, either rapidly or slowly. Her early novels were no great shakes, as she herself fully realized. There was discernible talent, yes, but a talent that had not found itself, and did not, until a lot of living and thinking had brought it to fruition. Her potential stature first became apparent with *Virginia,* published when she was nearly 40—the earliest age, as someone has remarked, at which a novel may be written which is worth the attention of mature minds. There have been exceptions, of course, but I think you can count them on the fingers of your hands, and you won't need both if you confine yourself to American literature.

While I do not place Ellen Glasgow among the world's greatest novelists—or any other woman, for that matter, fine as have been the achievements of that sex—I do rank her among the best we Americans have produced. In one respect she stands pre-eminent. She is the wittiest novelist in our history, bar none, and one of the best stylists.

This latter quality, as I have observed here before, is no indispensable quality of great fiction; it was not the possession, to name but two of the world's greatest novelists, of either Dickens or Tolstoy. Willa Cather was her superior in some respects, but she had neither wit nor humor, and Miss Glasgow had both.

What else did she have? A great deal. She had what all good writers about human life have had—a sense of the shadowy line between comedy and tragedy—a sense that cannot be alive unless the writer has, fundamentally, the tragic sense of life. It is a sense that can be acquired in only one way—by having lived below the surface of life. This she did, as any perceptive reader of *The Woman Within*—what might be called her spiritual autobiography—must realize. It was my good fortune to know her well. She was a woman of great courage (the quality she once described as "the only lasting virtue"), but for which she more often used the word "fortitude," because courage can be a flash in the pan, whereas fortitude connotes endurance.

It is a quality with which she more frequently endowed the women about whom she wrote, than the men. This was not merely because she had twice been disappointed in love; it was the just realization of a very feminine woman who happened to possess some of the attributes of the masculine mind, that her own sex is the one consistently schooled in fortitude; men have, of course, displayed it time and again, under stress of emergency; for women it has been a part of daily living.

She understood men to a degree not even surpassed by the novelist with whom she has most in common—Jane Austen. So far as I am aware, we know next to nothing about Jane Austen's intimate acquaintance with the opposite sex. Both women never married, both found their material in a provincial society, both were novelists of character and both wrote about men with a penetration seldom possessed by male novelists writing about women. Miss Glasgow wrote with special insight when she dealt with aging men: General Archibald in *The Sheltered Life* and Judge Honeywell in *The Romantic Comedians* are among her best creations.

Too much, perhaps, has been made of her role as a satirical critic of the Southern society into which she was born; that was one of her important functions as an American novelist—her exposure of the South's romantic tradition; but it is my belief that she will be remembered longer for her deeply considered reading of the human heart, studied by accident in the milieu she knew best, for her understanding of the age-old conflict between youth and age, and of the never-ending battle between the sexes.

John Buchan, the Graeco-Roman Scot

LONDON

John Buchan, later Lord Tweedsmuir, had many readers and friends on our side of the Atlantic, both in the United States and Canada, where, while serving as Governor General, he died in 1940. His fine autobiography, *Memory Hold-the-Door,* known to American readers as *Pilgrim's Way,* is admirably supplemented by a book I have just come upon—*John Buchan by His Wife and Friends.* It was published here by Hodder & Stoughton in 1947 and is still in print, but no American edition has yet been issued. Because of the intimate pictures it provides of a remarkable man, I am sure many admirers of John Buchan who are unaware of its existence will be glad to know about it.

He was a man of extraordinary versatility, strength of character and charm. One cannot read his autobiography and the subsequent memoir without being impressed by the degree to which he possessed these qualities. The two books bring one into contact with that increasingly rare phenomenon—a completely integrated personality. In him the man of action and affairs, the scholar and the artist, were strikingly blended. These capacities were accompanied by an outstanding human warmth, a never-flagging interest in and concern for other people, to the end that when he died, the editor of the *Times* (London) observed that never had that newspaper received so many tributes to a public figure.

As a writer, John Buchan's range was exceptional. Many readers know him only as the author of superior tales of adventure—thrillers, if you like—a field in which he has had no successor of comparable distinction. But the man who could toss off, by way of diversion, such stories as *Prester John, The Thirty-Nine Steps* and *Greenmantle,* much of them written on train journeys, was also a historian and biographer of eminence. Besides his history of World War I, he wrote lives among others, of the Emperor Augustus and Cromwell, and of his two great national heroes, Montrose and Sir Walter Scott, men whose characters are strongly reflected in his own. There are those who regard his Scott as the best portrait ever drawn of Sir Walter. Buchan published more than fifty books, including one volume of poems and such titles, even, as *The Taxation of Foreign Income, The Kirk in Scotland* and *The Royal Scots Fusiliers.*

How, one asks, was such a body of work produced—much of it memorable in quality—in a lifetime of sixty-five years, most of them crowded with other activities in which he achieved equal distinction? After the study of law, from which he turned away, he began his career as secretary to Lord Milner when High Commissioner for South Africa; he served through World War I in various capacities, including that of Director of Information; he was for many years a book publisher and a Reuter's executive; he served in Parliament; he represented the Crown first as Lord High Commissioner to the General Assembly of the Church of Scotland, and later as Governor General of Canada. He made innumerable speeches and worked on innumerable committees. And yet he found time to be an ardent mountain climber, amateur naturalist and fisherman, a tireless traveler, a dedicated friend, a devoted husband and father.

How was it done? The answers to my question—for there are more than one—may be found in his face and in *John Buchan by His Wife and Friends.* The face makes one conceive of a Scottish Roman; shrewdness, iron will and a driving force are all graven there. Those qualities provide one answer; the others are supplied by Lady Tweedsmuir and the testimony of his friends. He kept the sense of life as adventure to the end; he was, like many Scots, romantic and realist in one; he was self-disciplined to the nth degree; his interests flowed in many channels, and were unceasingly alive.

In his Preface to the memoir, the historian George M. Trevelyan observes that "we often say of a man that he was greater than his work; of another, that his work was greater than the man. It would be hard to place John Buchan in either of these classes. The man and his work run an even race. And the two seem inseparable." To call John Buchan a Scottish Roman is to use applicable words, but they do not sum him up. They are well supplemented by what one of his sons—Alastair—wrote of him, pointing to a quality which is Greek rather than Roman: the balance and inner harmony he achieved in his life, like his hero Sir Walter Scott. "Only twice in Canada," writes his son, "did I see the light go out of his eyes: once when endorsing a death warrant; and when signing Canada's declaration of war."

When he wrote his autobiography, he was still Governor General, and did not feel free to write of Canada at that time, as he meant later to do. He loved the country, which loved him in return. Much of his life there is, however, told in Lady Tweedsmuir's pages, which also evoke, with vividness and charm, other phases of their life together. To her memories of him are added those of such friends as A. L. Rowse of Oxford, Catherine Carswell (the biographer of Burns) and Leonard Brockington, who writes of Buchan's great contribution to Canada's understanding of herself.

Kipling I

It makes an interesting and possibly significant turn in literary events when T.S. Eliot, of all writers, places before us a selection from Kipling's verse and enters an earnest plea for his recognition as a great ballad-maker. It was time for such an effort as Mr. Eliot has made, and one hopes it may be followed by a similar espousal of Kipling's prose. For in Kipling's case the long and persistent detraction of a great writer had long since reached the point of absurdity.

Impatience with Kipling's politics was in large measure, though not entirely, the cause of this detraction, and Mr. Eliot has undertaken something of an apologia on this score. To do this, it seems to me, is only to obscure the issue. Kipling's politics, it has long been my belief, have very little to do with his contribution to English literature and will have still less as time goes on. What if he was a Tory. What if his attitude toward the British Empire was one that is not consonant with liberal thought? Kipling did not sit in Downing Street; his principality is in the wide, uncharted world of the imagination. He had the gift of magic, both in verse and prose, to a degree granted to few men of his generation. Let him be appraised for what he was: an artist of extraordinary endowment.

As Mr. Eliot insists, he was a great ballad-maker who sometimes achieved poetry. It was only occasionally that his politics ran away with his verse; the bulk of it has quite other claims upon our attention. If he could achieve the simplicity and force of the ballad form more completely than any other modern writer, he was also one of the most wide-ranging and skilled technicians in the history of English poetry. His accomplishment in that respect has seldom been adequately emphasized.

As a tale-teller he stands unmatched in our time. There is no one living who can write stories to place beside "The Man Who Would Be King," "Without Benefit of Clergy" and "The Brushwood Boy." And the *Jungle Books* and *Just-So Stories* have an immortality as secure as that of *Alice in Wonderland.*

Kipling wrote his own appeal to posterity in the lines which bring to a close the Definitive Edition of his verse:

> If I have given you delight
> By aught that I have done,
> Let me lie quiet in that night
> Which shall be yours anon.
>
> And for the little span
> The dead are borne in mind,
> Seek not to question other than
> The books I leave behind.

He is not the only writer of his period whose achievements have been belittled and will as surely be restored to their rightful stature. Conrad is another. He suffered, as Kipling did, from the inferior quality of his later books, but that in itself, as in Kipling's case, is not sufficient explanation of the shadow cast over his reputation. Again, as with Kipling, his eclipse had nothing to do with his powers as a writer. Conrad's start began to wane in a period when a negative attitude toward life was in the ascendant. It was purely accident—the fruit of his early life—that he wrote of the sea and the remote corners of the earth. Actually, he was primarily interested as a novelist in the souls of men; life held meaning for him only in terms of honor, loyalty and courage, and in a period when it became the literary fashion to treat such matters lightly or to ignore them, Conrad fell into disfavor.

In like manner Galsworthy came in for a pounding from the younger generation of critics. Here again the undermining of a reputation was brought about partly by a decline in the quality of the novelist's later work. It was the more serious in Galsworthy's case because in the novels which made up *A Modern Comedy* and *End of the Chapter* he was carrying forward the delineation of a social picture which he had opened so forcefully and revealingly in the novels which composed *The Forsyte Saga*. But he was suspect also because he hovered frequently on the border line of sentimentality. What his detractors failed to see was that almost always he avoided going over the line by a hairsbreath. He was not afraid of sentiment, and frequently his critics were unable to make the real distinction which exists between sentiment and sentimentality. In any case, "The Forsyte Saga" stands secure as the illuminating record of a social class and its complete attitude toward life. It will long survive the fluctuations of its author's reputation.

Such eclipses, partial or complete, are commonplaces of literary history. The greatest have not escaped them. They come with certainty, but they pass also just as surely.

Kipling II

Slowly, but with increasing momentum, Rudyard Kipling is being restored to his rightful position as one of the great writers of the modern age. Or rather, it would be more correct to say that he is only now being fully appreciated for the right reasons. For more than a generation his reputation has unjustly suffered because his political point of view was offensive to so many whose political attitudes were cast in a more liberal mold. So intense was the antagonism generated by this difference that most critics of this century were unwilling to grant him his most obvious literary virtues; they went so far as to place him, as a thinking person, on the level of a retarded adolescent. The truth is that he was a great thought not a supreme artist, as deeply conscious of his craft as Hemingway; a writer, moreover, with a genuinely tragic sense of life—one who reacted with extreme sensitivity to the human condition, or what we refer to more pessimistically as the human predicament.

Thus we are once more witnessing one of those inevitable swings of the pendulum, so constant in literary history, to which even Shakespeare was subject, and which few important writers have escaped: recognition, whether immediate or belated, followed first by rejection, and then succeeded by renewed recognition. This persistent phenomenon is presently exemplified by the even slower revival of Conrad's reputation, as it eventually will be by such a lesser writer as Galsworthy, although I think that in his case the re-evaluation will be limited to one fine piece of work—*The Forsyte Saga*. This restoration, I venture to say will not happen to H. C. Well as a social novelist (a fact of which he himself was unhappily conscious), and perhaps not to his American disciple, Sinclair Lewis, although I think Lewis has a better chance.

Let's get back to Kipling. The evidence in support of my opening paragraph was recently set forth in *Kipling's Mind and Art*, a selection of critical essays edited by Andrew Rutherford. It opens, appropriately enough, with an obituary lecture delivered in 1936 (the year of Kipling's death) by W. L. Renwick, the first, though tentative, effort at seeing him in true perspective. It includes eleven essays, nine by British writers, two by Americans. Several of them had been previously published; most were written for this collection. It impresses me as the most valuable book of its kind in recent years, because it offers a widely oriented approach to an assessment of a great writer.

I suppose the reassessment of Kipling began twenty years ago, with T.S. Eliot's (of all people) rather apologetic recognition of him as a poet, although Eliot insisted on a distinction between poetry and verse, in which he defended Kipling as a master in a lesser category. (Incidentally, Eliot, as a Harvard undergraduate, revealed, in an essay written for Prof. Copeland's course in English composition, a rather obtuse appraisal of Kipling's gifts as a writer of prose.)

So far as I know, there have been only two more than casual studies of Kipling by American critics—one by Edmund Wilson in 1941, the other by Lionel Trilling two years later. Both displayed intelligence but neither penetrated to a true understanding of Kipling as an artist. Both were blocked by diametrically opposed social attitudes and by insufficient perception of Kipling's powers. It is only fair to add that the editor of *Kipling's Mind and Art* states that Mr. Trilling asked him to say that if he were writing on Kipling now he would do so "less censoriously and with more affectionate admiration."

The space at my disposal imposes severe limitations. I would like to discuss several of these views of Kipling in detail, but that is impossible. One of the interesting things about this book is the arrangement of the contributions to it. They make a kind of crescendo. After Mr. Renwick's obituary lecture, they proceed through the somewhat grudging recognition of Kipling's genius granted by Wilson and Trilling to the more forthright encomiums contributed by contemporary British writers. Truly, I have not read another book of this kind that makes such a wide-angled approach to a writer of importance. In these essays, every aspect of Kipling, both as man and wirter, is considered.

Kipling's was not an attractive personality, political views aside. Partly because of that, his fierce integrity has been ignored. He never bowed a knee even to the Empire to which his name has been so understandably linked. He had little faith in its future, little, as a matter of fact, in the future of man. He was a remarkable realist in his conception of the roots of human behavior, of the conflicts that take toll of us all. And the vivid quality of his historical imagination (as in *Puck of Pook's Hill*) is truly exciting.

The Improper Bostonian

LONDON

The most obvious thing to say about John Marquand is at the same time, I think, the least understood fact about him. That is the love he had for what he satirized—one of the aspects of his work in which he resembled Sinclair Lewis. Their names are likely to be coupled in those histories of the American novel which are yet unwritten. They were the two most penetrating writers of fiction dealing with the American social structure of their time, and what was best in their novels was the product of an irritation under which lay a deep affection. Lewis' anger and Marquand's cool irony had different roots from the strong feeling which brought into being the novels of Dreiser or of James T. Farrell, or such a work as Dos Passos' *U.S.A.* trilogy, or Steinbeck's *Grapes of Wrath*. These were the product of a social indignation which was less a personal reaction than a mental attitude, though they too, were rooted in personal experience.

Marquand and Lewis shared other similarities. Both were irascible men who quickly responded to irritants. Both had an excellent ear for the speech of their countrymen; they wrote some of the most faithful to life dialogue in American fiction. Both had humor and compassion, qualities of which Dreiser and Farell possessed only the second. Steinbeck has displayed both, but tinged with a sentimentality of which Marquand and, to a lesser extent, Lewis, were free. Neither quality was a conspicuous element in *U.S.A.* In their failings also, Marquand and Lewis were alike. As time went on, they tended to turn out increasingly paler carbon copies of the works on which their reputation will rest. Neither attempted to answer the larger questions of human life as they observed it; their concern was chiefly with surfaces; these were sharply, bitingly reflected in their work, but neither plumbed far beneath them. I think Marquand saw the depths, but for one reason or another did not attempt them.

But enough of comparisons. John Marquand won for himself a distinctive place in American letters. In his own chosen area he was the master practitioner; he wrote the best novels we have about a certain segment of American society, and he brought back renewed vitality to fictional pictures of a region which for many years before the appearance of *The Late George Apley* had possessed no adequate interpreter. At the same time he rightly resented the tendency of many critics to make of him merely a regionalist. Most good novelists are to some extent regionalists, if we use the word in a not too restricted sense. So applied, it includes not only Hawthorne and Mark Twain, Willa Cather and Ellen Glasgow, Elizabeth Maddox Roberts and Edith Wharton but, even, Henry James. What deeply held Marquand as a novelist was the theme of frustration, as he found it expressed in the locale and among the people whom he knew best.

That he was fully capable of turning his sharp scrutiny upon other milieus than the one in which he grew to maturity is best exemplified, perhaps, in *Melville Goodwin, U.S.A.*, which is, to my mind, one of his best novels, to be placed beside *Apley, H. M. Pulham, Esquire, Wickford Point* and *Point of No Return*. Certainly nowhere else in our fiction has the military mind and the military life been more acutely presented and assessed. Somehow the same penetration and verisimilitude eluded him when, in *Willis Wade* and *Point of No Return,* he turned his attention to the world of business.

Marquand was deeply interested in the relations between men and women, particularly in the state of marriage, and everybody knows and remembers his wry reports of domestic conversation. For all his interests in the subject, which I know as strong because we once sat and talked about it for two or three hours after lunch, here too, some inhibition kept him from giving it more than surface attention in his work. Like Sinclair Lewis again, his handling of sexual relations was strongly reticent, and he never wrote a scene which, if read aloud to Queen Victoria, would have prompted her to say, "We are not amused."

There was a curiously hypnotic quality about Marquand's style; its strangely mesmerizing effect accounted in some measure, I think, for the wide popularity he won. There were other factors, of course, among them that he wrote about characters whom comfortably placed readers could meet without discomfort. I do not believe this restriction was intentional for that purpose; he chose merely to write about the people whom he knew best.

At the risk of ending with an observation as obvious as the one with which I began, let me repeat what has so often been said about Marquand—that his fiction and its central theme derived from the experience of his youth, as so much fiction does. It is conceivable that if Marquand's father had not been a poor relation, if his son had not felt cheated out of what he felt to be his social birthright, he might not have become the satirist he was. Be that as it may, he is assured of an estimable place in the history of American fiction.

The Other Johnson

Some time ago I remarked on the rather curious revival of interest in Samuel Johnson as a writer; interest in the man himself has been perennial. When an abridged edition of the famous Dictionary was published last May, that extraordinary work had been out of print for many years. In recent months two new volumes of selections from his prose and poetry have been issued, in addition to one more volume in the collected edition of his works launched by the Yale University Press in 1958. Last October Henry Darcey Curwen published *A Johnson Sampler* and now E. L. McAdam Jr., and George Milne, who collaborated on the abridged dictionary, have come up with *A Johnson Reader.*

The Johnson novitiate can now make his choice among these two most recent samplings and *The Portable Johnson and Boswell,* edited by Louis Kronenberger and *Johnson:Prose and Poetry,* selected by Mona Wilson, in the Reynard Library of the Harvard University Press. The Reynard Library volume is the most comprehensive; it runs to nearly a thousand India paper pages; the Kronenberger book affords the opportunity of reading between the same covers two writers whose names are indissolubly linked. Mr. Curwen's book differs from the others in that its selections are grouped under topical headings.

"A Johnson Reader" stands apart from its predecessors chiefly because it includes a liberal slice of the Dictionary, and a concluding section entitled "Johnson Talking," mostly taken, of course, from Boswell's life. Reading around in it, as I have been the last day or two, I was struck afresh by the vigor of Johnson's mind: its clarity; its forceful logic; a tolerance astounding in a man of many and violent prejudices; its consuming interest in human nature, for as I observed recently, Johnson's pronouncements on what is now called "the human condition," or "the human predicament," derive directly from life. You should not try to read him apart from his life; you must know first what the man endured. When Johnson holds forth on human conduct it is no cloistered scholar speaking; it is a man who has been intimate with hell from childhood.

Inadvertently, perhaps, I may have hit on the reason for this renewed attention to what he wrote. Johnson was a tough-minded character. It is a quality admirable in our era. We are annoyed by sentimentality (and thereby, too unappreciative of sentiment, its more honest brother). He, too, detested sentimentality, and so far as I know, was never guilty of it, but his sentiments were strong, as any feeling man's must be. His was a very masculine brain, and one of the best of his time. For that very reason, he missed the complete understanding of a mind like Shakespeare's—on whose work he was a deeply perceptive commentator—for Shakespeare had that extra gift of being able to understand women. Johnson gave himself away in this respect, when he made his often quoted remark about women's preaching: "Sir," he said, "a woman's preaching is like a dog's walking on his hinder legs. It is not done, well, but you are surprised to find it done at all."

But the man was extraordinary. In 1759, when his mother died at the age of ninety, Johnson was fifty. He had not, for many years, been an attentive son, in the sense of letters and visits, although he had, at great cost to himself, helped her financially. When she died, practically destitude, he was faced with the funeral costs, plus other debts, and sat down to write *Rasselas,* for two editions of which he received a little more than a hundred pounds. That book, we are told, was written in the evenings of a single week. Its length is not important though it ran to about 40,000 words. What is important is the power of mind it displays.

It was written in a particularly dark period of his life. No man ever feared death more than he; he was always thrusting the thought of it from him. A man of strong conscience, he was deeply troubled by what he considered the neglect of his mother, to whom he once wrote that he thought her the best human being he had ever known. Into that book he poured all the grief he felt, all the disillusionment about human conduct that years of battling against the world had brought him. He had planned to give it a happier ending in a sequel, but this, with his habitual procrastination, he never did. In spite of its dark conclusions about the human lot, its reluctance to look on any brighter side, it has a solid basis of bitter truth.

Besides this man, who knew the depths of human misery, I get damned impatient with those avant-garde writers who seem suddenly to have discovered (I have Samuel Beckett particularly in mind) that human life is not a bed of roses, as if it ever were. But the first man capable of sensible and sensitive reflection knew it as well as they. I supose every man must discover the fact for himself—and express it in the terms of his age. Nevertheless, I wish we had, among more writers, a little more of Sam Johnson's courage, a little more of his contempt for odds. He might rail, but he never cried in his soup.

VII

The Spirit of Place

IN SPITE OF his European visits and the first-hand knowledge of his country and his fellow Americans which exacting lecture tours afforded him, Emerson was contemptuous of travel. So, too, was Thoreau, whose ventures beyond the Concord River were fewer and less extensive. Both men prized the belief that Concord was a microcosm of the wide world. To a certain extent I share that belief (letting Concord stand as symbol for that place wherein one's life is normally centered), but I am also one of those who crave to see for themselves what lies on the other side of the mountain and who like to sense the particular spirit of place that informs the various corners of the earth. To me, travel brings a renewal and, I think, a deepening of awareness. You may ask, awareness of what? Of fundament differences and likenesses, I think, bringing with it, perhaps, a better knowledge of oneself by way of one's reactions to a new environment.

The pieces that follow have more to do with places than with books, although, since they were written for a literary column, books are necessarily a part of them. They are also, for the most part, about places for which I have a strong affection. I have written others about places for which I have a deep aversion: cities, for example, like Miami, Detroit, and Los Angeles, those enormous, spreading blots on the American landscape; or those faceless suburban developments that provoke wonder as to how their inhabitants are able to locate their own doorsteps.

There are times when I suspect that the literature of travel, which bequeathed us such entrancing books as Doughty's *Arabia Deserta*, Hudson's *Far Away and Long Ago*, Tomlinson's *The Sea and the Jungle*, Mark Twain's *Life on the Mississippi*, or the parochial excursions of Thoreau, to name a very few, is fated to be gone with the wind. Our cities, certainly, from New York to New Delhi, seem destined to an obliterating uniformity, and such landscape, as may remain, save for the Sahara, Death Valley, and our National Parks, to be reduced to narrow strips between the "freeways" (what irony in the name!) and the cloverleaves of the superhighways. Small wonder that we dream of outer space! If there is to be a travel literature of the future, after all of earth's inhabitants converse in a bastardized English and are all clad in Brooks Brothers' suits, from Canada's Northwest Territories down to Tierra del Fuego, surely it will have to be about localities light-years distant, which are as yet unbesmirched by man.

Maine Cookery

DAMARISCOTTA, MAINE

Only once before has this column had anything to say about cookbooks, and that innocent excursion got me into hot water. Thirteen years ago I made a brief stay in Key West, and as anybody at all familiar with that engagingly exotic island knows, its cookery is both delightful and distinctive. Stimulated first by the dishes I had sampled, and then by reading a cookbook published by the local women's club, I ventured some remarks—which included one to the effect that so far as I knew this was the only instance of a cookbook being issued by such an organization. In consequence, my mail for two or three weeks afterward resounded with cries of anger, dismay, pity and pain from women's clubs all over the country. Crow was the dish I had to eat during that period.

Now, properly chastened, but having chosen a similar topic for today's discourse, I mean to walk warily in the area of Maine cookery. In craven fashion, I shall put the burden of proof for what I have to say partly on the shoulders of Willan C. Roux, whose recently published *What's Cooking Down in Maine* will delight any dedicated Down Easter, part-time or otherwise. It will also, I guarantee, intrigue any outlander broad-minded enough to appreciate the qualities distinctive in the cookery of regions other than his own —even among such prideful connoisseurs as Marylanders, Philadelphians, Charlestonians, and San Franciscans.

As a frequent visitor to Maine, both inland and coastal, over many years, I have long been of the opinion that this state's cookery ranks among the best in the country. Not only that; I know no other state on the Eastern Seaboard where one can eat so well at so reasonable cost. I have told incredulous friends about the prime roast-beef dinner, complete with soup, vegetables, and dessert (the beef half an inch thick and eight inches wide) for which I paid $1.65 in a Bangor restaurant, only five years ago [1959].

Everybody knows, of course, or should, that until you have eaten Maine lobster on its home grounds, either at a lobster pound or at one of the specializing restaurants like the famous Boone's in Portland, you cannot know the gastronomic ecstasy lobster can provide. Beside lobster at its sublime best, chicken—in general—is a lowly, pedestrian meat, but Maine chicken begins with the advantage of being plumper, tenderer and juicier than any variety of that stupid bird I have elsewhere encountered. I refuse, however, to be drawn into controversy regarding the relative merits of Idaho vs. Maine potatoes. And this is in spite of the tender feeling induced by once having left an Idaho restaurant so laden with the dimes showered on me by a one-armed bandit that I walked out with a forty-five-degree list to starboard.

Enough of digressions. The first virtue of Mr. Roux's cookbook is that he not only writes interestingly about his recipes and the ingredients peculiar to Maine cookery—his recipes are clear and precise. You feel, after reading one of them, that you can go out to the kitchen and duplicate the masterpiece he has just described. That much cannot be said for some of the best-selling cookbooks. I have seen recipes that were as bewildering as a gobbledegook directive framed in a Washington bureaucrat's office.

What's Cooking Down in Maine has other virtues. Mr. Roux does not rely completely on his own predilections, to which every cookbook writer, like every editor, is entitled. (The theory is, what you like best and can be enthusiastic about, many others are sure to respond to.) That was a belief dear to the heart of Ellery Sedgwick, the editor who rescued *The Atlantic Monthly* from the doldrums, and a precept successfully followed by his successor, Edward Weeks. Mr. Roux has opened his arms to the notions of others who know something about Maine cookery, some who enjoy only a local reputation, others like the late Kenneth Roberts and Tristram Coffin and Margaret Chase Smith, whose fame extends beyond the state's borders. In that category one must also include such a contributor as L. L. Bean, proprietor of the nationally known outfitting store in Freeport—the only store in the country, I believe, that is open 24 hours a day, 365 days a year. (Maine has two remarkable stores—Bean's and Saunders' at Greenville, on Moosehead Lake.

Both are known to all fishermen and hunters, and Saunders' to any Easterner who ever paddled a canoe on a Maine stream.)

The basic ingredient of most Maine cookery, Mr. Roux observes, is salt pork. The number of recipes in which it plays a part is amazing to anybody except State of Mainers. Lobster dishes—and they are many—are exceptions, save for Mildred Hillman's lobster hash, which Mr. Roux describes as "a homely dish that has a real quality of greatness."

Maine cookery, as you will discover from reading this book, is unpretentious, yet individual. It is honest, like Hemingway's sentences. It may not be as subtle as the best French cuisine, but like its people, it has character.

Notes on Key West

Before getting down to brass tacks, a few flashbacks of Key West: the strange and delightful combination of burning sun made welcome by the fresh coolness of the steady blowing trades; the annual flower show, with its fine display of highly original shadow boxes, its wealth of tropical blooms, breath-taking in their coloring, and the fascinatingly worded descriptions of the herbs and simples and their uses, collected by the Negro exhibitors, which I regret not having jotted down; the most dilapidated taxicabs still capable of motion that I have ever seen; the dives of Duval Street, each with its gambling room in the rear; the little Puerto Rican strip-teaser at the Mardi Gras, with her Marijuana Dance, the like of which was never seen at the old Irving Burlesque; the drowsing *patios* back of the old houses; palms rustling at night, with their gentle surf-like sound, and over all the great night skies, with the huge, slowly drifting cloud masses seeming so near that one might climb a long ladder and touch them—these are a little of Key West.

And yet a few more: the clear aquamarine of the Gulf Stream, twelve miles off the Key, where Commander Close took me fishing in a Navy picket boat, and I caught my first shark; Elmer Davis, the caustically urbane, complete with precise black tie, reminiscing at his hard-earned ease over drinks at the Casa Marina; the lovely Sarah Palfrey Cooke, former women's national tennis champion, playing on the Casa's courts with that seemingly effortless ease which is the poetry of motion.

Then the youthfully venerable George A. Hough, most-painted of American newspaper editors, who broke me in as a cub on the New

Bedford *Evening Standard* more than thirty years ago, mixing his noonday pink gin before his evening switch to bourbon, while the tropics-loving Bob Thielen insistently shuts the window to exclude the chilling (to him) Key West air; mine host Harry James Mitchell of the Hibiscus, as gifted in his sensing of his guests' wishes as he is in the remarkable photographs of Key West's cloud-formations for which he will some day be better known.

But down to earth: once again this department finds itself chastened, due to its apparently incorrigible habit of sticking out its neck. As a tailpiece to my ungracious proposal for the submergence of a large part of the Florida mainland, I spoke of some of Key West's local literature, and remarked that, so far as I knew, the *Key West Cook Book* was the first volume of that kind to be published by a woman's club. Even the bright stain of Key West's sun cannot conceal my blushes. Detroit, a city to which I recently referred in terms which will never be quoted by its Chamber of Commerce, was, I learn, Key West's predecessor by several years, also by means of a cookbook.

As if that were not retribution enough, comes Prof. W. O. Farnsworth of Northwestern University, roused from his lolling in the sun at St. Simons Island, Georgia, to proclaim that a cookbook equally exotic and unusual (terms which I applied to Key West's product) was long ago produced by the members of the Cassina Garden Club of St. Simons Island. This too, was composed both of illustrations and recipes contributed by the cooperating members. The drawings, my correspondent informs me, "are both amusing and informative as to the colonial history of what Georgia has only recently begun to advertise as the Golden Isles."

The unkindest cut of all, however, comes from Samray Smith of the Virginia State Library, who, asking to be let in "near the head of the procession that will correct your belief that the *Key West Cook Book* is the only book, presumably of any kind, ever published by a woman's club," presents me with a list of five titles, which, with heaping coals, he introduces as "a few Virginia cook books published by women's clubs."

Relentlessly, Mr. Smith concludes by saying: "Far from being a rare or exceptional undertaking, the compilation and publication of favorite recipes would seem to be a favorite activity of women's clubs. I suspect that this is true in other states than Virginia." As for this department, it not merely suspects but is darn certain it will pick up the remainder of this week's mail with humility and trepidation.

Every writer of the ignobler sex, I suspect, would do well to submit whatever he has to say about certain matters to the searching eye of his wife, his daughter, his sweetheart, his female cousins, or his aunts, before publicly revealing himself as the well-meaning but blundering ignoramus that he is. Mark Twain, they tell us, submitted everything (well, nearly everything) to the solicitous inspection of his beloved Livy, but that, my friends, is another kettle of fish.

The Truth About Texas

All this to-do about Texas is getting mighty tiresome. For many weeks now the literary arena has been reverberant with reports of a threatened secession from the Union; one would suppose, from all the uproar, that Miss Ferber's new novel, *Giant*, had laid bare an astonishing and deeply disturbing new manifestation of American materialism. Why pin it all on Texas? How short can a people's memory be?

The whole silly business got off to a flying start during the war, when the notion took root that the tall tale was a purely Texan phenomenon. As a matter of fact, the tall tale is not only not indigenous to Texas; it did not even have its birth in the United States. Although it must be granted that we have used it far more lavishly than any other people, and even though Texans, during recent years, may have adopted a rather proprietary attitude toward that particular form of humor, their tall tales are really no taller, or broader, than those of the Rocky Mountain West, or those built about the exploits of Paul Bunyan.

What really sets me wondering about the national sanity is the excitement over Miss Ferber's indictment of the Texans' display of wealth. Nothing, I am sure, that Texas has turned up to date could possibly match in ostentation, and certainly not in inane vulgarity, the flaunting of their millions which, during the Nineties, gave such great delight to Eastern millionaires and their wives. What in the annals of Houston, Dallas and Fort Worth has approached the antics of the Four Hundred in Newport and New York? In the light of certain performances of theirs, Miss Ferber's shudders over DC-6's and lowly Cadillacs seem slightly exaggerated.

Might it not restore a little sense of perspective if we were to remind ourselves of such events as the Bradley Martin ball, the dinner party for dolls at which all those present were supposed to converse in baby-talk, the banquet for a hundred dogs, the one at which the guests assembled in the dining room on horseback? Have any of the new Texas millionaires presented quite as gaudy a front to the world as "Bet-a-Million" Gates or Diamond Jim Brady? What oil baron has 20,000 diamonds and wears them? Is there a man in Texas who could sit down to a dinner of four dozen oysters, a dozen hard-shell crabs, six or seven large lobsters, a huge steak, and four gallons of orange juice? Where has he been hiding?

All I'm trying to do is to pour a little oil on the troubled waters. I'm even willing to make a few admissions. Texas *is* big, as anybody knows who has driven across it; Texas girls *are* pretty, and Texas *does* have a history which considerably antedates all the furor about her new-found wealth. Skyscrapers rising from the mesquite aren't a bit more incongruous than The Breakers on Newport's shore, and the fervent desire to see and be seen in certain New York nightspots leaves little room for a superior attitude toward the social habits of those other Americans who are such a strange blend of South and West. I will spare you the Alamo, but I will mention the Rice Institute and Margo Jones' theater-in-the-round, and J. Frank Dobie, who has written more truth about the essential Texas than anybody before or since. Texas today is simply repeating an old American pattern, one so old and so constant that it should cause us no surprise.

Sometimes I despair about one part of the United States understanding another part. It comes up in every national election; it repeats itself over and over again in our literature. We are so much more diverse than the superficial commentators realize, when they accept as symptomatic the standardized appearance of Main Street from coast to coast. A literature which really represents them is easy for the British in their tight little island, but who, from what we say about ourselves, is really to know the United States? That is one of our troubles in the world today; we are unable to present a coherent picture of ourselves, and in consequence, we are the most misunderstood people in history.

One of the great differences between individuals and between peoples is the difference in tempo. That, incidentally, explains our inability to reach a real rapprochement with the South Americans. But it is also a key to our misunderstanding of one another. We are really a very complex people. In illustration of that, I should like to quote from Mr. Dobie, in a preface he wrote for the Southwest edition of B. A. Botkin's *Treasury of Western Folklore*. "The tempo of the Southwest," he wrote, "is compounded of the leisureliness of the Old South, the *manana*-ness of Mexico and the waiting quality of the Indian. One driving slowly through certain parts of New Mexico and Arizona may spot an Indian up beside a rock looking away and away; if one halts to watch for movement by that Indian, he may have to wait until sundown. Genuine range people—among whom are not to be included oil millionaires who have bought ranches and hire somebody else to run them while they themselves operate in air-conditioned office buildings—have a limitless capacity for reserving their energy."

Texan Tale-teller

HOUSTON, TEXAS

On a recent visit to the University of Texas at Austin, I was taken to call on the dean of Texas letters, who is also one of the few living princes of storytelling—and the tall story in particular—J. Frank Dobie. College professors of the younger generation may sometimes be mistaken on a first encounter for bank presidents, All-American tackles, ward politicians or anything else outside the academic fold; Mr. Dobie, who is of my own generation, could be mistaken for a rancher. But after all, that's small wonder, for he was born on a Texas ranch seventy-four years ago, and for a couple of years during a career in which the writer, the scholar, and the outdoorsman have happily intermingled, he was, indeed, a ranch manager.

No living American has made a more authentic or interesting contribution to regional literature. Our first meeting had been at a Kenyon College convocation in honor of Robert Frost's eightieth birthday, and I found myself reflecting after my visit the other day, on certain similarities between Dobie and Frost. Neither could possibly be taken for anything but an American; in both one found a native wisdom now too infrequently met, and a keen interest in other human beings, not as symbols or case histories, but as fellow creatures; both were teachers with the common touch, not intellectual autocrats or condescenders. One such on a campus is a gift from God.

On the plane back to Houston from Austin, I began reading Mr. Dobie's *Singers and Storytellers*. It had to do with the storytellers Mr. Dobie has met and listened to since, as a boy on a ranch in Live Oak County, he was spellbound by a man from up the

Nueces River, who dropped in one evening and reeled off story after story about panthers. "He shivered my timbers," writes Mr. Dobie, "in a way from which I have never recovered or wished to recover."

That evening saw the beginning of our good fortune, so far as much of Mr. Dobie's writing is concerned. The Texas frontier, of which large remnants may still be found (as I learned on a visit to the Big Bend country on the southwest border), lives in his pages. The longhorns may have vanished, along with the mustangs, but you can see them again in Mr. Dobie's books about them, just as you can see much else that was Texas, through his observant eyes. Not all of it has gone, by any means; there are still coyotes in plenty, wild turkeys and havolinas (wild pigs), and owls in the live oaks that say, "I cook for myself. Who cooks for you-all?"

The visitor from up the Nueces River triggered what was to become for Mr. Dobie a lifelong quest—a search for folk tales that took him not only over most of his native state and down into Mexico, but up into country better known to me, Arizona, New Mexico, and the high plains of Montana and Wyoming. In *Singers and Storytellers* he writes of Nat Straw, "golden liar of the golden West," who rode a tamed grizzly; the dancing Negro he met up with near the Grand Central Station in New York, who was just back from France, and could tell "a bigger lie than anybody in Europe" and Bill Cole, who seemed to believe his own tall stories.

Allow me to express my agreement with the observations which conclude his recollections of the storytellers he has known: first, that he never heard a really good talker who could not narrate. (The pity is, let me add, that so few of them can write—and, vice versa, that so few skilled fiction writers today can or will narrate.) One of the best talking storytellers I ever heard was the late Bob Flaherty, genius of the documentary film; he was long under contract for an autobiography, unfortunately never written. It could have been produced in only one way—with Bob and a couple of cronies, plus a bottle, seated beside a tape recorder.

Herodotus is Frank Dobie's favorite historian, as he is mine, "because Herodotus never allows fact to get in the way of narration—or truth." I can even go most of the way with this pronouncement: "When Chaucer comes with his tales and John Aubrey with his character anecdotes, ideas and causes fade away. All of Samuel Taylor Coleridge's metaphysical theories, spun out of philosophy-befogged intellect, are forgotten; his sure passport to immortality is that tale called 'The Rime of the Ancient Mariner.' I have enormous respect for thought. I surrender all to a storyteller—if he's good enough."

And speaking of storytellers, sooner believe the tallest tale ever spun in Texas that swallow whole some of the cracks that have been made by provincial Easterners about the Lone Star state. Texas can't be defined in terms of oil gushers, Cadillacs, and Neiman-Marcus luxury items. Houston, for example, may boast more handsome homes to the square mile than any other American city, but don't forget that its symphony orchestra has been led by two of the greatest living conductors, or that over in Austin is one of the best of university presses, a quarterly that is not only the largest of its kind, but beautifully designed and intelligently edited. The university has a growing collection of literary documents any Ivy League college might covet.

Thoreau and His River

Rivers have fascinated me all my life, and that is the prime reason, I suppose, why today's column concerns a new selection from the writings of Thoreau. *The River,* arranged and edited by Dudley C. Lunt, is drawn from the Journals, and gives us, in seasonal sequence, the story of Thoreau's association with the river he knew and loved best—the prevailingly placid Concord that flows through his native town. Small as our rivers go, and unspectacular, it nevertheless partakes of the essence of rivers—reminders as they all are of the passage of time, yet curiously reassuring too, in the manner of the ebb and flow of the tides to which they are eventually joined. Ponds and lakes can hem us in, as much as city streets, but rivers never.

The Concord, which the Indians called Musketaquid or Musketacook, is formed by the confluence of the Sudbury and the Assabet near the town of Concord, Massachusetts; thence it flows northeasterly to join the Merrimack as it comes down out of New Hampshire; at Lowell the Merrimack turns east and flows past Newburyport to the sea. The Concord is what we call a "dead water" stream; its flow is gentle, never precipitous, though in spring freshets it has been known to spread mightily over its encompassing meadows.

It reminds us, like the neighboring Charles, of so many English rivers; like them, it stimulates contemplation and generates peace. They are the kind of streams that Izaak Walton knew, and I wonder if the similarity did not have some bearing on the delight with which the Massachusetts traveler has always regarded the English scene; not in Thoreau's case, to be sure, for in his memorial address Emerson reminded his hearers that Thoreau's "preference of his country and condition was genuine, and his aversation from English and European manners and tastes almost reached contempt." But Thoreau was a thorny man, and sometimes a perverse one.

His devotion to the Concord was passionate and unswerving. He knew its every reach and turn as he knew the palm of his hand. He knew it in every season and at every hour of the day or night; he would rise sometimes at one or two in the morning and go down to its banks. Year after year, as winter approached its end, he waited impatiently for the day when the river was sufficiently free of ice for him to launch his boat and go a-venturing—sometimes alone, often with his friend William Ellery Channing, who also accompanied him on his excursions to Cape Cod.

As Mr. Lunt observes, "It is when Thoreau is out on a river that he reaches the peak of his power as a descriptive writer." He did not know many, for his travels were, by inclination, small in compass, though *multum in parvo.* Nobody has as well described the Maine rivers he came to know, the Penobscot and the Allagash. I wish sometimes that he had gone farther afield; that he could have known the curious majesty of the Mississippi and the treacherousness of the Missouri; that he had followed the Hudson from source to mouth, or the Housatonic or the Connecticut. I wish he might have stood on the summit of Mount Revelstoke in western Canada, and seen the Columbia approaching its Great Bend. I wish he had seen other Western rivers, though I would save him those of the South, except for the Rio Grande.

Forgive the outburst. I shall never describe any river as well as Thoreau described his, and perhaps that is why I wish he had seen some of those I have known and loved. He would have delighted in the Quinault, on Washington's Olympic Peninsula, and in the Indians who took me in a cedar dug-out, past the great rain forests, down to the Pacific.

Thoreau makes you humble. He makes you see so much where without his guidance, you see so little. Nothing escapes him. He is alive to all forms of life, to all colors, all sounds, all movements. Where did I read the other day that the best American writers are distinguished (Hemingway for one) by their transmission of what they receive through their senses? It is true, and it puzzles me that

Hemingway could not read Thoreau, in whom the testimony of the senses was brought to a keener pitch than in any American who ever wrote—perhaps because Thoreau, in spite of this capacity, was not a sensual man. Comfort seemed to mean nothing to him. Yet sight, hearing, taste, smell—I'm not so sure about touch—were, in him, extraordinarily developed.

To read Thoreau is to realize how many parts of us are but half-alive. I think of myself as one who loves Nature, yet he makes me conscious of how much there is in her that escapes me—how much I do not see or hear. I think I catch the principles; I know I miss the details, and sometimes they tell a great deal. I also know this: that in Thoreau, and in his mentor Emerson—as much as any man could be Thoreau's mentor—there is healing for much of our contemporary malaise, for they bring us close to the main stream of life, to our part as members of the natural world, from which we seem intent on divorcing ourselves.

The Changing Face of New England

We are likely to think of New England, in its essential aspects, at least, as unchanging. Most Americans, wherever born, and even if they have never been east of the Hudson, have a definite picture of New England in their minds—a picture composed, usually, of a white-steepled church on a village green, backed by forested hills. Nor is anything more deeply imbedded in the American mind than its idea of the character of New England people. Can you think of any other city of whose inhabitants the rest of us have such clear-cut—and sometimes erroneous—impressions as we have of Bostonians? Even New Yorkers are more nebulous in the nation's eye. Of late years the novels of John Marquand have reinforced this conception, but it had taken firm root among us long before *The Late George Apley* was written. One reason for the response to Cleveland Amory's *The Proper Bostonians* was that it dealt amusingly with an already established view.

These reflections and others have been prompted by an unusual little book, appropriately called *The Changing Face of New England,* by Betty Flanders Thomson, a transplanted Middle Westerner who teaches botany at Connecticut College. Miss Thomson is not concerned, as her title might indicate, with such recent phenomena as the removal of New England's cotton mills to the South, or the passing of so many of her dwindling farms from the Yankee hands that made them.

Hers is a longer view—the longest, in fact, that can be taken—for her book has for its basis the geological history of New England. Do not, however, let that fact deceive you. This is not a technical treatise, but a book written primarily out of love for the New England countryside. To this she has added an informed interest in how it came to be the kind of countryside it is. I think her book will have an appeal for anybody who knows and loves New England. All the physical aspects are touched upon—its mountains, its forests, its lakes and streams, its open spaces, its seacoast—and about all of them she has interesting things to say.

Did you know, for instance, that there was once a great lake, named Hitchcock for a geology professor at Amherst who was one of the first to realize that it had existed, which stretched from mid-Connecticut up through Massachusetts, and halfway up the dividing line between what are now New Hampshire and Vermont? Its formation was one of the results of the glacial drift that began a million years ago and which was eventually to make the physical New England that we know.

Lake Hitchcock, writes Miss Thomson, was formed "when a mass of rocky debris accumulating from the melting ice formed a dam across the valley near Middletown, Conn., just at the end of its rocky gorge section. The appearance of this blockade had far-reaching effects. Water was impounded from there northward all the way to the retreating edge of the ice. The resulting lake eventually reached as far north as Lyme, New Hampshire, a distance of 137 miles. In Massachusetts and Connecticut the lake was as much as twelve miles wide; farther north it narrowed to two or three miles."

The shoreline of that ancient lake can still be traced. Even the beaches are visible in certain sections. The geologists believe that the lake lasted for more than four thousand years, coming suddenly to its end when water burst through the dam below Middletown during the floods of spring.

New England's mountains, including even Washington and Katahdin, although they have their aspects of grandeur, seem puny to us when matched against the peaks of the far younger Rockies. Long ago they were loftier, but much as the geologists are able to read—and it is amazing how detailed their deductions can sometimes be—we do not know the original height of these mountains. As Miss Thomson observes, although the general course of events which brought them into being is not hard to understand, "when it comes to ancient details, a geologist may prefer to talk of other things, and to send his students to the newer Rockies, where the workings of the earth seem by contrast clear and simple."

Even if Mount Washington lacks the soaring upthrust of the Grand Tetons, it has other no less arresting claims on our attention. Though you can reach its summit by railway and by road, it has taken the lives of many more climbers than any other mountain in the United States—more than any, I imagine, in the whole Eastern Hemisphere. According to Miss Thomson, the scientists who have worked on both Washington and in the Antarctic say that the summit of Washington can offer the worst weather in the world. The highest wind velocity ever measured, 231 miles an hour, was recorded there.

Whatever your favorite corner of New England may be—and I say this out of long acquaintance with every one of her states—the chances are that Miss Thomson has been there, and that she can tell you something about it you had not known. I suspect she has seen less of the Maine woods than of any other New England region, but no matter—one can always turn to the pages of Thoreau, whose book about them remains unsurpassed.

Thoughts on Canadian Lakes

LAC SEYMOUR, P. QUE., CANADA

For a week now, the war and the world of books have been incredibly remote. It is amazing how quickly and how far one's most serious concerns can recede once these North Woods have closed about you. A few days ago, on Lac La Pin, I had the feeling, momentarily, that there was nothing beyond the jagged skyline made by the spruce and pine standing on the little hills that rim the lake. La Pin lies high enough above the country immediately surrounding it to give the impression of being wholly alone and apart. The waters of the lake itself, the curving shore and the wooded hills that rise abruptly from it—these were the world, and there was nothing else. Nothing but that profound silence peculiar to the North—a silence so complete on a windless day that, to one fresh from the never-ending noises of the city, it seemed, by a strange reversal, to be thunderous in its impact.

The French-Canadian guides can paddle so silently, when the lake waters lie unruffled, that the deep quiet is not broken even by the stroke of the blade. It was good, though, to hear once more a sound I had not heard for several years—the eerie and once heard, never forgotten, cry of the loon, that bird which seems to share with the eagle a passion for solitude. I have been hoping, too, to hear the crash of a bull moose breaking through the brush, but though we have come several times upon fresh tracks of both moose and bear, we have yet to sight either.

We returned to the main camp of the Mastigouche Club today, after seven days on the outlying lakes and the portages. What little news of the war we learned seemed strangely unreal, and one had a renewed realization of what a nerve center New York is—and also of what tensions it imposes upon one's own nerves. "The world is too much with us," said Wordsworth, standing upon Westminster Bridge in the comparative quiet of the time in which he wrote his most famous sonnet; what would he write today, caught in the maelstrom of Times Square, in the most portentous period, perhaps, that the world has ever known?

I brought no books with me on this trip, except my fly-book, and I have done very little reading in any others. Two manuscripts went into my brief case, but they stayed here at the main camp, and have thus far been untouched. The clubhouse has a small library, and there is usually a shelf, or at least a handful of books, in each of the outlying camps. The other day, in camp at Lac Grand Noel, I picked up, as closest to my mood and immediate interests, one of Arthur Stringer's tales of the North Woods. This one was called "Heather of the High Hand," a pleasing yarn about a Scotch-Canadian lassie who, following her father's death, runs a salmon-fishing club whose existence is imperiled by the invasion of a power company—symbolized, naturally, in the person of a personable young man. He and Heather, who is a girl after my own heart, are locked in a battle of wits before they are locked in the embrace that solves and settles everything. This, for your correspondent in his present frame of mind, represents the Higher Literature.

Some day I must go back to the books of Stewart Edward White (those which he wrote years ago, before he became preoccupied with psychic phenomena) and see if they are as good as they seemed to me when I read them as a boy. How they whetted my appetite for the woods, for the little ardors and endurances of the trail! They were grand reading for a boy whose tastes ran to the outdoors—that much I know. Books like *The Forest* and the tales of the lumber camps carried me into a world I had not known, but which I felt, with a certainty that was later realized, I some day would.

Maps make the best reading on a trip like this, particularly when they are on a large scale; they are good to pore over before you set out to cover a new bit of country, and good again after you return, when the dotted lines of the trails, the contour lines and the lakes and streams that lie along them have taken on a fuller meaning. And they will be still better this winter and next spring, when these two weeks will have become no more than a pleasant memory. Maps never let you down; they will bear rereading as only the best-loved books can do. They are as suggestive, as stimulating to the imagination, as a fine poem. And whatever your mood may be, maps will find their way to meet it, whereas how many times, when the right book is not at hand, one finds it difficult to read.

But my companion is eager to be off, and is thumping vigorously on his pack to flatten it for his comfort. The fishing has not been too good, for the lakes have stayed unseasonably warm, but yesterday a blustering wind swept down from the north, and last night the thermometer dropped to 34 degrees. The trout will soon be venturing up from the deeper water where they have taken refuge, and a three-pounder, perhaps, even now has a rendezvous with a Parmachenee Belle, a Silver Doctor, an Alexandria, or a buck-tail streamer waiting for him in my fly-book.

Rocky Mountain Trails

FORT WASHAKIE, WYOMING

Fifty miles south of here, in what is now the ghost town of South Pass City, one of the great revolutions of modern times had its birth in 1869. At a tea party (sic) in one of the houses then sheltering 6,000 gold seekers (present population can be counted on the fingers of two hands), began the movement resulting in woman suffrage. I visited South Pass yesterday, and the neighboring ghost town of Atlantic City, where, incidentally, it is still possible, at the Carpenter Hotel, to sit down to an old-fashioned Western dinner for 75 cents. Both towns lie at an elevation of about 7,000 feet, in the foothills of the great Wind River Range. West of them stretches some of the wildest, most inaccessible country left in the United States.

One of these days some writer will do for Wyoming and its history what Joseph Kinsey Howard did for the neighboring state of Montana. The material is equally rich, equally interesting, but so far it has had, for the most part, inadequate handling. And Esther Morris will be part of the story. In the pamphlet written by Fred D. Stratton Jr. (descendant of one of the first settlers) and sold by him at his general store in South Pass City, she is described as a large, forthright woman whose plain talk and friendly helpfulness made her a favorite with the miners who were thronging into the town.

Esther Morris had of course her predecessors in the struggle for equal rights, but hers was the first tangible victory. Its strategy was planned at that tea party in 1869. The first Wyoming territorial election was to be held in September, and Mrs. Morris arranged for the women of the community and the two local candidates for the Legislature to meet at her cabin for tea. "We would like to have from you," she told Colonel Bright and Captain Nickerson, "a public pledge that whichever of you is elected will introduce and work for the passage of an act conferring upon the women of our new territory the right of suffrage." Both men gave the pledge, and shortly after his election to the Wyoming Senate Colonel Bright drafted the bill which became law that year—the first to give the vote to women anywhere in the world.

They still mine for gold ore in the hills surrounding Atlantic City (I had the fun yesterday of panning out a little dust myself), but the oil wells that now dot the Wyoming landscape will bring in more wealth than was ever taken out of the quartz rock of her mountains. That fact doesn't disturb the geologist and mine operator who showed me over his holdings; oil doesn't interest him, but aside from his hopes for the Diana Mine he gets a curious satisfaction out of the knowledge that the rock stratum into which he is boring dates back a billion years. He likes to think he is monkeying with something considerably older than anything else in Wyoming.

But the writer who takes this state for his province will have much more to bring to life than the ghost towns of the Wind River foothills and the single-minded determination of Esther Morris. He will have, among other things, the savage wars of the cattle and sheep men; he will be dealing with territory criss-crossed by more of the famous old trails than any other in the West. A few miles from where I write is the grave of Sacajawea, the Shoshone girl who served as guide on the Lewis and Clark expedition. The route of the Pony Express lay across Wyoming; indeed, the attacks of the Shoshones, now living on this reservation, closed that brief but stirring chapter in the history of the West. Independence Rock in Wyoming was the most famous landmark on the Oregon Trail. Brigham Young led his Mormons along the Sweetwater and over South Pass, and two years later, between May and October, more than 30,000 Forty-niners came that way. North and south, east of the Big Horns, ran the Bozeman Trail; just south of here, east and west, lay the route of the Deadwood stages.

Up this valley, called by the Indians Valley of the Warm Wind, came the Conquistadores, bringing the horses that had so profound an effect on the lives of the Plains Indians, and eventually on the whole history of the West. The French knew it too; down from Montreal in 1733 came Sieur de la Verendrye and his three sons, as far south as the region where I now am. This is the country of Father DeSmet, greatest of mediators between Indian and white; Jim Bridger and Captain Bonneville knew this country as Boone knew Kentucky.

The most stirring story of all, perhaps, is that of the Stuart expedition of 1812. Robert Stuart and his six companions, who had sailed from New York, round Cape Horn and up to the mouth of the Columbia in 1810, were, on their tremendous journey east, the discoverers of South Pass, due to become the great gateway through the Rockies. Such were their privations that they escaped cannibalism only because Stuart was a man of iron will and fierce resolve. Yet even their trek was matched by the journey in 1836 of Dr. Marcus Whitman and his wife, Narcissa, one of two white women who were the first of their sex to go over South Pass and to cross the continent. Almost it may be said that with them the westward movement began.

Thoughts on the Southwest

SANTA FE, NEW MEXICO

Four flags have flown over the Palace of the Governors in the old plaza of Santa Fe—Spain's, Mexico's, the Stars and Stripes, and briefly, for two weeks in 1862, the flag of the Confederacy. Although there are other American cities as old or older, in none other is the far past so pervasive or its presence so immediate. The reminders are everywhere and constant: in its ancient buildings, in the fact of its Indian and Spanish natives, in this valley through which Coronado passed four centuries ago. And now, thirty miles to the northwest, in Los Alamos, stands a cradle of the incalculable future.

There is, it seems to me, an arresting irony in that proximity; that here, where time has moved in such a slow stream, where so much has resisted its passage, there should have come into being this hatchery of science holding within it the promise either of man's doom or his great betterment. About fifty miles northeast of the Los Alamos atomic plant lies the pueblo of Taos, where life has followed an almost identical pattern for centuries—for just how many we cannot be sure.

The junction of past and present has always proved stimulating to writers. The fact that the Southwest, especially Arizona and New Mexico, makes one conscious of time—not in the clock sense, but in somewhat the same way it is felt when we live beside the tides of the sea—accounts in some measure, I think, for the attraction it holds for the creative worker. Its wealth of material, its dramatic and colorful history, are only the outer wrappings of this attraction. Nor is it only because the Southwest deepens in us the sense of time, of the long perspective, that artists of one kind or another have found here food for the spirit. It is the kind of country which quickens man's curiosity about the important things, which carries his mind back to origins and causes, pricks him into speculation about the fundamentals of life and death.

It stimulates, too, his sense of wonder, that capacity which it is so important for the artist in whatever form to retain. Sophistication, which might almost be described as a numbing of the sense of wonder, always results eventually in a loss of depth, in a preoccupation, however cleverly expressed, with the surface of things; you can trace that development in the history of any literature. It is only natural that religion and art, stemming from the sense of wonder, should have so great a part in the life of the Indians.

For that sense is fed in so many ways by the character of the physical environment: by the hugeness of the land itself, with the Grand Canyon at the apex; by the extreme violence of its climatic disturbances; by the blazing depths of its night skies. This is the kind of land that cradled the great religions of the world, and out of which came the great poetry of the Hebrew prophets and psalmists. It will be surprising, I think, if it does not in time yield a literature of greater depth, perhaps, than any we have had.

What has been written so far—and a great deal has been written—has been for the most part, I think we might say, in preparation for that literature. The bibliography of the Southwest is already bewilderingly large, and I doubt whether that of any other region of the United States matches it in variety. Because it is a land that bears so deeply the imprint of the centuries, it has been the source of a growing body of scientific literature; the archaeologists, the geologists, and the ethnologists have found it rewarding ground. Its history has been copiously but not fully written; much spade-work, I understand, remains to be done for the decades immediately preceding occupation of the region by the United States.

During recent decades there has been a great outpouring of descriptive writing about the region, much of it excellent. It has been more interpretive in character than most of our other regional writing, partly because of the three strata of population—Indian, Spanish, and Anglo, as they say here. More than half the population of New Mexico today is Spanish-speaking, and I wonder how many people in other parts of the country know that New Mexico's Legislature is still bilingual—the only one on the Continent except for the Province of Quebec.

Everyone who comes to the Southwest goes away with the desire to know more about it, and as with any country that fires the imagination, the prospective visitor does well to prime himself beforehand with a few books that will heighten his response to what he sees. My own acquaintance with the literature of the region is sketchy enough, but there are a few books known to me which I think will be profitable for any reader of this column who may be coming out here for the first time.

Erna Fergusson's *Our Southwest* serves well as a general introduction to the whole region; both she and her brother Harvey Fergusson, whose *Rio Grande* is saturated with the feeling of the country, write as natives to the land; Haniel Long's *Pinon Country* is a sensitive and informing book about northern Arizona and New Mexico; Ruth Laughlin's *Caballeros* deals understandingly with the Spanish half of the population. And, of course, no one should set foot in Santa Fe without having read Willa Cather's *Death Comes for the Archbishop*.

P.S. There was one unpardonable omission from the concluding paragraph of this column. I failed to mention the many fine contributions to the literature of the Southwest made by the late J. Frank Dobie. And, since it had not yet been published, there was no reference to Paul Horgan's outstanding work, *Great River: The Rio Grande in North American History*.

Death on the Little Big Horn

Big Horn, Wyoming

A week ago, on one of those crystalline August days when the intensely blue sky heralds the approach of fall on the high Western plains, I spent the morning riding and walking over the hills above the Little Big Horn, where "Glory-Hunter" Custer, with 225 officers and men of the Seventh Cavalry, fell before the encircling Sioux and Cheyennes on June 26, 1876. In this, the outstanding battle of our Indian wars, the enemy loss has been estimated at less than forty. Though the whites were vastly outnumbered in what has too long been misleadingly called the Custer massacre, it is also true that they were outgeneraled, if not outfought.

From my guide, a young Crow veteran of the war in the Pacific (the battlefield lies within the boundaries of the present Crow reservation in Montana), I heard one explanation of the disaster which I have not seen recorded in any of the considerable literature on the subject. Though the story is probably apocryphal, I repeat it because Three Irons, now tribal policeman on the reservation, says it was told him by several old men of the Sioux. I prefer not to credit their story, because it diminishes the gallantry which we associate with the "last stand." The old men, Three Irons told me, insisted that Custer's troopers were roaring drunk.

Drunk or not, it was to prove the soberest day of their lives. All too soon they must have realized, when the overwhelmingly superior strength of the Indian forces dawned on them, that they would not see another sunrise. The story of their desperate effect to save themselves is written for the visitor to read, in the widely scattered stones that mark the places where they fell. Though there is one big cluster within the enclosure where their leader lies, the trail of attempted escape is plain, and sad to see. They died with prospects of great beauty stretching out before them, with the Big Horns and the Wolf Mountains ringing the horizon.

Like another field where a lost cause ebbed out in blood—Culloden, overlooking Moray Firth in northern Scotland, where the Duke of Cumberland, the "Butcher," slaughtered the clans under Prince Charlie, the Custer field looks much the same today as it must have appeared to the eyes of the men who died there, save for the gravestones, and below the gentle rise, in the broad valley, a few green squares on the farms of the Crows.

When will we learn to think of them—these Indians of the plains, of the desert pueblos and the Eastern lakes and forests—not merely as savages (whose savagery twentieth-century Western man has more than matched) but as the possessors, not only of the land from which we uprooted them, but of a way of life whose human dignity, spiritual strength, and awareness of beauty contained elements for which we may envy them?

I have just been reading, with much interest, the Indian songs and stories collected by Natalie Curtis in a volume called *The Indians' Book,* published by Harper in 1907; whether it is still in print, I do not know. I hope so, because it is a book of great value to amateurs in American ethnology and to anyone who wishes to learn something about the true nature of our predecessors on this continent. As Theodore Roosevelt, in the days before Presidential reading was confined to official reports, mystery stories and westerns, remarked in a brief foreword to the book, "These songs cast a wholly new light on the depth and dignity of Indian thought, the simple beauty and strange charm—the charm of a vanished elder world—of Indian poetry."

It is not commonly realized—due in part to the stupidly distorted picture of Indian character and temperament which most of us drew from our school reading—how very large a part was played by song in the life of the Indian. We had heard about the death chant, and the song of exultation in victory, but we were not told about the permeation of song through every aspect of his everyday life. Most of his sons were religious, but by no means all; there was, as Miss Curtis observes, "scarcely a task, light or grave, scarcely an event, great or small, but had its fitting song." Nor should it be forgotten that while in Genesis the creating word is spoken, in nearly every Indian myth the creator *sings* things into life.

Reading some of our literary pundits, one might suppose that symbolism was the invention of "modern" poets. But just as in Indian design—some of which has extraordinary beauty—the cloud-form, for example, is no copy of a cloud, but a conventionalized image that is a symbol *meaning* cloud, or a wavy line means water, so in Indian poetry one word may be the symbol of a complete idea that would require a whole sentence in English for its adequate expression. Note also that the Indian had the good sense to make his symbols universal, not private.

Of the songs in Miss Curtis' book, I append here a brief one which I single out because of its striking parallel with the Twenty-third Psalm. This morning song is one of the oldest Cheyenne melodies, sung by old men, often from the summit of a hill at dawn:

He, our Father,
He hath shown His mercy unto me.
In peace I walk the straight road.

Indian Sign

FORT MACLEOD, ALBERTA

Twenty miles south of this old frontier post, on the buttes that rise above the Belly River, the Bloods of the Blackfoot Confederacy have assembled for their annual sundance. Their tepees and tents form a great circle in the center of which stands the framework for the sun lodge. This table-top on the prairie, in the heart of the great Blood Reserve, swarms with gaily dressed children and the mongrel dogs inseparable from every Indian camp. Horses crop the prairie grass; now and then a band of youngsters, riding bareback, gallop by with easy grace; for many generations they have been born to the saddle.

The women work at their manifold chores or gossip in the lodge of their society. Most of the younger men are busy getting in their hay or wheat; some are working within sight of the camp, the Belly River winding below them, the sharply serrated peaks of Glacier Park behind them, rising abruptly from the plain. The old men, still wearing braids, doze or sit about in little circles, exchanging stories of the vanished days. Some are talking sign, their faces impassive, all expression gathered in the fluid movements of their hands.

As an adopted member of their tribe, I am being taught sign-talk. Trying to learn it is a pleasure because, aside from poetry itself, it is the most imaginative form of communication I have yet encountered. Regrettably, it is used today only by the older men; few of the youngsters will take the trouble to learn it. Like all the arts, it is best learned by practical apprenticeship; the best way is to sit beside a skillful sign-talker and repeat his movements as he shows you the signs for various objects, feelings, thoughts and actions. Part of its beauty stems from the manner in which the signs are made; the beginner is likely to move his hands jerkily, far from the easy, rhythmical gestures of the practiced signtalker.

In preparation for my own attempts, I bought a copy of William Tomkins' *Universal Indian Sign Language*. This manual has been described by M. W. Sterling, chief of the Bureau of American Ethnology at the Smithsonian Institute, as the best work of a practical nature that has been written on the subject. It is, moreover, at the present time the only published work dealing exclusively with Indian sign-talk that is readily obtainable. Ernest Thompson Seton's *Sign Talk* includes also many of the signs used by the deaf and dumb.

The first valuable work on the subject was a book by Maj. Stephen H. Long, published in 1823, and long since out of print. More than fifty years later Lieut. Col. Garrick Mallery, under the auspices of the Smithsonian, produced two works which are also out of print. Regarded as the most authoritative handling of the subject is Capt. William Philo Clark's book, published in 1885, and now very difficult to obtain. Three other books, published in the late Eighties and early Nineties by Lewis F. Hadley, a missionary in the Indian Territory, round out the list. These too are very scarce.

Two striking differences divide Indian sign-talk from that employed by the deaf and dumb. The latter make much use of facial expression, the Indian none; the other difference is that Indian sign is much more richly symbolic, more closely identified with natural phenomena. Some of its imagery is startlingly beautiful and delightfully apt. For example, if I wish to sign that I am going home in the autumn, I do it as follows: first pointing to myself, I make the signs for going and for home, then I make the sign for tree; that is, I hold my open left hand, thumb and fingers spread, back outward, about the height of my shoulder and move it slowly upward, thus indicating growth. Then I make the sign for leaf and draw my hand down with a fluttering motion.

If I wish to convey that I am feeling sad, I point to myself, and then, having made the sign for heart, draw my hand down and away in the direction of the ground. If I wish to say that I am happy, having indicated my heart, I make the sign for sunrise. This last, properly executed, is a finely suggestive and graceful gesture. Most of the signs indicating natural phenomena have a high content of poetry. Imagery enters also into the designations for animals; there is more than one way to sign mountain lion, for example, but the most vivid is to make the sign for lightness, and then the one for walking forward.

Accomplished sign-talkers can convey their meaning more rapidly and with as fine nuances as they can with words. Long stories are told in this manner, sometimes punctuated by hearty bursts of laughter, for contrary to the notions of our schoolbook days, Indians are among the most humorous of peoples, and great teasers and kidders.

It is extraordinary that though there are great differences between the spoken languages of the Plains tribes, to the point where verbal communication was impossible, yet all the tribes of the plains were able to converse easily by sign. There are minor variations geographically, but basically Indian sign can truly be described as a universal language and, incidentally, as the only one which was completely developed on this continent.

Notes on the Northwest

BILLINGS, MONTANA

Yesterday, as I came down through the great Judith Basin (onetime stomping ground of Charley Russell, the Montana cowboy artist, many of whose paintings—the most authentic ever done of the old West—enliven the lobby of the Norther Hotel here) I fell to thinking that maybe I shot a bit wide of the mark in what I said two weeks ago about "the homogeneity which, as a nation, we once had, and lost." Have we ever really been a homogenous people? We were once, to a far greater degree than now, in our racial components, but were we ever fully so in our attitudes and in the values by which we lived?

In America there has always been a frontier (it lies today in Alaska, into which new settlers are pouring steadily)—and there has always been conflict between the frontier and the older settlements. Their ways have never been alive; their values, save for the love of freedom and the belief in American destiny, have never been the same. Until North and South took divergent paths economically (an industrial vs. an agricultural economy), which led them to civil war, they were actually more homogenous than were their eastern and western divisions. They are becoming so again as the South enters its present phase of industrial expansion, but the cleavage between East and West remains. It was not this cleavage, peculiar to ourselves, that Kipling had in mind when he wrote that never the twain should meet, but one wonders sometimes whether the phrase is not equally applicable to the United States.

Certainly I have been made to believe so on this journey, as I always am whenever I come West again. Another civil war in the United States seems to us unthinkable and, no doubt, lies beyond the margin of probability, but if an economic gulf as deep as that which separated North and South should arise, it could be, Our daily press doesn't do enough to bridge the differences by way of mutual understanding, and the writers of our fiction do little more. Out of this deep-seated separation between East and West rises, of course, the question of isolationism and the equally urgent question of the relative importance for our future of Europe or the Far East. As you travel west the importance of Europe diminishes in popular conception; that holds all the way to the West Coast, even though the West Coast cities are not Western in the sense that Spokane, Denver and the smaller communities of Wyoming, Montana and Idaho are. If the West Coast looks back to the Eastern seaboard culturally, economically it has always been conscious of the lands across the Pacific.

One of the inevitable reactions of the traveler in the Northwest is a sharpened sense of the fundamental unity underlying not only the states which compose it but embracing also the Canadian provinces of Manitoba, Saskatchewan, Alberta, and British Columbia. The range and direction of their interests are identical; they are parts of a gigantic and rapidly growing whole. They feel with a mounting intensity that their problems and even their attitude toward life are not understood in the East and that the capital of the United States is steadily being moved from Washington to Europe. They are as aware as anyone else of the contracted world we live in and of this continent's unavoidable global involvement, but their ideas of how we should conduct ourselves in this new situation are far from identical with those prevalent on the Eastern seaboard.

We find it hard to understand the Russians (or, more accurately, perhaps, their masters), but it seems to me we are in equally urgent need of understanding one another, and the chief burden of that need, I think, rests on the shoulders of the East. The East simply doesn't know enough about the West and makes insufficient effort to learn. In the same way the Canadians are far better informed about us than we are about them; we forget that the kid brother is getting to be a big boy now. Too many of us are ignorant of the fact that he is handling some of the problems we have in common more fairly and more intelligently than ourselves (as was the case with rationing in World War II and has always been the case in his treatment of that most trampled upon minority of them all, the American Indian).

What I have been saying is, I know, very general in character, much too lacking in specific detail. This column is not the place for the elaboration that is needed. My reason for writing about these matters at all is that I believe the writers of this country, by moving in on a new literary frontier, can do a great deal to spread information and understanding where it is needed. Now and then, regularly as the equinoctial disturbance that has been messing up the weather, some critic in London or New York announces that the novel is on its last legs. Though I'd prefer a somewhat ruder and more vulgar comment, "Stuff and nonsense!" must do. If a few more novelists would get over their green-sickness and stop fiddling with best-seller formulas or figuring out new ways of shocking the daylights out of a remarkably shock-absorbent generation, and turn their attention to some of the really meaningful phenomena of our time and country, the general falling-off in fiction sales might not be so painfully apparent.

Our Most Abused Minority

Big Horn, Wyoming

On my desk as I write this piece lie two Indian dogtags, brass checks stamped with the date June 1909, when they were issued to two second-class citizens named Charles Longjaw and John Badger, Cheyenne Indians then living on the Tongue River Reservation in Montana. I was given them last week when I went over the state line to visit the agency which our benevolent Government, champion of the world's minorities, maintains at Lame Deer. Today, on that Northern Cheyenne Reservation, which adjoins that of their hereditary enemies, the Crows, there are living, in abject poverty, nearly 2,000 Cheyennes, 60 per cent of whom are full-bloods. Eighty per cent live close to starvation; most of them are miserably housed.

The agency superintendent at Lame Deer, Carl Pearson, is one of the competent and dedicated men in the Indian Service. He does what he can, but the problem he faces is a tough one. The land on which we expect the Cheyennes to make a living is not adequate either for profitable farming or cattle-raising; when, during the depression, the Government staked each Cheyenne family to ten head of cattle, they were, necessarily, slaughtered one by one for food; any stockman will tell you that no matter how hard you work you can't get anywhere with a herd of that size.

These facts are by way of prelude to reporting on an examination I have been making of the manner in which our treatment of the Indian has been handled in the history textbooks used in our schools. Most of them are, in that respect, badly in need of revision. Most of them present a misleading, distorted picture or pass over almost entirely the shameful pages of the record. We all know, or should, how nations lie about themselves in their histories, and those used in the schools are the chief sinners. Our own performance may look guileless beside that of the Russians, but it is far from being above reproach.

To school children here in Wyoming and Montana, Indians are not merely part of a romantic past, as they are to Eastern children. They are everyday objects, indifferently encountered: shabby and often dirty members of a still discriminated against minority. The other day I saw a teen-age white girl close to tears because her white high-school classmates actively disapproved of her friendship with two Indian girls. Even today Indians are refused admittance to many stores and restaurants in Western towns. We shout ourselves hoarse over the discrimination practiced against larger and more powerful minorities. What about this one, against whom our sins are heavier and more numerous than against any other? Have Americans lost the capacity for anger? Are we shameless?

How many American school children know the story of the Sand Creek massacre in 1864, when a Colorado militia colonel named Chivington shot down in cold blood hundreds of Indian men, women and children, peaceably assembled at the command of their white betrayers? Out of a dozen or more history textbooks I have looked into, that incident, or others like it, is mentioned in only one; the only one, moreover, in which I have found a completely fair and sufficiently comprehensive account of our relations with the Indians in the conquest of the West. I take off my hat to its authors, Mabel B. Casner of the Washington School in West Haven, Connecticut, and Ralph Henry Gabriel, Professor of History at Yale; at least these were their positions when their book, *Exploring American History,* was published by Harcourt, Brace & Co. in 1931.

By way of contrast, permit me to quote from a textbook used in the schools of this state—a descriptive and historical treatment of *Wyoming: Frontier State,* by Velma Linford, issued by the Old West Publishing Company in Denver. "Wyoming was red man's domain until 1860. Through a series of treaties, the United States gave the plains and Rocky Mountain country to the Indians. There the tribes fought with each other and developed a culture of their own. After 1860 the white man saw Wyoming as a country he wanted; first merely for a trail, then for a pasture land, and finally for a home.

By treaties, battles, and overpowering numbers the white man pushed the red away from the great grasslands to Indian reservations."

No mention, you observe, of the *breaking* of those treaties, the lies and the betrayals, the indignities heaped on a proud but prostrate people, of which the dogtags I mentioned at the head of this column may stand as symbols. White justice! Within this year a starving Indian on a neighboring reservation stole one or two cattle from a white rancher's herd, and promptly landed in jail; shortly afterward another white rancher made off with a herd of Indian cattle; months have passed, and he has not yet been brought to trial.

We offer ourselves to the world as moral mentors and we do not even teach our children the truth about how we waxed fat and great. What, in Heaven's name, is the use of teaching them that we live in one world, where all men are bound together in a common destiny, unless, by knowing the truth, they approach that world with dispassionate, unprejudiced eyes?

P.S. The foregoing column was guilty of such gross injustice toward one of the textbooks therein discussed, that in a subsequent piece I made such amends as I could. An unfortunately worded paragraph in Miss Linford's *Wyoming: Frontier State* led me to accuse her of suppressing the facts concerning our government's relations with the Plains Indians. Elsewhere in her book she had given full recognition to the many betrayals of our trust. Although the column was written fifteen years ago, I believe its overall criticism of what our school-children are taught about our treatment of the American Indian is still justified. Indeed, the whole content and slant of our history textbooks calls for the close examination it is beginning to receive. It is my hope, incidentally, that one beneficial by-product of our present concern with civil rights will be a reassessment of our attitude toward a minority more gravely abused, in some respects, than any other.

Hymn to Western Montana

CALGARY, CANADA

From a hill above this city, then a sprawling prairie town, I had, in the summer of 1913, my first glimpse of the Rockies. Fresh from college, I had come West over the C.P.R., headed in a somewhat roundabout fashion for the Presidio at San Francisco, where I had enrolled for the Plattsburg camp to be opened there that summer. But my funds, scanty to begin with, fell short. I wired Uncle Sam my regrets and found myself a job carrying a rod on a Government survey crew which was mapping the foothills of Mount Rainier.

On First Avenue in Seattle I had my never-to-be-forgotten induction into the ways of the West. Light-hearted improvidence had reduced my slim capital to something like $7 or $8. Job in hand, I walked into the first outfitting store I came to, bought a flannel shirt and a few other needed articles, and was then faced with the fact that the piece of equipment I needed most—a pair of high hobnailed boots in which to negotiate the rough and heavily timbered country I would be working in—was beyond my reach; they cost $12. When I explained my plight to the proprietor, he smiled and said: "That's all right son. Take 'em along, and when you come out at the end of the summer come in and see me."

When something like that happens to you at twenty-one, you don't forget—that is if you had grown up, as I did, on the Eastern seaboard—and, more specifically, on Manhattan Island. Each time I come West the memory of that heart-warming little experience travels with me. It is always in part a sentimental journey, both for that reason and for others; the present one more so than usual, because it was from Calgary that I first saw part of that fiercely upthrust backbone of the continent along which I have been traveling intermittently for two weeks past, and because soon I shall drive on to Seattle, where I have not been since I left it in the spring of 1917.

If you are beginning to fidget and ask what has all this to do with the present state of literature in the U.S.A. and elsewhere, I beg you to be patient; the application will be apparent, I hope, before too long.

In Seattle and on my return to Montana, from which I have just come, I shall start on the working leg of my journey, and that part of it which concerns this page will touch on the literary aspects of the Northwest—one of our regional areas whose literary potentialities, no less than its material ones, are still far short of full development. In the meantime, may I direct your attention to the two quotations which fill the Treasure Chest for today—two tributes to Montana, which, aptly enough, bears the proud nickname of the Treasure State, as every Montana automobile license plate reminds you. Though I suspect Montanans sometimes wish they had thought first of the bucking horse that adorns the plates of neighboring Wyoming, they have so much to boast of that they can well afford to be indulgent toward the cocky Wyoming insignia.

Don't be too ready to label the late Joseph Kinsey Howard's paragraphs as smacking of the purple patch, nor to accuse Donald Culross Peattie of merely making a neat and aptly sounding synthesis. Don't do so at least if you have never traveled in western Montana. Having said so much, I shall now jump overboard myself. Some hint of what to expect may already have reached those of you with sensitive antennae; to mix metaphors more than a little, I shall ride with as tight a checkrein as possible, bearing in mind also that what I say may grieve my friends in Wyoming. Anyhow, off with the old love, on with the new! I still have great affection for Wyoming, and hope I may yet have many happy days there, but——

Until this present journey I have never seen western Montana, except briefly and unrepresentatively, from a train window, many years ago. There is a popular and smoothly worn cliché to which many Westerners are addicted; they like to speak of "God's country." As to that, every man must find his own, and many never do, but I *have* found mine. I first felt the new infatuation (but I know in my bones and deep in my gizzard that it is more than a passing fancy) when I drove up out of Yellowstone with the Gallatin Range to my left and the Absarokas on my right; I felt it when I went over to Three Forks and stood alone by the headwaters of the Missouri (shades of Lewis and Clark!); it deepened when I came into Missoula through Hell's Gate (where the Blackfeet laid in ambush for encroaching tribes); waxed warmly when I fished in the early morning on Flathead Lake, and burst into something not too remote from ecstasy when I entered Glacier Park for the first time. I cannot trust myself to write about Glacier—not yet. Let me instead make a bald statement: It is, to my mind, the most magnificent recreational area in all the United States. But to say that is to say nothing of what Glacier *really* is. Those who know it well would not exchange it for any other million acres on the face of the earth.

The Languors of Charleston

CHARLESTON, SOUTH CAROLINA

When I was last in Charleston—October, 1932—this most charming of American cities was physically down at heels, but was happily experiencing a kind of literary ferment. The occasion for my visit, as a matter of fact, was a Southern writers' conference which had been organized by Du Bose Heyward and others then active in the city's cultural life. Among those who came were Julia Peterkin, whose *Scarlet Sister Mary* was one of the forerunners of the South's literary revival since witnessed; Lawrence Stallings, whose *What Price Glory?* was still fresh in memory, Gerald Johnson, better known today than then, Irita Van Doren, and Struthers Burt. Ellen Glasgow had planned to come, but couldn't. Besides Du Bose and Dorothy Heyward, the Charleston writers included Josephine Pinckney, Archibald Rutledge (not present), and Herbert Ravenel Sass, who wrote with distinction about the natural beauties of the Carolina Low Country.

The picture today is in reverse. Literally, Charleston is in the doldrums; there have been no notable successors to the group I have named. But in outward appearance Charleston has brightened much. No city in the country that I know has with equal stubbornness maintained its distinctive character. That remains, even if the old street cries like "Gyarden on mah haid" have mostly been silenced. My first impression, as I came into the old part of town and recognized familiar landmarks, was the lavish presence of fresh paint. When I first saw the city in 1927, and again in 1932, the grace and dignity and charm were there, but she was a Southern belle whose beauty had faded, or more accurately, whose clothes were in disrepair. All that has changed, and today she wears a shining face.

As one who loves her, I wish as much could be said of her literary fortunes. Possibly they have suffered because of her tenacious regard for her past. She remains the somewhat ghostlike embodiment of all that was best in the South's tradition—now so denigrated and bescoffed—of gracious living. It lives on in her colonial and ante-bellum houses, of which, probably, she has kept more than any other American city, in her almost unchanging skyline (the spire of old St. Michael's still dominates the town) and in the leisurely pace of her normal life.

Is she then out of step with today's literary tempo and out of tune with its attitudes? Depending on your point of view, that would be a debit or credit. I have not been here long enough to report with any accuracy on the prevalent attitudes of such aspiring young writers as Charleston may have, but I suspect that the deficiency is due simply to the lack of a cluster of talent, plus the fact that Charleston is not a university town,—and it is in university towns that most of today's literary activity (New York aside) is centered. Besides, Charleston remains a small city, with a population now of about 70,000, and not nearly as intent as such Southern cities as Atlanta or Jacksonville on great increase.

Her literary lagging certainly is not due to indifference to cultural matters. She has a symphony orchestra and an interesting art gallery; displays of contemporary painting by local artists are frequently on display in the lobby of the Fort Sumter Hotel on the Battery. Her vigorous morning newspaper, the *News and Courier,* carries a book page. She is, moreover, very much a cocktail-hour town; her residents travel abroad in larger numbers than at any time since the Civil War, and when a writer like Auden or Sir Osbert Sitwell comes to town, Charlestonians turn out. She has her Dock Street Theater, and interest in the drama runs high.

Today her best-known writer is a transplanted Northerner, Paul Hyde Bonner. Most of the writers who were part of her brief literary revival are dead, including the author of one of the favorite books of my childhood, John Bennett, whose *Master Skylark,* a tale of Shakespeare's time in which he engagingly appears, is I hope, still in favor among those youngsters who can be induced to read anything other than space yarns or those proliferating books about the problems of that separate race, the teenagers. And speaking of them, my Charleston friends tell me that their youngest generation—in a city which has prized family descent—is, like its contemporaries elsewhere, disgustedly scornful of such outmoded concerns.

The literary attitude of Charleston's writers—when she had them—was prevailingly romantic and nostalgic. None, so far as I know, was subject to the Faulknerian miasma, nor did any write with Faulkner's power. Josephine Pinckney, I think, made the closest approach to a realistic stance. Du Bose Heyward, the most gifted of them all, writes with delicacy and charm, and as everybody knows his tale of the Negro cripple, Porgy, brought into being the only American folk opera that we have. He remains the one enduring literary reputation that South Carolina has contributed to our century, and Catfish Row is one of the first things tourists ask to see. For more resounding names, we must look to Virginia, Kentucky, North Carolina, Georgia, and Mississippi, the states which have contributed most to the South's literary renaissance.

Mountains vs. the Sea I

This may prove to be an unprofitable discussion, and I begin it simply because the thought which provoked it never occurred to me before, and I am curious to see where it leads. Since it was a thought which has probably entered the minds of many people besides myself, to pursue it may have a more general interest than the satisfaction of my own puzzlement. The thought was this: Why has the sea played so much more of a part in literature than mountains have? Why has it stirred the imaginations of men to a so much greater degree?

The mountains and the sea are the two outstanding aspects of man's physical environment. Both have affected his history profoundly, Nations are what they are because they had access to the sea or because they were hemmed in by mountains. In some cases, as in our own, a people has been subject to the effect of both, and it would be difficult to say which of the two had played the greater part in determining the character of that people,

If the sea and the mountains have affected great groupings of men, they have also had an impact on us as individuals. Most of us are predominantly attached to one or the other. Someone once suggested to me that this attachment is largely determined by the conditioning imposed by our early years. If one's childhood was colored predominantly by either mountains or sea, the attachment is likely to persist, My own experience inclines me in favor of that theory. My summers as a child alternated between the two, and in consequence, it seems to me, my allegiance is divided. If I am absent long from one or the other, I feel a need for the balance to be restored.

The theory, however, is by no means airtight. People born far inland yearn for the sight of the sea, and if I am not mistaken, Navy enlistments are heavily weighted by applicants from the midland states. And one thinks, naturally, of writers like Joseph Conrad. As a boy in Poland, he told us, he put his finger on a spot in Africa, and said, "I shall go there." No other writer's work, with an early background so definitely inland, has been so dominated by the appeal of the sea.

Perhaps I asked myself this question because I am subject to both appeals. Certainly the sea spoke to men before mountains did—centuries earlier. Although the sea can be more terrifying than mountains, except for the summits of the highest peaks, early man stood in more awe of them than he did of the waters on which he so courageously embarked. Mountains did not enter literature until the arrival of the romantic movement. Indeed, it was possible for Samuel Johnson to define a mountain as "a considerable protuberance."

The literature of the sea is enormous: the stories which have it for background, the poems which have touched upon it in every one of its multifarious aspects. Yet mountains are capable of affecting the minds of men as profoundly as the sea. Even more so, perhaps: did not the Psalmist write, "I lift up mine eyes to the hills, whence cometh my help." Much as the sea has stirred the imaginations of men, much as they have loved and hated it. I do not think it has ever been pictured, as the mountains have, as a spiritual resource.

Both have in them the element of challenge. Man has not been able to look upon either without wanting to know what lies beyond. Now, of course, when every sea has been charted and we know what lies behind every mountain range, the challenge has been diminished. Our minds turn toward outer space, and our imaginations are engaged by the thought that we may in time be able to reach other worlds than our own. But though we have penetrated every sea, and sail them all with confidence, one mountain at least, the highest of them all, still defies our efforts to conquer it. The summit of Everest remains unreached. (I do not, let me add, mean to suggest that man has conquered the sea; he has not really conquered anything in nature, much as he may pride himself on splitting the atom.)

Recently the sea, in the books that have been written about it, has particularly engaged our attention. I do not begrudge that attention; Rachel Carson and others have richly deserved our interest, but I should like to see mountains less in the shadow. Perhaps the balance will be somewhat restored by the forthcoming publication of *Annapurna,* the story of the French expedition led by Maurice Herzog, the author of the book, which reached the top of the highest mountain yet climbed by man. Nothing in the sea's annals, not even the astounding voyage of Captain Bligh, can surpass, as a record of human endurance and fortitude, this account of what men will suffer for a deeply prized objective.

No one yet has written the book about mountains in general which would treat imaginatively and factually the part they have played in human history. It would not be an easy book to write, but someday someone will undertake it.

Mountains vs. the Sea II

On the point of continuing the discussion recently begun here on the question of mountains vs. the sea in literature, a bevy of inconsiderate bacteria laid me low. The enemy has now been routed, and I return to the question fortified by some interesting opinions offered by readers of this column. Partisanship in the matter, it seems, is strong. I had confessed, as one whose affections are divided between mountains and sea, some difficulty in understanding why the sea has played so much larger a part in literature. Mountains, I maintained, were deserving of more attention than they have had. Most of my correspondents, however, champion the sea.

When I wrote as I did I was well aware that during the past century there has been a vast and growing body of what may be called the literature of mountaineering. Particularly in Great Britain, the number of books dealing with mountain climbing has been large. But my query was not concerned with that kind of writing, excellent though some of it is. What I had in mind, and perhaps failed to make sufficiently clear in the first article, was the degree to which literature in general had been infused by feeling for either mountains or sea. In all so-called creative writing the sea has by far outbalanced the mountains.

Several readers make much of the fact that, compared with the sea, mountains are static. We are fascinated, they say, by the change, fullness and capriciousness of the sea. But is not the difference more apparent than actual? The mountains' changes in form are more fundamental than the sea's, though they take too long for us to observe them; that, however, need not affect our consciousness of change, even in them. (Read the Rocky Mountain poetry of Thomas Hornsby Ferril.) And certainly in the play of light and shadow produced by sunshine and cloud, the mountains surpass the sea in variety of aspect. As for capriciousness, any mountain climber can tell you how unpredictable mountains can be above the timber line.

One reader offers as an obvious explanation—and one, certainly, with some sound sense behind it—the fact that with some notable exceptions "centers of culture have been on or near the sea and not in the mountains. Until comparatively recent times, writers were to be found in proximity to the sea—or at least to people who knew the sea—and not to mountains. This is not to say that mountain-dwelling people were not stirred by their surroundings, but they were not of the sort given to writing about them." This same correspondent, Mr. Edgar B. Nixon, further remarks that mountains can only be truly experienced by getting on and into them, whereas the sea has been more easily accessible to greater numbers of people.

From Boulder, Colorado, where the mountains loom large, Mrs. Harrison Thompson remarks that "Surely the sea is more exciting because it is essentially, to man's seeming, a 'way,' while a range is a barrier." She sees it as "more dramatic because it offers a wider gamut of terror and delight, sensuous intimacy and stern desolation, vitality and deepest death. The mineral mountains speak less to the blood, they do not sigh or thunder through dreams, they have no powerful rhythms, no rippling reflections, no tang, no peacock hues, no infinity of creatures, no power to cast up delicate or fearful surprises. The imagination is sooner done with masculine mountains than with the calms and commotions of the female sea." (Eloquent though Mrs. Thompson is, I cannot go all the way with her.)

The suggestion is made by another correspondent, Mr. George Groskritz, that the sea's preponderance in literature may be accounted for by the fact that it has more seriously involved the working lives of human beings and has been the source of more tragedy in the loss of life. One or two readers, naturally, mention man's biological kinship with the sea—his derivation from it and its persistence in his blood. May I, in this connection, remind you of Ridgely Torrence's fine poem on that subject, called "Sea Dream"? It is too long, unfortunately, for reprinting in the "Poets' Column."

Miss Miriam Blumberg calls my attention to a passage in Thomas Mann's *Buddenbrooks,* in which Thomas Buddenbrook meditates on the difference in our homage to mountains and sea. It lies, he says, in the way we look at them. "It is a strong, challenging gaze, full of enterprise, that can soar from peak to peak; but the eyes that rest on the wide ocean and are soothed by the sight of its waves rolling on forever, mystically, relentlessly, are those that are already wearied by looking into the solemn perplexities of life—health and illness, that is the difference. The man whose strength is unexhausted climbs boldly up into the lofty multiplicity of the mountain heights. But it is when one is worn out with turning one's eyes inward upon the bewildered complexity of the human heart that one finds peace in resting them on the wideness of the sea." Miss Blumberg thinks the distinction drawn by Mann may explain contemporary interest in the sea. But Mann's distinction seems too subjective to me for broad application.

The Queen of Islands

MARTHA'S VINEYARD, MASSACHUSETTS

We are, as everybody knows, a nation of migrants, as well as immigrants; we were a people on wheels even before Henry Ford devised the Model T—buggy wheels and prairie-schooner wheels, to be sure, but we were always on the move. What other people have made homes in so many different places in the land of their birth?

This phenomenon is now still more marked than it was in our beginning and during our early growth. The rise of the chain stores and the multiplying of great corporations with offices or plants in a dozen different cities have made us in large part a nation of transients; even our academic men flit, during their early years, at least, from college to college.

There are, however, a few places—even a few regions—where roots are still deep, and prized besides. In spite of the Southern Negro's migrations, the South—especially the Deep South—is such a region. So are Vermont, New Hampshire, and Maine, and so too are some of our islands. Not Long Island certainly, nor Manhattan itself, but to find the tradition of rootedness at its strongest (save for the Appalachian mountaineers) one must turn to the islands of Nantucket and Martha's Vineyard, plus some of those off the coast of Maine.

Islanders here, or anywhere in the world, are a special breed, and their unifying trait is independence. Consider for a moment, before I get down to literary brass tacks, the amazing history of the great island peoples of this world. They are three, or possibly five in number. First, ancient Greece; though properly a peninsula, one thinks of the Greeks as an island people, which they essentially were; then England, once master of the greatest empire mankind has known; then Japan, for a time so nearly master of the Far East. On the fringe are Ireland and, if not geographically, certainly in character, Scotland—both peoples (originally one) who have made themselves felt throughout the civilized and not so civilized worlds.

I write this column from an island loved by many thousands of Americans who were not born here; fifteen minutes distant by air lies another which has at least an equal number of devotees—Nantucket. I will not stick my neck out and proclaim the superiority of one over the other; their rivalry is old and unending. They are among the last outposts of a sane manner of life in these United States, and happy is he who knows them.

I call your attention today to a little book concerned with the life lived for generations by one family on the island of Martha's Vineyard. It is by a native Vineyarder whose roots on the island reach back for three hundred years. *It Began With A Whale: Memories of Cedar Tree Neck* is for the present, at least, obtainable only in certain shops on the Vineyard, or by writing to its author, John Tobey Daggett, at Marblehead, Mass.

Perhaps the most interesting single fact in Mr. Daggett's book is the price paid by his grandfather for the two-centuries old Daggett Homestead. With about 100 acres, which include a half-mile or more of shorefront on Vineyard Sound, looking across to the most feudally maintained area in the United States—the island of Naushon—the purchase price a century ago was $1,800; today the property would bring at least a quarter of a million.

This is a simple story filled with homely but often fascinating details about the kind of life lived by these island folk since the Vineyard was settled over 300 years ago. Its beauties are shared today during the summer months by some 34,000 people; the population then drops to 6,000. Part of the Vineyard's charm derives from its variety; it has hills and woods and moors (though these last lack Nantucket's heather); it has great beaches on the open sea, pounded by a magnificent surf, and smaller ones across the island, on Vineyard Sound; it has multicolored cliffs that are steadily consumed by the hungry Atlantic; sheep meadows and ponds and lagoons.

Mr. Daggett's father was a commercial fisherman who combined farming with his fish traps, as did other island men, and as a few still do, although the fish are no longer so plentiful as they once were. So too have the sheep herds dwindled. The heath hen, once native to the island, is now extinct, but the deer are many, and Canada geese make stop-overs on the island ponds during their migrations, as do many varieties of songbirds—and always, of course, there are wheeling gulls that smash open their clams on the island bridges.

The book offers intimate glimpses of the life the islanders led through many generations, when to cross the island and back over the dusty roads was a full day's journey instead of a half-hour's motor trip; Mr. Daggett tells of their simple, happy recreations and the warm neighborliness of the island life. Some of this remains, and any part-time Vineyarder will tell you how the island and its ways have worked into his blood. For my own part, it is the only place in the world where I have seen that aphoristic phenomenon, a blue moon.

Our Regional Differences

REVELSTOKE, B. C.

The dateline is correct so far as the postoffice is concerned; actually this is being written nearly 5,000 feet above the town of Revelstoke, at a place called Heather Lodge, located on the summit of Mount Revelstoke. I doubt whether there is a more beautiful spot on the North American continent. It is completely encircled by the various ranges that make up the Selkirks; Alpine meadows, from which, unfortunately, the wildflowers have by this early date almost vanished, compose the foreground. The lodge, incidentally, comes honestly by its name; heather grows here in profusion, as well as the Indian paintbrush.

When I woke yesterday morning a great white blanket of cloud lay at the 5,000-foot level (the lodge stands at 6,350), so that I looked from my windows across a feather-soft lake to the steep slopes of the Clachnacudainn Range. Then, bit by bit, rifts in the blanket appeared, revealing long prospects of pointed fir; while away to the north the Columbia, dropping down through deep gorges, gleamed in the sun like a silver snake. There is only one way to write about books amid such surroundings, and that is to turn your back upon them, which is what I have done this morning; my table faces the door to my room.

But I don't want to write about books; I want to write about my journey along the Big Bend of the Columbia (where a speeding Greyhound bus nearly brained me when its rear wheels flung a rock up from the gravel road and cracked my windshield into a spider-web design); about the she-bear that chased me on the banks of the Athabasca when I took a few incautious steps toward one of her cubs; about the fat marmot who emerged from the rockslide to look me over as I puffed along the trail.

Enough of this nonsense. This column is, I believe, entitled "Speaking of Books." What good books have I read recently? Let me recommend to you the excellent "Guide to Glacier National Park," by George C. Ruhle, naturalist in the National Park Service —a model of its kind in text, in illustration, and in arrangement. And although my reading has been largely of maps (touched upon last Sunday), I have greatly enjoyed making the acquaintance of Joseph Kinsey Howard's *Montana Margins: A State Anthology,* which I missed upon its appearance in 1946.

If I may characterize this volume in the same way as the Glacier Park guide book, it, too, is a model of its kind. I did not learn of Mr. Howard's recent death until my reference two weeks ago to his glowing description of the Treasure State in his *Montana: High, Wide and Handsome.* He was among the best of our regional writers, and his untimely going is a great loss to the budding literature of the Northwest.

With no immediate access to a good library, and my memory being the treacherous thing it is, I cannot be certain as to what extent

Mr. Howard's performance in his state anthology has been duplicated. The idea behind it seems to me as valid as those underlying the Rivers of America or the American Folkways Series. If it were to be as generally applied the results would, no doubt, be as variable as they have proved to be in the case of the two very successful enterprises I have mentioned. I suppose, for example, that the Nevada anthologist would need to rely largely on sources little read except by historians of the West; the same would be true, say, of Utah, Idaho, the Dakotas—or, to go much farther East, of Tennessee, Delaware, New Jersey, even. On the other hand the compiler of the literature native to New York, Massachusetts and Connecticut, or of Ohio, Indiana and Illinois, of South Carolina, Georgia and Louisiana, would be faced by an embarrassment of riches from which to choose.

In any case, it is a project I would much like to see undertaken. Its *raison d'être* would be much sounder than that underlying many contemporary anthologies; and in each instance a reasonably good local sale, at least, would seem to be assured. And it would help, among other things, to dispel the much overemphasized conception, so dear to the hearts of visiting Englishmen and others, of these United States as a monotonous waste of cultural uniformity. In spite of assemblyline Main Streets strewn across the continent, any reasonably observant traveler, as he goes from region to region, or even from state to state, must be aware of differences not too subtle, though they may not be as marked or profound as those which separate Canada's Maritime Provinces from her Northwest Territories.

Our awareness of these differences can add much to our understanding of the variable texture of American life; and nowhere is an increase in such understanding more needed than among those Americans who live on the Eastern seaboard. I think we can get nowhere in our international relations until we have a better knowledge of ourselves and recover in comprehension, if not in fact, something of that homogeneity which, as a nation, we once had, and lost.

The Spirit of Place

EDINBURGH

After these months abroad I find myself in even heartier agreement than I would otherwise have been with Lawrence Durrell's contention that "the important determinant of any culture is after all the spirit of place." Mr. Durrell's article in the issue for June 12 was an eloquent plea for conceiving of character as almost a projection of landscape. A people—and the individuals composing it—can truly be understood only as expressions of the land that formed them. As Mr. Durrell has demonstrated in his own novels, it is not essential for a writer to be one with the people he writes about—not if he has been able to absorb, by a kind of osmosis, the spirit of place by which they have been created. What is essential is the capacity for identification. He ended his article by asserting—truly, I think—that not enough attention is paid to the sense of place as a literary criterion, though nearly all the best fiction, including our own, bears testimony to its importance.

In lesser measure, poetry too draws veracity and strength from identification with place. For that reason I disagree with much that Donald Hall said in his recent report on the present British literary climate. He expressed annoyance with the younger English poets partly because they are concerned with place and with intimate, daily life. They are wrong, he thinks, because in our contemporary world regions no longer really exist, and because, for related reasons, the best poetry of the modern world involves sophistication and cosmopolitanism. Let us not, I say, be deceived by surface uniformities, for underneath the apparent obliteration of regional lines produced by mass products and mass media, the spirit of place lives on. For all our talk of one world, national consciousness intensifies everywhere.

As for sophistication and cosmopolitanism, are they really important to poetry? Surely the essence of poetry is in seeing things as if they were observed for the first time. "Every word was once a poem." Poetry is the antithesis of sophistication, and cosmopolitanism is in direct opposition to the spirit of place. "If only regional poetry can be written now," wrote Mr. Hall, "or only poetry that comes exclusively from daily situations and emotions, very little good poetry will be written at all, and nothing will be written that we will call great." How is it, then, that most of the great poetry we have came from precisely such sources as these?

The abuse to which the word "regional" has been subjected is a great pity. It is constantly applied in the narrowest sense. When one considers how much in the great literature of every tongue is regional in its roots, and continues so age after age, to use the word as if it meant no more than the reproduction of a local dialect is to spread confusion and to do injustice. Where can one find a more regional book than Chaucer's *Canterbury Tales,* or modern poetry that draws more from regional effects than "The Waste Land," to choose an example less obvious than many others? The spirit of place dominates the whole range of English literature no less than Edinburgh Castle dominates its city.

And what of ourselves? The best book that Mark Twain wrote—*Life on the Mississippi*—and the best parts of *Huckleberry Finn* are drenched in the spirit of place. If Hawthorne were writing now, he would risk dismissal as a regionalist. What was best in Henry James, in Whitman, in almost every major writer we have had, found its sources in the sense of place. It is the one capacity every writer of fiction must possess, if his work is to have veracity and enduring life. Those in whom this capacity is most strongly developed are able to carry it with them wherever their lives may be lived. Hemingway is an outstanding example. If Willa Cather could write with complete understanding of the Nebraska prairie folk among whom her most impressionable years were spent, the sense of place did not desert her when she turned to the Southwest and wrote *Death Comes for the Archbishop.* If Edith Wharton, in *The House of Mirth* and *The Age of Innocence,* could memorably recapture the particular New York world in which she grew up, her sense of place enabled her also to write, of an alien environment, what was perhaps her most notable achievement—*Ethan Frome.* O. Henry was a writer of many and serious faults, yet he, most of whose life had been spent in the South and West, was able to reflect, as nobody else has done, another New York of Edith Wharton's period—the New York of the "Four Million" rather than the New York of the "Four Hundred."

How is it done? By a kind of surrender, I think; by not trying to take our country or region with us when we leave home, by trying, however ineffectually, to merge ourselves with the life of which we are temporarily a part. What all this matter of the sense of place comes down to, I suppose, is a species of sensitivity. The best novelists are more awake to the differences between people, and more interested in them, than the average person. That is one reason why they become novelists. Even that type of fiction, so common among first novels, which is a sort of self-purge, derives from the writer's need to distinguish himself from an environment with which he finds himself in conflict. It comes out of an awareness of differences.

Citadel of Courage

Just a year ago [1960] I was in the midst of a stay of several weeks in London, after not having been there for twenty-four years. In spite of the havoc wrought during World War II, of which only a few scars remain, in spite of the greatly risen tide of traffic and the advent of some monstrous cubes of glass and steel, I felt no shock of unfamiliarity; this was still the London I had known and loved—the London so well reflected in a book I have been reading—Ivor Brown's delightful anthology, *A Book of London.*

No doubt I would have had the same reaction had I returned to Paris instead, after an even longer lapse of time. But two years before my London visit of last spring I returned briefly to an American city where I had lived many years before and, though my absence had been even longer than from London, I was not prepared for the bewilderment I felt on seeing Seattle again. It took me two days to orient myself. Yet none of these cities has altered in essential character, whatever the outer changes, comparatively slight in London and Paris, enormous in Seattle, have been.

I took Ivor Brown's book down to Princeton last weekend, and read it sitting by a window in the Princeton Inn which looks out on a prospect happily appropriate: a gentle parklike landscape (actually a golf course) divided by a grassy-banked stretch of placid water, complete not with swans but with ducks and Canada geese, and with the square Gothic tower of the Cleveland Memorial rising abruptly from the green, much like Fountains Abbey or Salisbury Cathedral.

A Book of London is the latest addition to the excellent series of National Anthologies issued by William Collins Sons & Co., English publishers who maintain a branch office in New York. Previous volumes were devoted to England, Scotland, Ireland, Wales and Australia; another on Canada is to come. All are illustrated by numerous photographs and are attractively bound and designed.

Anthologies of this type demand particularly skillful editing, for what they should convey is not only the spirit of place, in itself an elusive thing to catch, but the character of the people as well. In accomplishing these aims the Collins anthologies have been outstandingly successful. Mr. Brown, who is well known here for the series of "word anthologies" he published during and after World War II, was the editor of *A Book of England,* and to *A Book of London* he has brought the same discriminating and illuminating taste which distinguished the earlier volume. The new book contains more than fifty photographs.

One of the things that most impressed me about Mr. Brown's selections is the feeling they communicate of that essential, unchanging character so marked in so many cities and countries. I suppose no city in the world has changed outwardly more continuously or more strikingly than the city of my birth: New York has been transformed since I was born in it a block away from where I now live, yet its essential character (with which I am not in full sympathy) has remained the same since the days of Philip Hone. Its prevailing air has always been commercial, complacently provincial, ruthless, ever welcoming of change whether for better or worse. It discards its past, and always has, like yesterday's newspaper, less to remind one of its three centuries of history than any city of equal or greater age in the world. And yet O. Henry's stories about New York, in their human content, have as much validity today as when he wrote them half a century ago.

But this piece is supposed to be about London. You cannot read Mr. Brown's book without realizing, if you hadn't before, that it has always been a city—I had almost written, a citadel—of courage; a city whose people have also been sustained, as they still are, by a lively sense of humor, which, next to courage, is the most precious of human qualities. He who has them both is blessed among men, for they reinforce one another, and make their possessor impregnable. Beside them, intellectuality is insignificant.

Mr. Brown has put together his portrait of London, past and present, by selections from poets, novelists, essayists, diarists, dramatists, biographers and historians. He has not disdained, bless him, to use also those anonymous and unpretentious writers who are sometimes so revealing of a people's inclinations and character—the popular ballad makers whose equivalent we have in the cowboy songs collected by Mr. Lomax, in such a tale as that of Frankie and Johnny, or, on a higher level, in the Negro spirituals.

The book runs from Chaucer and Shakespeare down to Galsworthy, Priestley, and Aldous Huxley. I find no trace of the "angry young men," but I do not think this invalidates Mr. Brown's book in any way, for the angry young men have nothing to do with the essential character of London and of Londoners, any more than the San Francisco beatniks have anything to do with the essential character of the United States and its inhabitants. They are merely froth on the top of the wave; the power and the impact are contained in the water beneath.

The New York of Fiction

Really, New Yorkers don't know what life is all about. (Neither, for that matter, I suspect, do Bostonians or Philadelphians, or even Chicagoans.) I believe I am fairly entitled to a word on the subject, since I was born within a stone's throw (well, a long stone's throw) of the street in which I write. Primarily, I am talking about those who were born and grew up in these great cities, unless they met life at first hand in one of the little neighborhoods in which most citizens of great cities live; even there, they are part of a much larger community, whose members are insulated against life as the citizens of a small town or a village are not. Those who come to the cities from the towns and villages have had a better education in humanity.

What set me off on this topic—which will presently become literary—was an obituary published on the front page of *The Vineyard Gazette,* regarded by some perhaps prejudiced observers as the best weekly newspaper in the United States. It announced the death of the Island's oldest resident, Theodore S. Wimpenney of Edgartown, who, had he lived until December, would have rounded out a full century of life. Many of the facts in that life are of interest only to Vineyarders—the four-year whaling voyage on which he embarked at the age of seventeen, his later work as a carpenter, and his long years of service as court crier. But Vineyarders or not, all readers can enjoy the fact that on his ninety-eighth birthday, which he had to spend in bed, he flexed his right forearm and said, "I believe I could still strike a pretty powerful blow!" One likes to learn, too, that at the age of sixteen "he could earn the wages of a man because he could do a man's work."

The story of his funeral, as carried in the Gazette's next issue, began by recording the fact that the bell of the Congregational Church in Edgartown slowly tolled ninety-nine times, once for each year of his age. His former pastor, who spoke the words of tribute, had this, among other things, to say: "He had in him something of the straightness and simplicity of the age whose spirit built fine clean houses like this old church in which we gather to remember him. He had something of the staunchness and fundamental honesty of the ships on which he and his fathers sailed and of the houses which his workman's good hand builded. New times have come and we are too busy to seek for the right simplicity, but we pray that enough of his kind of heritage has entered into us to hold us if 'the hurricane' comes."

From this kind of community experience the big city resident is too often cut off. The obituaries which he reads in his morning paper are too often the stories of lives which have never touched his own. What was it gave such poignancy to William Allen White's famous account of his daughter Mary's death? It was a tragedy in which a whole community closely shared. What was it made the pitiful story in last week's New York papers, about the poor child who took her life because the boy she was expecting did not call, moving only as something that we read in a book may move us? Only to her family's neighbors did it come really home.

Perhaps we have here the reason why so few native New Yorkers have been able to write with truth and feeling about the city of their birth. Henry James's New York was the New York of the great world; so, too, was Edith Wharton's. Who are the New Yorkers born who have made the city live in fiction? Can we name one who has caught and held in his pages the myriad facets of its life, in whose work we find reflected not only the teeming tenements of the lower East Side, or the roaring Forties, but also the placid Brooklyn streets, the huge steel and stone packing-cases of Park Avenue, the crush and the loneliness of the subway, the Central Park of the lovers, the bird-watchers, and the hoodlums? A bit here and there by this man or that; that is all.

We fare a little better when we think of O. Henry, who, say what you will about the contrivances he employed, and the blight he is supposed to have laid on the American short story, did manage surprisingly well to catch the feeling and the atmosphere of the New York of his time. (And let us not forget that at a moment when the phrase, "The Four Hundred" was stock material for every Sunday supplement, he called the collection of stories for which he is best remembered, *The Four Million*. But he was a boy from Greensboro, North Carolina.

The most successful effort at a kaleidoscopic picture of New York in fiction was Dos Passos' *Manhattan Transfer*, but he was born in Chicago and spent a good part of his childhood abroad. The best nonfiction piece about New York that I know (with a very definite bow in the direction of Henry Irving Brock of this newspaper) is E. B. White's magnificent summing-up in the current Holiday. But he was born in Mount Vernon at a time when, as I well remember, you could, after not too long a walk, come to woods where the chestnuts could be shaken down.

Tom Wolfe must not go unmentioned, for he wrote pages about New York and its people which had great power; there were others, but space grows short. And what have we now, from the bright young men who come to town from Kansas and Iowa, from Oklahoma and the Carolinas, to work in publishers' offices, on newspapers and magazines and in advertising agencies? Stories about writers and publishers, about newspaper and magazine tycoons, about the big shots of the advertising world. How much are they of New York? More about this, perhaps.

VIII

Ships and Shoes and Sealing Wax

As the title indicates, the pieces included in the section that follows are nondescript in character. They discuss such matters as I have touched upon in "Borderlines"—what separates the great from the merely good in writing, the merely sensuous from the pornographic, the sometimes shadowy dividing line between romance and realism—the contradictory qualities that exist in all human beings, and that must also exist in the novelist's depiction of them. I have considered here such questions as the kind of book best adapted—if there is one—to reading in bed, some observations on book titles, on that infamous literary category, "Teen-age reading," on the union of art and science in the creative process, the national passion for quantitative measurement and its bearing on the literary scene—these, and as many more.

Borderlines

Borderlines fascinate me. Whether precisely drawn, as they are on maps, or when they exist more vaguely in the mind, they tease us into attempts at definition of what separates this from that. In terms of our own geography, where does the West begin? A sentimental song tells us, "Out where the handclasp's a little stronger." There is a modicum of truth in that, but we cannot accept it as a satisfying definition. Even such a realistic dividing line as the hundredth meridian, valid though it is in terms of rainfull for most of the country west of the Mississippi, does not hold when we reach the Pacific coast. For me the West begins when I reach the long roll and swell of the Nebraska prairies. That line of division is more or less subjectively drawn, and so it must be, I think, when we try to make certain literary distinctions.

For these, too, cannot have the precision of the map that tells you where France ends and Belgium begins. Recently I talked about the impossibility of scientific criticism—of, even, objective criticism. They are impossible because all of us, whether professional critics or not, approach a painting or a book subjectively—that is, with certain innate preferences and prejudices. We may be conscious of them, and endeavor to allow for them, but try as we will, they are sure to affect our judgment. I do not believe a completely objective piece of criticism has ever been written.

There is more to be said on this subject—much more than I touched on three weeks ago, and I may return to it. But today I want to pursue a little further this matter of borderlines. Obviously, the critic must sometimes deal with them. If he likes a book or a picture, he may call it good or he may call it great. Where is the dividing line? Who can precisely define what constitutes a great book? We can feel it is that, but can we prove it? The only really trustworthy arbiter is time, and even time, which has buried so much that is inconsequential, not infrequently preserves the trivial.

In this matter of the choice between "good" and "great," I grant that we use the second word more indiscriminately than it was used in the past. Ours is an age of superlatives. We talk, in this country particularly, more about the bigness of things—as if there were some inherent virtue in mere size—than people of other centuries. I know it is not a characteristic peculiar to the twentieth century, but it first became noticeable in the nineteenth, and has become steadily more emphatic since. It is qualitative as well as quantitative; such a word as "colossal" was found insufficient as an adjective of praise for Hollywood spectaculars, and so we were given "super-colossal."

The dividing line between good and great is only one of many. Where, for example, does light verse end and serious poetry begin? Confining ourselves to modern instances, there are poems by Auden, Frost, and Eliot, all serious poets, in which the distinction would be difficult to make, and the same holds true of certain poems by Phyllis McGinley and Ogden Nash, who are regarded as writers of light verse.

Where is one to draw the line between what, in writing, is merely sensuous and what is pornographic? Where does romance end and realism begin? Most definitions of either are unsatisfying, though I have always liked Bliss Perry's definition of realistic fiction: "that which does not shrink from the commonplace or the unpleasant in its effort to depict things as they are, life as it is."

This matter of borderlines enters into the novelist's depiction of human character. Somerset Maugham has written, "I have been accused of making men out worse than they are. I do not think I have done this. All I have done is to bring into prominence certain traits that many writers shut their eyes to. I think what has chiefly struck me in human beings is their lack of consistency. I have never seen people all of a piece. It has amazed me that the most incongruous traits should exist in the same person."

The novelist, if he is to present a credible picture of human life, must reckon with the inconsistency which impressed Maugham as so outstanding in human nature. He must have the ability to show the contradictory elements in character and to make them plausible in spite of their seeming irreconcilability. It is not an easy thing to do, and that is one reason why so much fiction fails to carry within it the truth of life.

John Galsworthy once observed that in his depiction of character the novelist has two choices: he can proceed romantically and stress the virtues of his characters, or he can look character straight in the face and show what men might be by giving due prominence to their defects. It is by such a method, of course, that the great characters in fiction have been created. The novelist's difficulty may be measured by our own when, as so often happens, we find it hard to put ourselves in the place of someone we know. One cannot say that the novelist's people are merely creatures of his imagination, and that he can do what he pleases with them. Something of people he has known and something of himself goes into their making as well. And no one, more than he, is concerned with borderlines.

Reading in Bed

This is a casual piece about reading in bed. I began wondering the other night whether there are certain kinds of books more suitable than others for that hour when consciously or not, you are composing your mind for sleep. Are there books which should be avoided? My suspicion is that these are not very sensible questions, in the face of individual differences in temperament and habit, but I ask them because I am interested to see where they will take me.

Perhaps I should begin by saying that reading in bed has not been a long-established habit of mine. I think I have done more of it during the past year or two than in all the rest of my life. For much the greater part of it I have been one of those fortunate people who, having decided to put the day behind them, are able to do so in five or ten minutes. Evidently, then, I can pretend to no authority born of long first-hand experience. Even if I could, the conclusions drawn from my own experience might have no validity for you.

The sociologists, along with their offspring, the pollsters, the rating diviners, and the motivational research men, have undertaken surveys of almost everything we do or think or like. They have explored our sexual habits, the nature and quantity of our reading, our taste in other entertainment and in cars, our interest in sports, our opinions on public matters, and many other aspects of our daily lives. So far, however, they have not tried to determine where and when we do our reading. I am one of those who have small faith in their findings, and still less in the efforts of the quiz-masters who attempt to measure intelligence and aptitude.

Be that as it may, I suspect that if such a survey were made, it would indicate that the number of persons who do the major part of their reading in bed make up a large proportion of the more literate population. Our days are more fragmented than those of our forebears; there are more intrusions on our daytime and evening hours. Nor would I discount the impact of the popularity of twin beds; I would bet that when the double bed was in almost universal use, the habit was less widespread. Not everybody was as ingenious or determined as the ancestors of a friend of mine who rigged a curtain along the center of their double bed so that one of them could read without disturbing the other.

Lacking the dubious findings of the pollsters, it would seem from what I have heard and read that a great many people—I have no idea how large a proportion of the bed-reading population—find the release they seek in mystery stories. Now I may be wrong, but to me this is a contrary practice, calculated to defeat what I assume to be the chief purpose of reading in bed—the achievement of composure. Perhaps that opinion is partly due to my lack of addiction to the whodunit, though I have read a good many mysteries with enjoyment. Nevertheless, from where I stand—or lie, rather—it seems to me that no form of reading is less likely to induce that composure or plain weariness which precedes sleep. If the mystery writer knows his business, you won't want to put the book down until you have arrived at the solution. You might argue, of course, that if you have rightly guessed it, you then swim in a quiet sea of self-satisfaction, and go promptly to sleep. But what if you have been hood-winked?

There are other books which should possibly be excluded—hotly controversial ones which may leave you irritated and angry, and very dull ones which induce boredom and thereby prevent composure. A dull book makes me fretful and restless; it does not sooth me for sleep. Is this an idiosyncrasy, or is it a common reaction?

It is now evident that I am mainly asking questions. My first was whether certain books are more suitable than others for reading in bed. It seems to me that much can be said for the kind of book that can be opened anywhere and read with enjoyment—books from which you can easily detach yourself because they are not tightly knit. Because I have recently been reading in them I mention as belonging in that category Boswell's Johnson and Pepys' diary. Any one of the great letter writers would belong there also. A good anthology is helpful in the same way, particularly one of a reflective or contemplative kind.

Also I would say that the hour before sleep is the best time for the rereading of old favorites. You know precisely where you are and what to expect, yet you may have the pleasure of coming upon a particularly good passage the full flavor of which had previously escaped you. There can be a tingle of excitement in that, but not so strong as to set your mind racing.

But maybe your day has been so dull that you seek a little vicarious excitement before turning out the bedside light, and so regretfully I reach the conclusion that there are no precepts in this matter which are worth keeping in mind. I am sorry to have taken you on a fruitless excursion.

A Book By Any Other Name . . .

The happiest of all book titles, it has long seemed to me—and I do not mean that in any optimistic sense—is W. H. Hudson's *Far Away and Long Ago*. In memorability, in sound, and in apt descriptiveness, it achieves perfection. The gift for giving things an appropriate and appealing name is a very special one, and curiously enough many writers otherwise skilled in the use of words do not number it among their endowments. Usually, when a misleading title provokes some comment by the reviewers of a book, the publisher stands suspected of the fault. The author, it is suggested, was probably bullied into it. He sometimes is, but there are occasions too, and, I suspect, more frequent ones, when the publisher saves him from making a fool of himself.

The importance of titles is, of course, a highly debatable matter. They can play a considerable part in launching a book on a successful career, and they can place it under a handicap, yet it is doubtful whether any truly remarkable work was ever denied its ultimate audience for lack of a helpful christening. Run-of-the-mill books, yes, but not those that have sent out widening circles. I can think of no more unappealing title than *Critique of Pure Reason,* yet every educated person is familiar with it, though he may never have opened the book.

Novelists, from the beginnings of fiction, have frequently been content to name their books after the story's chief character, and I should say, at a rough guess, that at least half the most famous novels, from the eighteenth century down, were so titled. Serious novelists today are, for the most part, inclined to avoid that ancient practice; most of them find their titles in a quoted phrase of poetry or prose which seems to them symbolically apt for the tale they have to tell: *For Whom the Bell Tolls; Look Homeward, Angel; From Here to Eternity.*

The name title has its pitfalls. Several years ago, on the occasion of the Scribner centenary, Roger Burlingame wrote a history of that house which might serve as a model for similar projects, because of its emphasis on the human side of publishing, which, with the gambling factor, is its most interesting aspect for the general reader. Mr. Burlingame had many good stories to tell about the relationship between publisher and author, and some of these revolved around the choice of a suitable title. (This, incidentally, is as good a time as any to say that anyone who would enjoy a glimpse of what actually goes on inside a great publishing house can do no better than to read *Of Making Many Books.*)

One of Mr. Burlingame's stories concerns Harold Frederic, a well-known novelist of the Nineties, who, in suggesting a title for his new book, wrote to Scribner's, "Isn't it true that to give a personal narrative the name of its chief figure is to help individualize it in the public mind?" He went on to mention some of the obvious instances, such as *Tom Jones, Henry Esmond,* and *David Copperfield.* He then proposed that his novel be called "Douw Mauverensen." The entire Scribner staff, Mr. Burlingame relates, shuddered in unison. Maybe in upstate New York, where the story had its setting, there would be no resistance, but what about the Deep South, the Middle West, and New England? When his suggestion fell upon deaf ears he came forward with "Where the Mohawk Gently Glides."

Whereupon the publishers countered with *In the Valley,* under which title the book made its appearance.

Another, and earlier battle which was happily concluded by firmness on the publishers' part, took place in the Seventies, when Scribner's began publishing George Washington Cable. He wanted to call the book "Jadis," and when that, understandably, evoked no enthusiasm, he came up with "Prose Idylls for Hammock and Fan," "Half Hours for Hammock and Fan," and so on. Even for the period, these were pretty dreadful, and were followed by others just as bad, like "Odors from the South." What finally emerged, at the publishers' suggestion, was *Old Creole Days.*

Even more amusing, it seems to me, was the struggle over the title for Scott Fitzgerald's best book. He had suggested "Trimalchio in West Egg," "Trimalchio," "On the Road to West Egg," "Gold-Hatted Gatsby," and "The High-Bouncing Lover." All these were sensibly frowned upon by the Scribner editors, who then suggested *The Great Gatsby,* and received Fitzgerald's reluctant consent. The book had been printed and bound, and its publication date set, when a frantic cablegram arrived from Capri. It read, "CRAZY ABOUT TITLE UNDER THE RED WHITE AND BLUE STOP WHAT WOULD DELAY BE." It would, the reply came from Maxwell Perkins, be fatal. And that was that.

Why do otherwise sensible men become publishers? For a very simple reason. Practiced on its higher levels, there is no business in which the necessarily dominant profit motive is so entangled with human interests and considerations.

The Teen-Age Book

It is a reasonable assumption that during recent weeks salesmen in bookstores were being subjected to the usual seasonal requests for something that might interest an uncle who likes to read history, an aunt who has the strangest interest in pirates, or a brother who reads everything that touches upon the home life of the bumblebee. They are not unreasonable requests, and I have no bone to pick with the makers of them, but I am out of patience with the people who wander into a bookshop and ask for something suitable for a "teen-ager" to read.

If I were asked for a list of symptoms pointing to what is wrong with American education and American culture, or to the causes for the prolongation of American adolescence, I should place high on the list the multiplication of books designed for readers in their teens. I am not certain whether demand or supply came first; that is not a matter easily determined, if it can be at all. There is no doubt whatever, though, that the supply is now enormous and the demand considerable. So far as I know, ours is the only country in which the writing of books (other than textbooks) for adolescents reaches sizable proportions.

The existence of this phenomenon had not occurred to me until the other day, when, at a meeting of the Books Across the Sea Committee, I heard Mrs. May Lamberton Becker report on the activities of the organization in England. Among other things, she noted the almost complete nonexistence in English publishing of the so-called teen-age book.

This, incidentally, may be as good a time as any to refer to the work of Books Across the Sea. Carried on under the auspices of the English-Speaking Union. It undertakes an interchange of books between the two countries, the selections on either side being made with a view to the promotion of better mutual understanding. It may, by the way, surprise readers of this column, as it did me, to learn that less than 3 per cent of new British books are made available in American editions. The proportion of American books published in England is today very much greater; I do not know the figures, but the gap is a very wide one.

Be that as it may, my concern at the moment is with this matter of books written for boys and girls at the adolescent stage. It is one of the most formative periods in any life (the other being the years before the age of six), and the ideas and attitudes with which we are brought in contact at that time are likely to have an important and often decisive effect upon the ideas and attitudes by which we are governed throughout the remaining years. For my own part, I know that the writers I read in my late teens left more of a mark on me than those I have read since. Later reading may have changed my opinions about many things, what I have in mind is something deeper, more unconscious than mere opinion: those underlying attitudes which set the pattern for our whole approach to life.

The teen-age book, it seems to me, is a phenomenon which belongs properly only to a society of morons. I have nothing but respect for the writers of good books for children; they perform one of the most admirable functions of which a writer is capable. One proof of their value is the fact that the greatest books which children can enjoy are read with equal delight by their elders. But what person of mature years and reasonably mature understanding (for there is often a wide disparity) can read without impatience a book written for adolescents?

It seems to me most desirable that there be no intermediary stage between the book for children and the book for adults. There have been, it is true, a few writers whose work would seem to have been appropriately addressed to readers in the adolescent years. One was G. A. Henty, whose stories were eagerly devoured by the boys of my own generation. But a boy who could enjoy Henty could also enjoy Dumas, who did not write for an age group. He could certainly enjoy the *Iliad* and the *Odyssey,* if they were not thrust upon him as tasks to be performed and to be catechized over. There are many books, written without age groups in mind, simple enough to be appreciated by youngsters, and yet with a power of suggestion, because they were not written down to an arbitrary level, which make the artificial and limited horizon of the teen-age book the wasteful superfluity that it is.

For readers of any age, it is a good thing to make the acquaintance of books that they do not completely or immediately understand. Life does not come to us like that; neither should books. If development is not to be impeded, there must be some teasing of the mind, some reaching out for meanings and significances that are not at once apparent. I think that writers—and I have in mind particularly those addressing themselves to an adolescent audience—who are careful not to overreach what they conceive to be the mental group of those for whom they write, are doing their readers a disservice.

Mathematics and the Muses

With something not far distant from fear and trembling, this department pulls itself together to approach a topic about which, probably, it has no business to be writing at all. Three Sundays ago, in reporting on the Kenyon College conference held in honor of Robert Frost, I ended by saying that in my opinion the most interesting contribution to the conference was a paper read by the eminent mathematician, Marston Morse, entitled, *Reflections on Evaluations in Mathematics and the Arts,* and that I proposed to make it the subject of another article.

Even if the mathematics with which Professor Morse is concerned were on the high-school level, I should be starting with a heavy handicap, remembering, as I vividly do, my almost complete incapacity to deal understandingly with the elementary concepts of algebra and geometry; but worse still, Professor Morse, a colleague of Einstein at the Institute for Advanced Studies in Princeton, is one of those men who sail serenely through the mathematical stratosphere, in that lofty region where poetry and mathematics become sisters under the skin. In any case, the reflections set forth in this column will be, for much the most part, his, not mine. I undertake to summarize them because I think they are deeply suggestive concerning the underlying unity with which the human mind operates creatively, whatever kind of creation it is, whether in science, philosophy, and religion, or the arts.

The widest-ranging minds have always been aware of that unity; Leonardo's for one, Goethe's for another. It was Goethe who gathered strength as a poet from his scientific consideration of Nature, and who contended that if art undertakes to create works which can compete in truth and beauty with those of Nature, the artist must "learn at least to some extent from Nature the way in which she proceeds in the forming of her works." As Prof. Karl Vietor has pointed out, Goethe's work reveals how "his insights in one field clarify and confirm in another."

Was it not his recognition of this unity which caused Robert Frost once to remark that "a poet must lean hard on facts, so hard, sometimes, that they hurt?" And is there not in Frost's much-quoted and profound remarks about the figure a poem makes more than a slight resemblance to a mathematical theorem when he says that a poem "begins in delight and ends in wisdom. . . . It begins in delight, it inclines to the impulse, it assumes direction with the first line laid down, it runs a course of lucky events, and ends in a clarification of life—not necessarily a great clarification, such as sects and cults are founded on, but in a momentary stay against confusion."

Professor Morse, as a matter of fact, uses Frost's conception of the figure a poem makes as evidence of the first essential bond he finds between mathematics and the arts: the fact that "discovery in mathematics is not a matter of logic." Rather, he contends, it is "the result of mysterious powers which no one understands, and in which the unconscious recognition of beauty must play an important part. Out of an infinity of designs a mathematician chooses one pattern for beauty's sake, and pulls it down to earth, no one knows how. Afterward the logic of words and forms sets the pattern right. Only then can one tell someone else." This is much what Frost was saying of writing poetry: "I tell how there may be a better wildness of logic, than of inconsequence. But the logic is backward, in retrospect after the act." And, "For me the initial delight is in the surprise of remembering something I didn't know I knew. I am in a place, in a situation, as if I had materialized from cloud, or risen out of the ground."

These statements were compared by Professor Morse with the accounts given by the great mathematicians Poincaré and Gauss, of how they came to make some of their discoveries. I wish there were space for me to quote from them. Previously he had drawn similar evidence for his contention from the work and statements of Albrecht Dürer, the geometer-artist, who, as Professor Morse observed, more than any other artist "formulated the rules of symmetry, perspective and proportion, and used them in his art."

The underlying unity of creation between mathematics and music, which is more generally accepted (being more obvious), was also touched upon by Professor Morse, who framed his thesis in these words: "The basic affinity between mathematics and the arts is psychological and spiritual and not metrical or geometrical."

Also, he found further evidence of this affinity in the comparative history of the arts, which he described as "the history of recurring cycles and sharp antitheses. These antitheses set pure art against mixed art, restraint against lack of restraint, the transient against the permanent, the abstract against the non-abstract." These antitheses, he pointed out, are found also in the history of mathematics.

He ended by regretting that science is so often attacked without perception of its creative unity with the arts; that it is so often viewed "without its penumbra or its radiance." The creative scientist, he argued, "lives in 'the wildness of logic' where reason is the handmaiden and not the master. . . . It is the hour before the break of day when science turns in the womb."

Words of the Bible

Now that the dust of controversy rising from the publication of The New English Bible has begun to settle—so far as it ever will—I should like to offer a sampling of the reactions by which this ambitious work has been greeted, and to offer a few personal ones. Also, I should like to call your attention to an interesting volume published last year, which has not a little bearing on the subject under discussion. It is *The Bible Word Book: Concerning Obsolete or Archaic Words in the King James Version of the Bible.* The authors are the late Ronald Bridges, a former president of the Pacific School of Religion at Berkeley, and Luther A. Weigle, dean emeritus of the Yale Divinity School. Their book contains 827 brief articles concerning that number of words used in the King James Version which have been affected by changing English usage. It explains what the King James translators meant by them, and shows by what words they were replaced in the Revised Standard Version.

Concerning The New English Bible's New Testament (the Old will not appear for many years, judging by the time taken to produce this volume), suppose we mention the pleasantest things first. Certainly it is an attractive volume physically, as one might expect of a joint product of the Oxford and Cambridge University Presses; it is tastefully bound, printed on good paper, typographically elegant, and presented in easily readable form. That is, in paragraphing and chapter headings, it resembles any other well-edited, well-produced book. There has been no adverse criticism on this score; neither has it been argued that the work was unnecessary.

Where there has been sharp and wide difference of opinion is over the quality of the translation. Like its immediate predecessors—the R.S.V. and the K.J.V., the N.E.B. is the product of collaboration by a large number of scholars and writers. In this respect the text of these three translations differed from such one-man performances as those of Tyndale and Coverdale, or more recently, Msgr. Ronald Knox. One of the objections raised against the N.E.B. has been that while the K.J.V. maintained a remarkable unity of style, for all that it was written by a group of men, the N.E.B., to an even greater degree than the R.S.V., is lacking in any such individuality. Incidentally, while the translators of the K.J.V. accomplished their magnificent job in four years (both Old and New Testaments), the N.E.B.'s New Testament has occupied its scholars and writers since 1946. It is true, of course, that the K.J.V. was a less complicated undertaking, since it was not so much concerned with changes of meaning; the K.J.V. came less than a century after the first translations into English.

One of the harshest judgments on the N.E.B. was that of Robert Graves, who reviewed it in *The Observer* (London). He found it verbose, often unclear, and undistinguished in style. The most interesting review I have seen, of those published in this country, was that of Garry Wills in The National Review for May 6; it was captioned, "Water in the Wine." Mr. Wills regards the N.E.B. as merely "another step in the clearing process." Martin E. Marty, associate editor of The Christian Century, who reviewed it for this newspaper in the issue for March 19, was more favorably impressed. He called the N.E.B. "an achievement of first quality." The same view was shared by Gilbert Highet, who, in answer to expected complaints that the new translation "lacks the poetry, even the magic of the old," observed that "the traditional versions of the New Testament often over-elaborated the original, made it sound nobler in English than it is in the Greek." Mr. Highet's review in *Horizon* was counterbalanced by a blast in the same magazine from William Harlan Hale, who thinks the N.E.B. was phrased by a group of men all with "a tin ear," whose English is "the jargon of official hand-out writers and lower-echelon bureaucrats." It sounds to him like Newspeak.

Personally I do not care for it either. I have no doubt that in many instances it has struck closer to the precise meaning of the Greek originals and that as a scholarly effort it is commendable, but it has no tang or, even, flavor. I find it a wishy-washy approximation of current English, and I wait with some trepidation for the N.E.B.'s rendering of some of the great Old Testament passages in the K.J.V. Will it repeat such a mangling of the Twenty-third Psalm as was committed by the R.S.V., when "thou anointest my head with oil, my cup runneth over," was made to read, "my cup overflows"? I choose a little thing purposely, because it points up the insensitivity of the modern translators more sharply, perhaps, than a more heinous assault would do. But if you want a real humdinger, see what the N.E.B. does to "I will give unto him that is athirst of the fountain of the water of life freely." This becomes: "A draught from the watersprings of life will be my free gift to the thirsty."

I have a suspicion that these labors, whatever scholarly corrections they may have established, will not dislodge the K.J.V. from its vantage point. If we read the Bible for the delights of language, we will not forsake its noblest version.

Those Frightened Philistines

Most people, in the course of an argument, are content with setting up one straw man, but Mr. James T. Farrell, who apparently finds it impossible not to work on a large scale, creates a league of them. In the essay from which his new book takes its title, *The League of Frightened Philistines,* he blows into being a bogy army of literary critics whom he represents as a group which has dedicated itself to an attack upon "serious writers." Since Mr. Farrell has included me, along with Van Wyck Brooks, Archibald MacLeish, John Chamberlain, and Bernard De Voto, as a member of this company of strange bedfellows, and since his conception of what some of us, at least, are about is curiously unperceptive, this department cannot pretend to a studied indifference.

Mr. Farrell, as many persons have remarked before me, is a very honest man, and a very earnest one. He appears to have a passion for truth, and I respect that in any man. Unfortunately, however, this unrelieved earnestness of his sometimes gets in the way of a clean approach to his objective. Not only does it become difficult for him to see the woods for the trees; he sometimes seems unable to distinguish between the tree trunks and the underbrush.

It seems that this League of Frightened Philistines is, to begin with, unappreciative of the terrific struggle which these "serious writers" have made to prevent themselves from becoming "hired writers." Mr. Farrell appears to believe that any honest writer living in a capitalist society must guard his virtue as anxiously as any Victorian maiden. Indeed, he takes as his text a passage from the Communist Manifesto, in which Messrs. Marx and Engels solemnly assured us that "the bourgeoisie has stripped of its halo every occupation hitherto honored and looked up to with reverent awe. It has converted the physician, the lawyer, the priest, the poet, the man of science into its paid wage laborers."

This is the fate worse than death that has overtaken the Pasteurs and the Wassells, the Darrows and the Willkies, the Wesleys and the Niemoellers, the Goethes and the Frosts, the Curies and the discoverers of penicillin. Wage slaves all, who might have benefited the human race had they had the good fortune to arrive at maturity in a regimented state.

Somehow it is a trifle difficult for at least one member of the League of Frightened Philistines to grow apprehensive of the shackles that lie in wait for every honest writer in these benighted United States. It seems to him that our novelists and our poets, our playwrights and our pamphleteers have experienced no great difficulty in speaking out their minds for many years past, and in not a few instances being handsomely paid for doing it. The American public is a very indulgent public; it will even pay good money to have its intelligence minimized, to have itself insulted. What envious eyes these poor, honest writers of ours have cast toward the states in which the Molochian bourgeoisie was no longer a menace, and where a writer could so freely celebrate the heaven on earth that was to be!

Worse still, this League of Frightened Philistines believes that art should be democratic; they look with disfavor and distrust upon writers who demand a password before granting admittance to those who would read and understand them. They seem not sufficiently aware that it is difficult for men who have not bread enough to eat to appreciate the values of the spirit. (Writers with "security" and bulging pocketbooks are so frequently spiritual leaders!)

A vicious lot, this League of Frightened Philistines. They honestly think that American society in the Twenties and early Thirties had a few bright patches which Mr. Dos Passos failed to include in a series of books to which he gave the somewhat comprehensive title, *U.S.A.* They honestly believe that the people of this country were not quite so rotten as the novelists of that period commonly pictured them.

And worst of all, the members of this dangerous League actually believe that writers have a burden of responsibility. They have the effrontery to imagine that writers can actually put courage in the hearts of men in place of hatred and despair; they are so stupid as to believe that you can lash out at injustice, hypocrisy and cant in a novel, and still introduce a human being or two worthy of men's respect. They are so short-sighted as to "superimpose life in general over modern society in particular"; in other words, they have the quaint notion that there is some continuity in human experience, and that certain principles which held good in the Athens of Pericles or the England of Shakespeare might conceivably have some application to the problems which confront us now.

But alas! one of them, at least, the writer of this column, "has always been a literary conservative." He has been so misguided as to suppose that, in the midst of the experimentation we must always have if art is to remain a vital force, we can check the experiment's value against the experience of the race. He has the audacity to reject some experimentation, to refuse to believe that *Finnegans Wake* marks the creative peak of our time. And as for his part in "discovering that God is a principle of literary criticism," that one is much too deep for him. Mr. Farrell, I fear, has lost his way in the underbrush.

Masculine and Feminine

In those provocative reflections on women as writers which Virginia Woolf set down in *A Room of One's Own* she entertained the idea of the union of masculine and feminine elements as essential to the highest flights of creative writing. It was that kind of fusion in the mind, she guessed, that Coleridge must have meant when he said that a great mind is androgynous.

"Coleridge certainly did not mean," she reflected, "that it is a mind that has any special sympathy with women; a mind that takes up their cause or devotes itself to their interpretation. Perhaps the androgynous mind is less apt to make these distinctions than the single-sexed mind. He meant, perhaps, that the androgynous mind is resonant and porous; that it transmits emotion without impediment; that it is naturally creative, incandescent and undivided. In fact, one goes back to Shakespeare's mind as the type of the androgynous, of the man-womanly mind, though it would be impossible to say what Shakespeare thought of women."

What would we say, offhand, were the feminine elements which contribute to such a fusion in the mind of a masculine writer? Would they not be, perhaps, intuition as a supplement to logic or abstract conception, sympathy as a corrective to detached perception? There are others, no doubt, but these would probably be basic. Something of the sort may have been at the back of Coleridge's mind when he wrote elsewhere, in comparing Fielding's handling of character with that of Shakespeare, of Fielding's dependence upon what he had actually seen.

Coleridge had great admiration and affection for Fielding as a writer, and praised highly the truth and humor which he achieved by observation, but pointed out, quite justly I think, that where Fielding could not help himself by copying what he had seen, where it was necessary that "something should take place, some words be spoken, or some object described which he could not have witnessed (his soliloquies, for example, or the interview between the hero and Sophia Western before the reconciliation)," he becomes unnatural and forced and lacking in psychological truth. It was, on the other hand, the measure of Shakespeare's completeness that no situation seemed alien to him, no character closed to him, whether of man or woman.

Fielding, of course, is one of the most masculine of writers, and beyond question one of the great novelists; but would he not have been greater still had there been a dash of Jane Austen in his composition? One thinks at once of Scott in the same way, as completely masculine in his mental fiber as Fielding, and though widely separate in the character of his work, hedged by the same limitations. To come closer to our own time, one thinks immediately of Kipling, although in his case the line becomes slightly blurred; definitely masculine though Kipling was in his quality and in the appeal of most of his work, he could hardly have written such a story as "The Brushwood Boy" without some infusion of the feminine elements. Hemingway, of course, is the obvious contemporary descendant in the Fielding line, and in him the limitations imposed by his overemphasized masculinity have been severe.

Mrs. Woolf safely surmises, I think, that "No age can ever have been as stridently sex-conscious as our own." No period has been so self-consciously insistent that certain books and certain writers are definitely masculine or feminine in their appeal. And I cannot imagine that the Thurber cartoons, or the Thurber thesis of the war between the sexes, could at any previous time have had the edge and point that they hold for us today.

It all comes down to this, in Mrs. Woolf's opinion: that if the theory of the two sides of the mind holds good, then "virility has now become self-conscious—men, that is to say, are now writing only with the male side of their brains." And when they do that, she concluded, women, at least, find them lacking in the power of suggestion; the experience so often encountered in reading a writer like Coleridge, in whom the masculine and feminine elements were fused—of having a sentence explode in the mind and give birth to all kinds of other ideas—is not to be had. And that, she rightly observes, "is the only sort of writing of which one can say that it has the secret of perpetual life."

It is absurd, of course, to touch so glancingly upon what is one of the basic issues of the age we are entering—the subject matter of a book that has never been written: the reconciliation of masculine and feminine qualities which has been made so difficult by the economic and social pressures under which we now live. It will, increasingly, I think, become the theme of writers. They will come round in the end, perhaps, to the concept ascribed to Aristophanes in the *Symposium* of Plato: that "human nature was originally one and we were a whole, and the desire and pursuit of the whole is called love." Or, in mythological terms, that the gods separated man from woman, and that they have ever since been trying to effect their reunion.

How Much, How Many, How High

One of our great American passions is for measurement. How much, how many, how high, how long, how wide, how deep, are matters that somehow have always concerned us more than they have other people. Probably there is a satisfying explanation for this obsession, although I am not sure what it is. Possibly the initial impetus derived from the fact that in the beginning we came from a country of little distances to a land of great ones; certainly there is no more potent factor in the thinking of a people than the character of its geographical environment; if it were the only one, Russia and America could have no misunderstandings.

This delight of ours in measurement was all very well and harmless enough so long as we confined it to material things—to the length of rivers, the height of mountains, the size of towns (though even there a certain confusion of values set in), but when we began to carry over the passion for measurement into the realm of those things that cannot satisfactorily be measured—then the mischief began. That was the beginning of one of the great American fallacies, of our naive faith in statistics. About the time we began to put our trust in intelligence tests we began to think less clearly.

These reflections were prompted by a recent review in these columns of *The Great Dilemma of World Organization,* by Fremont Rider. I have not had an opportunity to read Mr. Rider's book, and my reference to its thesis rests upon the reviewer's presentation. From this it appears that "the great dilemma" of Mr. Rider's title lies in the inability of the nations to agree as to the share of power which each would have in a world state. Various proposals have been made as to the basis of such an allocation. Finding none of these satisfactory, Mr. Rider proposes that education be made the yardstick.

Well, you say, that doesn't sound too bad; there could be worse ways of allocating power. But how are we to determine the relative standing of the nations in this respect? Alas, that is where our new national obsession raises its comical head. What Mr. Rider terms the "relative total of the educational accomplishments of all the citizens of each country" would be arrived at in this fashion: each nation would be allowed a fixed number of years of "accomplishment credit" for each member of its population who has completed some stage of formal education. The barely literate, I gather, would receive one year of credit, and so on up to nineteen years for a holder of a doctoral degree.

It is all so simple—and, to my way of thinking, quite preposterous. If the possession of a formal education were an adequate measure of intelligence, one might take such a proposal seriously, but as it is I would as soon put my faith in an agreement to measure each citizen by the size of his hat.

Recently a plan was put forward for testing the readability of a book. I do not recall it in detail, but the idea is something like this: you count the number of subordinate clauses, the number of periodic sentences, the number of unusual words, and so on; then you multiply by seven and divide by five, or some such abracadrabra, and you arrive at a figure which supplies a kind of literary batting average. I protest that it is time to call a halt. If this sort of thing continues to gain momentum, I can envision a future state in which all citizens will be graded like eggs, only with an infinitely larger number of gradations. Some of the marriage counselors are busy laying the foundations for that tidy Utopia: a little simple arithmetic and you are guaranteed a perfect mate.

Buffeted by the various schemes of these determined measurers, I have been finding some measure of relief in Don Marquis' approach to *The Almost Perfect State,* and I shall close this column on a totally inconsequential note. Pondering the question whether the A.P.S. could be realized before our world became too cold for comfort, Don Marquis affirmed his optimism in this wise: Man, he decided, will either heat the planet artificially or he will grow fur.

The latter seemed the more likely: "It has not been so many millions of years since his ancestors had fur, and he can grow it again when he needs it. Indeed, some men are able to face the cold partially unclothed, without fur, even now. It has only been a short time since the Highland Scots went generally bare-legged through the snows, and to this day thousands of Scotsmen, while they have their coats, vests and trousers made of cloth that is all one color and pattern, nevertheless insist that their trousers be constructed of material very much thinner and more open in weave than the coats and vests. They can scarcely bear to have their legs covered at all and even in the bitterest weather wear no underclothing over these portions of their anatomy. It is possible that the Highland Scots really have fur covering the parts of the leg which their grandfathers exposed, but that it is invisible because it grows under the skin instead of on the outside. Unfortunately, there is no authentic information on hand to determine the truth of this supposition. But the immunity from cold which the Highland Scot enjoys as to his legs can certainly be acquired by a whole species if necessary."

P.S. Much—some would say, far too much—has happened in the world of measurement in the nearly twenty years since this was written. We need no longer think; we have the computer!

Who Said It? I

A part of this page is customarily given over to quotation, and recently I have been giving thought to quotation as a practice and even, if you will, as a minor form of art. Like every other art, major or minor, it has its abuses, and like most practices, its uses as well. Harsh things have been said about it as a practice. Emerson, who was not above contradicting himself if what he thought one morning was at variance with what he thought the day before, could say, "I hate quotations. Tell me what you know," but he could on another occasion remark, "Next to the originator of a good sentence is the first quoter of it."

Quotations are, of course, frequent provokers of controversy. Those in most common use, and some which are not, are inevitably garbled from time to time, even to the extent of belying the meaning they were originally intended to convey. And all too often they are attributed to the wrong person. Several years ago, in this column, I began a piece with a reference to that frequently encountered observation about the man who makes a better mousetrap than his neighbor. Correctly, I named Emerson as its creator, but I was at once taken to task by readers who claimed the remark for Elbert Hubbard. When I did get round to checking the dictionaries of quotation, I found I had been right, but there are still people who insist it was Hubbard who had said that people would beat a path to the inventor's door.

The trouble in this instance arises from the fact that the statement about mousetraps, although it bears the Emersonian stamp, can nowhere be found in his writings, and also because Elbert Hubbard claimed its authorship. What actually happened was this: a Mrs. Sarah S. B. Yule, who in 1889 published a book called *Borrowings,* there credited the saying to Emerson; many years later she explained that she had copied the remark in her notebook on hearing a lecture given by Emerson. She had written down this: "If a man write a better book, preach a better sermon, or make a better mousetrap than his neighbor, tho' he build his house in the woods, the world will make a beaten path to his door."

By way of parenthesis, I can't help adding that when Emerson made this optimistic remark, something less than a century ago, the Madison Avenue boys and all the other "hidden persuaders" were as yet unborn. One fears that today, if the book were not sanctified by book-club choice or a high-powered promotional campaign, if the sermon were not broadcast over a national network, and if the mouse-trap were not promoted by pictures of a bosomy feminine mouse-catcher and a series of wacky ads, the book would be soon remaindered, the sermon forgotten, and the mousetrap tossed into an auto graveyard, there to rust away with the bodies of Detroit's current monstrosities.

Let me bring up another interesting case, which concerns a saying no less—indeed, even more time-worn—than the one about mouse-traps. Everybody has heard that "No man is a hero to his valet." It is also one of those quotations that have been distorted from the author's intention. The remark is also one of those obscured in a cloud of controversy. Most people think of it as something Goethe said; he did, but he himself was remembering what he had somewhere read.

In Bartlett, the saying is given first place in point of time to Marshall Catinet, but there is also quoted from the essays of Montaigne, "Few men are admired by their domestics." The editors add: "This phrase, 'No man is a hero to his valet,' is commonly attributed to Mme. de Sevigné, but on the authority of Mme. Aisse . . . it really belongs to Mme. Cornuel." In Burton Stevenson's *Home Book of Quotations,* the comment by Goethe on this saying is traced to Goethe's "Wahlverwandschaften," for a translation of which I am indebted to the Century Association's omnivorous librarian, Theodore Bolton: "It is said that no man is hero to a valet. But that is simply because a hero is recognized only by a hero. The valet, obviously, can know only the merits of his own kind." (A remark not greatly to Goethe's credit.)

What interests me most about this whole matter of observations commonly regarded as worth repeating is the chain of indebtedness to what somebody else had said years and often centuries before. No remark has been more widely quoted in our time than Lord Acton's on power, which, curiously, is absent from Mencken's *Dictionary of Quotations:* "All power corrupts, and absolute power corrupts absolutely." The thought is many centuries old; perhaps Acton put it more succinctly than most. But it's in Thucydides, and it has been repeated, in varying forms, century after century, as it needs to be.

The same goes, of course, for the remark by Franklin Roosevelt which at once electrified and reassured a nation in 1932: "All we have to fear is fear itself." It was most aptly used, and with great effectiveness, in his first inaugural, but it was no more original with

F.D.R. than the thought about power was original with Lord Acton. Thoreau had said it, and centuries before him, so had Montaigne, with many another in between. Verily, verily, where human truth is concerned, what is there new under the sun?

Who Said It? II

One of the more unusual reference books I have encountered is the Kenkyusha *Dictionary of English Quotations,* published in Tokyo by the Kenkyusha Press. It is not as comprehensive as Bartlett, Mencken, the Home Book, or the Oxford Collection, but it undertakes something which they do not. Its purpose is to show by example the use which has been made by modern authors of well-known passages of prose and verse. To this end its editors collected some 15,000 examples from English and American writers. Of these, about two-thirds were used. So far as I am aware, no comparable collection has hitherto been published.

In these 10,000 examples, ranging from the eighteenth century to the present, some 3,170 quotations appear in one form or another. The Bible, as we would expect, leads the list of most frequently quoted books. There are 1,351 quotations from it, 773 from Shakespeare, and 1,046 from miscellaneous other sources. Of these, Milton takes third place, Wordsworth fourth, Tennyson fifth, Pope sixth, and Shelley seventh. Genesis is the most frequently quoted book of the Old Testament, with the Psalms a close second. The largest number of Shakespearean quotations comes from *Hamlet,* with *Macbeth* second, and *Othello* third.

The editors note that among the more recent English writers a particularly liberal use of quotation is made by Samuel Butler (especially in *The Way of All Flesh*), Anthony Trollope, who is rich in quotations from Shakespeare, Aldous Huxley, and P. G. Wodehouse. They found the use of quotation to be much more common among English than among American writers, especially those of the present time. Contemporary Americans, though making frequent use of quotation in their titles, otherwise avoid it. The reason for this, the editors suggest, is that "they are interested in evolving a new and personal style of writing, and dislike therefore quoting from Old-World writers." It seems to me there are other reasons as well, among them the fact that the average British writer is better read, and with a stronger feeling for the tradition of the language.

Most of us are aware of the many Biblical phrases which have worked their way into our daily speech and writing. It is seldom difficult to identify them. Though Shakespeare has permeated the language almost as much, it is always somewhat surprising to find how many phrases in common use have their source in him. I am not thinking so much of the great passages as of such oddments as "foregone conclusion," "as good luck would have it," "we have seen better days," "eaten out of house and home," "must give us pause," "to the manner born," "the seamy side," "pomp and circumstance," "more in sorrow than in anger," "the smallest worm will turn," and "a king of shreds and patches," which usually turns up as "a thing of shreds and patches."

Though on the basis of this collection, Milton, Wordsworth and Tennyson would appear to be more frequently quoted by subsequent writers than Pope, I believe he would take rank after the Bible and Shakespeare as the writer whose phrases have become most deeply imbedded in the spoken language. What phrases have had wider currency, for example, than those beginning "fools rush in," "hope springs eternal," "the proper study," "as the twig is bent," "speed the parting guest," "to err is human" and "a little learning"?

We do not customarily think of Sir Walter Scott as the source of phrases in common use, yet he is the author, for example, of "one crowded hour," "tell that to the marines," "my native heath" and "a ministering angel." I had forgotten, if I ever knew, that "Hell is paved with good intentions" is not a proverb in the sense of being an anonymous piece of wisdom, but is one of the many examples of Dr. Johnson's illuminating common sense. Nor did I remember that we owe "handsome is that handsome does" to his friend Goldsmith.

Quotations, like individual words, pursue a life of their own. Sometimes, with continued use, they are deflected from their original meaning. A curious instance of this is the use which has been made of Shakespeare's "more in sorrow than in anger." He used the words to describe the countenance of the ghost in *Hamlet*. They were used in an adjectival sense, but when they appear in quotation they are almost invariably employed adverbially. We use them to say that someone spoke or acted more in sorrow than in anger.

In taking note of these sea-changes, the Japanese editors of this dictionary are sometimes led astray. They think, for example, that the much-quoted "milk of human kindness" has been distorted to mean compassion or sympathy, whereas Shakespeare used it as a figure to denote the weakness of human nature. The context, however, supports the use to which the quotation has always been put.

For Lady Macbeth goes on to say, "Thou wouldst be great,/Art not without ambition, but without/The illness [that is, the wickedness] should attend it."

There are times when I think that the ideal library is composed solely of reference books. They are like understanding friends—always ready to meet your mood, always ready to change the subject when you have had enough of this or that.

The Profession of Humor

When I read a piece like Frank Sullivan's lament on our vanishing humorists, I am forcibly reminded of how old I am, and, in this case, of how old Mr. Sullivan himself must be. That is not a crack; his writing is as lively and spirited now as it was when, longer ago than any of you can possibly remember, we were neighbors at 280 Broadway, he on the staff of *The Evening Sun,* I on what had just a few weeks before been the old morning Sun and had temporarily, in the clutches of a haddockeyed gentleman named Frank Munsey, become *The Sun and Herald.*

Yet it seems only yesterday that I rode up Fifth Avenue behind an elephant (imagine what *that* would do to traffic in these days when a wheelbarrow abandoned at the wrong spot can tie midtown Manhattan into a Wagnerian knot) in a cab occupied also by Mr. Sullivan and a gentleman of many adjectives named Dexter Fellowes, whose straw hat, as our journey progressed, became festooned with those long straws used in the consumption of soft drinks. The purpose of our journey was to deposit the elephant, Old John, in safe and permanent retirement at the Old Elephants' Home in a Westchester town whose name I have forgotten. Or could it have been Somers?

Possibly it was this incident which gave rise to my long cherished ambition to ride a bull moose up Fifth Avenue—an objective which, as time goes on, seems ever less likely of accomplishment. In this mood of reminiscence, which will shortly pass, I also wonder whether the piece which Frank wrote about his substituting one day for one of the freaks in the basement of the old Madison Square Garden during circus time, ever found its way into a book. Whether he was for the time being the Lion-Faced Boy or the Bearded Lady, I can't remember, but it was a good piece.

Mr. Sullivan has called the roll of those humorists who, since 1920 (the year to which I have been referring) have gone to their reward in what we must hope has proved to be a happier place than the one they left. It was truly a staggering list, and one which by no effort of the imagination can be counterbalanced by the one Mr. Sullivan also offered, composed of their survivors and successors. Every night I kneel by my trundle bed and pray for the emergence, in these days of My God What a World Fiction, of another Harry Leon Wilson. In the spring of 1917, when soldiers could still sing and Homo sapiens seemed a little more salvageable than now, three of us at Plattsburg, snatching our Sunday ease on the shore of Lake Champlain, laughed ourselves to the border of hysterics over *Ruggles of Red Gap*.

As Mr. Sullivan remarked, the climate is not propitious for humor, and yet, like him, I am a little distressed and a little puzzled that the crop of new humorous writers is so disappointingly thin. As he reminds us, people *have* laughed at wakes before this, and, I would add, there is some reasonable ground for doubt whether there is actually a corpse in the room. And even if there is, he may, like the corpse in an Irish one-act play the name of whose author I have forgotten, suddenly galvanize into life and confound us all. The subject links itself in my mind with this column's topic of two weeks ago, for there is, I think, some connection between humor and guts. Maybe that's where we got the word "belly-laugh." Don't tell me that George Washington, whom I cited in that piece, was, however indomitable, without a sense of humor. That's part of the plaster image; he could roll on the ground with laughter, as Owen Wister tried to remind us in a long-forgotten book, *The Seven Ages of Washington*.

In discussing the long and solemn faces of our younger novelists, Mr. Sullivan mentioned their frequently clinical treatment of the matter of love. I'm not quite sure whether he was talking about sex or love, but in any case, it occurs to me that a humorous handling of that source of so many troubles and satisfactions can be expected only from either a primitive people, such as the American Indian, or an old and *deeply* sophisticated people (which we are not), like the French, the Italians or the Chinese. Youngsters in the world, like ourselves or the Germans and the Russians, get into a terrible dither about love, at least in that aspect of it which concerns the relations between male and female.

What puzzles me deeply is the fact that humor in our literature has been so much confined to the professional humorists like Mr. Sullivan himself, or Mr. Thurber, or Artemus Ward or Mark Twain.

The English are a little older than we, though not as old as they like to think, and so there has been more humor in the English novel than there has been in our own. Think back, and look at the record: Hawthorne, Melville, Henry James, Dreiser, Sherwood Anderson, Howells, Edith Wharton, Frank Norris, Stephen Crane, Wolfe, Farrell, Faulkner, Willa Cather, Dos Passos, Hemingway—how large, how pervading, is the content of humor?

P.S. There have been a few—a very few—encouraging signs or signals (the current vogue word) since this column was written. One is the emergence of Art Buchwald, who is, in my estimation, the best contemporary American humorist. He has restored something to American journalism that has been painfully absent since the death of Will Rogers. He is the welcome antidote to the world-savers who besiege us on every editorial page from one side of the country to the other. Today's columnists, by and large, offer us either vacuous gossip or, assuming the mantle of Moses, they give us solemn directions for leading us out of Egypt. Mr. Buchwald has the true humorist's gift of being correctively funny about serious things. So too, in less marked degree, have James Reston and Russell Baker of the New York *Times*. In Mr. Reston's case, it should be added, his humor is supplementary to his acutely intelligent appraisal of national and world affairs.

The Cult of Originality

The fundamental human truths are all men's property. Whether or not we live by them, we all know them, with a deep instinctiveness. In the realm of human conduct, I don't suppose it is possible for any man, however acute or profound his mental processes may be, to say anything bearing the stamp of universal truth that many other men, in equivalent words, have not said before him. Back of each of us there are those many thousands of years of race experience.

When Franklin Roosevelt, in his first inaugural address, said that the only thing we had to fear was fear itself, he said precisely the right thing at precisely the right time, and the phrase, coming when it did, had enormous effect. But the thought it contained had been expressed from time to time, in almost identical terms, for centuries past.

The fear of saying what has been said before is one of the least formidable fears a writer has to face, and yet I believe it to be one that has often blocked the development of young writers, and that it frequently does so today. The history of literature, the history, indeed, of any of the arts, is a history of borrowings and adaptations, even when they are being most "modern," but that fact does not minimize the achievement of those who have really assimilated and turned to their own uses what they have found of value in the work of their predecessors.

In a foreword which he wrote for *The Sea and the Jungle,* H. M. Tomlinson spoke of the debt he was conscious of owing to Thoreau. Once, going through a book dealer's catalogue, he found listed a first edition of his own book, and on the same page, at a considerably lower price, one of Thoreau's. He felt embarrassed. "I am not," he wrote, "a collector of old books and first editions, but I rescued this volume of the Eighteen-fifties at once, for very shame. Why, the light of that work had penetrated clear through the years, and was reflected in my own effort beside it. Here I feel I ought to acknowledge my debt, for it would be idle to pretend that an author, unlike a ploughman, can be born out of the blue; the lines of the old furrows driven by his forefathers show in the ancient earth, and he must use as his handful the seedcorn which has descended from harvests that were reaped long before history began."

As a matter of fact, Tomlinson is more conscious of his debt than is his reader. He himself remarked that none of his reviewers had detected the presence of Thoreau's influence. And it is, indeed, hard to discover. The experience recorded in *The Sea and the Jungle* had passed so completely through his own personality that the book is his, and nobody else's.

The determined effort to achieve originality has led many a writer into stony pastures. That urge, certainly, has been responsible for a vast amount of bad poetry. It was once pointed out by T. S. Eliot that it is not in his personal emotions that the poet is in any way remarkable or interesting, these being the common property of mankind, provoked by similar stimuli through untold generations. One error, he remarked, of eccentricity in poetry is "to seek for new human emotions to express, and in this search for novelty in the wrong place it discovers the perverse. The business of the poet is not to find new emotions but to use the ordinary ones."

And yet, dealing in this ancient and fundamentally unchanging material, poetry, through the centuries, has managed to renew itself, to recover freshness, to achieve over and over again a true individuality, because, as A. E. Housman observed, "Poetry is not the thing said but a way of saying it." And so, too, in the hands of those who refuse to be bulldozed by the fear of what has gone before, do other forms of literary expression, even the novel, whose imminent end is every now and then predicted, renew themselves and arrive at a true individuality.

They, too, if they are not merely to discover the perverse, must draw their strength and the capacity for renewal from the ordinary stuff of human life, precisely in the way that Nature herself is forever using the same old materials over and over again and with them achieving her endless variations.

That was what Emerson told himself when at the age of thirty-five he wrote in his journal: "Consider that the perpetual admonition of Nature to us is, The world is new, untried. Do not believe the past. I give you the universe new and unhandled every hour. You think in your idle hours that there is literature, history, science, behind you so accumulated as to exhaust thought and prescribe your own future and the future. In your sane hour you shall see that not a line has yet been written, that for all the poetry there is in the world your first sensation on entering a wood or standing on the shore of a lake has not been charted yet. It remains for you, so does all thought, all object, all life remains unwritten still."

Art vs. Science

Ours is a time in which the diverse claims upon our attention of the scientist and the artist are in conflict as never before. The strange thing about it is that fundamentally both are in pursuit of the same objective, which is truth. They approach it differently, and if we are to understand the separation between them we must make an effort to see where their paths diverge. In spite of the fact that the great triumphs in both science and art are often achieved by an unconscious effort of the imagination, the compulsions leading up to that effort are of a different kind.

These compulsions were never better described than they were by Joseph Conrad in his preface to *The Nigger of the Narcissus.* He was insistent upon the underlying unity of aim shared by the artist, the thinker and the scientist. All are intent upon arriving at truth, but the artist, as opposed to the thinker or the scientist, takes off from a different base.

Art, thought Conrad, might be defined as "a single-minded attempt to render the highest kind of justice to the visible universe, by bringing to light the truth, manifold and one, underlying its every aspect. It is an attempt to find in its forms, in its colors, in its light, in its shadows, in the aspects of matter and in the facts of life, what of each is fundamental, what is enduring and essential—their one illuminating and convincing quality—the very truth of their existence."

The basic difference in art's approach to truth, as against that of philosophy or science, is that it is made, as Conrad observed, through the senses. It is that fact which creates the close relationship between the various forms of art. If literature strives to encompass the other arts, to include within itself the primary concerns of sculpture with form, of painting with color and composition, of music with suggestion, the same may be said of them, in varying degree. Literature, it seems to me, aims at the broadest synthesis of them all; it has always encroached, more than the others, upon the functions which they are best fitted to fulfill.

But our concern is not so much with the point at which the arts separate—sometimes a shadowy one—as with that at which science, philosophy and art diverge. For though they share a common objective in their concern with truth, their paths soon separate. The thinker, in his preoccupation with ideas, the scientist with facts, make an appeal to us which is valid and important, but which is divorced from that of the artist. When Conrad says of the thinker and the scientist that "they speak authoritatively to our common sense, to our intelligence, to our desire of peace or to our desire of unrest; not seldom to our prejudices, sometimes to our fears, often to our egoism—but always to our credulity," and then remarks that it is otherwise with the artist, I think he draws too sharp a line.

For the artist, too, often makes these same appeals, or most of them, but he makes another—the one which Conrad very properly emphasizes—the one to our less obvious capacities, "to that part of our nature which, because of the warlike conditions of existence, is necessarily kept out of sight within the more resisting and hard qualities—like the vulnerable body within a steel armor. His appeal is less loud, more profound, less distinct, more stirring—and sooner forgotten. Yet its effect endures forever." Then comes the penetrating flash that really defines the distinction Conrad is trying to make.

The thinker and the scientist, he points out, are confronted by a condition from which the artist is exempt. As the generations pass, ideas are discarded, as when Copernicus supplants Ptolemy. Facts are questioned, theories are demolished and replaced by others. "But the artist appeals to that part of our being which is not dependent upon wisdom; to that in us which is a gift and not an acquisition—and, therefore, more permanently enduring. He speaks to our capacity for delight and wonder, to the sense of mystery surrounding our lives; to our sense of pity, and beauty, and pain; to the latent feeling of fellowship with all creation—to the subtle but invincible conviction of solidarity that knits together the loneliness of innumerable hearts, to the solidarity in dreams, in joy, in sorrow, in aspirations, in illusions, in hope, in fear, which binds men to each other, which binds together all humanity—the dead to the living and the living to the unborn."

Could it not be, perhaps, a breaking down of the distinction which Conrad here makes that has led increasingly to the separation of the artist from the common need? Too often, it may be, he has allowed his own function to be merged with those of the thinker and the scientist. He has made himself the vehicle of ideas and facts to a degree that has overshadowed his capacity to speak to our capacity for delight and wonder. This is why, I think, so many contemporary novels, for all their close observation and parade of simulated fact, are basically unsatisfying. We live in a period when ideas are more insistently and freely communicated than ever before, when facts are set before us more rapidly than we are able to absorb them. But the other and more enduring need of which Conrad spoke is less often filled.

Innovation and Tradition

The roots of the perennial conflict between tradition and innovation in literature and all the other arts were never more clearly exposed or their nature more simply stated than they were in a story told by Alice Marriott in a book about the American Indian called *The Ten Grandmothers.*

The story to which I refer was not introduced in the book for its bearing on the questions to which I am applying it. It is there simply to illustrate the opposing forces in the Indian's struggle for adjustment to a changed way of life. The time is 1871, and two young men are talking—Eagle Plume and his friend Wood Fire. Eagle Plume's father has died, and he has asked Wood Fire to help him perform some of the ceremonies which tribal custom demands.

In accordance with one of them, the dead warrior's horse must be killed where he is buried. It so happens that the Kiowas have been going through a difficult time, and Wood Fire argues against killing the animal. "That's a good horse," he says, "and people will need good horses." But Eagle Plume is determined to do what he feels should be done. "This is what my father would want," he insists, and cuts the horse's throat.

Afterward the two friends sit by the fire and continue their argument. Wood Fire says, "That is the end of one kind of living. I think all the old things will be dead soon." Eagle Plume, while he dries some sticks to put on the fire, answers: "I think the old things won't die so easy. I think there are still some people who love them and think they are right." But Wood Fire is not convinced. "There are always some people," he remarks, "who hang on to the things that should be buried, just because they can't stand to give them up. That's the way some people are."

"Well," says Eagle Plume, "There are some people who know they have to keep things alive for the other people. Some people have the right to keep the old things going." Wood Fire is equally stubborn. "Well," he says, "some people have the right to get new things started."

Eagle Plume then made a final effort to explain what was working in his mind. "You have to have new things," he said. "You have to have new springs to make the grass grow. But grass grows out of the old earth. You have to have old things for new things to have roots in. That's why some people have to keep old things going and some people have to push new things along. It's right for both of them. It's what they have to do."

Eagle Plume, it seems to me, got to the heart of the matter when he said, "It's right for both of them." The principle he drew from the earth at his feet, of the interacting forces out of which all stable growth is produced, is one that both the traditionalists and the innovators tend too often to forget. Actually, taking his analogy direct from nature as an Indian would, Eagle Plume was saying much the same thing that André Gide reported himself as once thinking: "It suddenly seemed clear to me," he wrote, "that if there were no names in the history of art except those belonging to the creators of new forms, there would be no culture; the very word implied a continuity, and therefore it called for disciples, imitators and followers to make a living chain: in other words, a tradition."

Or, as John Buchan once put it, if a man regards the past "as the matrix of present and future, whose potency takes many forms but is not diminished, then he will cherish it scrupulously and labor to read its lessons, and shun the heady short cuts which end only in blank walls. He will realize that in the cycle to which we belong we can see only a fraction of the curve, and that properly to appraise the curve and therefore to look ahead, we may have to look back a few centuries to its beginning."

So far as literature and the other arts are concerned, it is when we have, as we so frequently do today, an almost absolute intolerance of the representatives of one force for those of the other, that we get the dry rot of sterile repetition or the gross exaggerations by which the hidebound traditionalist or the intolerant innovator proclaims his disregard for the interaction of which Eagle Plume, André Gide and John Buchan were all so aware. The conflict has never been more intense than during the time in which we live. It has been marked not only in the arts but in almost every area of human activity. If only more of us who are involved in one way or another could keep always in the forefront of our minds the knowledge that "it's right for both of them," we might rid ourselves of a lot of waste motion.

P.S. The only addition I would make to the foregoing column is its application to politics. In our time, *conservative* has become a dirty word. But the role of the conservative in government is as essential as that of his counterpart in art, and for the same reasons. Nature, in her processes, strives for balance. It is a lesson we seem slow to learn. If we could, man's tenure of his planet would seem assured. Something in man, unfortunately, pushes him to extremes. He wants to have his cake and eat it too. He may be a stepson, but he needs to heed his mother.

The Interlocking Arts

As time goes on, I find myself increasingly aware of the parallels and divergences between literature and the other arts, and more and more interested in their manifestations. Often, if they are not pushed too far, these likenesses and differences help to explain how a particular work succeeds or fails in its purpose; they sometimes make possible a more concrete understanding of the qualities which distinguish a certain piece of writing. To take a simple example: if we speak of a novel as having a kind of symphonic structure, we can indicate more clearly and briefly, by using the analogy from music, the kind of effect which the novelist has been able to obtain.

But these parallels and divergences have to be used with care; if we summon them too freely or give them too much importance, they can lead us far astray. There are, in the provinces of the arts, boundary lines that cannot quite be crossed. All forms of art, for example, can establish and communicate a mood, but music, I think, can do this more completely and more hauntingly than any other. Yet it can be done to very tangible effect both in writing and in painting, in somewhat less degree in sculpture, and even, to some extent, in architecture.

We speak of composition with particular reference to painting; it plays a great role in all forms of art whose appeal is primarily to the eye, but its parallel can even be found in a piece of writing where pattern is made important. Mr. Marquand, for example, is outstandingly skillful in his use of what we call the "flashback." Pattern is the essence of this device, and without stretching the term too far, we can speak here of composition in the sense in which it is applied to painting. The use of color, naturally, lies at the heart of painting, and while the writer can, in this respect, achieve *something* with words, he is, essentially, confronted by one of the boundary lines of which I have been speaking.

The writer, in some respects, is, in the use of his medium, the freest of all the workers in the arts. To a greater degree than any of the others, he can borrow from them. If he has an ear, he draws from music, and can incorporate in his work some of its effect. If he has the recording eye which is one of the greatest gifts that can be bestowed upon him, he can range in the province of the painter. If the structural sense is strong in him, he can create obvious and striking parallels with the work of the composer or the architect. No other of his fellow artists has as wide a range.

His advantage shows up especially in the matter of structure or form. That is everything in architecture. Structure is tremendously important in music and sculpture, and less so, but still potent, in painting. Literature stands alone among the arts in the fact that although structure can greatly enhance it, literature can achieve greatness without benefit of that powerful component in the appeal of all the arts.

It would be wiser, perhaps, not to make that an absolute statement. Structure, in writing, begins with the sentence, extends to the paragraph, the stanza, the chapter, the part of one kind or another, and ends with the whole. Some kind of structure in the sentence, at least, is essential, both to our understanding and our pleasure. The farther it can be extended, so that it embraces not only the parts, but the whole, the greater, for some of us, at least, is the pleasure. Yet the fact remains that some of the most prized works of literature, taken as a whole, give no satisfaction to the structural sense. They sprawl, they leave things at loose ends. When the pattern is too evident, when the ends are too neatly tied together, we are likely to complain that this is not life, but merely art. We do not raise the same objection about a piece of music or sculpture, about a painting or a building. There the form is paramount.

Could the reason for this be that literature is closer to life? The symphony, the statue, the landscape, the cathedral, somehow achieve an entity divorced from the personality of their creators to an extent which is not possible for the work of the writer. That is still entangled with life, drawn more directly from it than the others. We identify ourselves more easily in the reflection of life which it gives. Could this be the reason why we seem to be more interested in the lives and personalities of writers than we are in the case of other artists? Perhaps one reason why the architect's name is not known or remembered, lies in the fact that his creation is so impersonal. The best books are, in effect, like letters written to us. Music, painting, sculpture, architecture, all speak to us, but in a somewhat different way.

Notes on Winslow Homer

Two weeks ago in this column I remarked on certain similarities between Robert Frost as a poet and Winslow Homer as a painter, observing that they both possess "that unfrantic vitality which has always been the possession of first-rate artists in whatever medium, proceeding from a masculinity which has no need to proclaim itself." Today I should like to enlarge on that statement, in its bearing on certain characteristics of contemporary writing and painting, and also to comment briefly on the very interesting essay which Albert Ten Eyck Gardner, Associate Curator of American Art at the Metropolitan Museum, wrote for the Winslow Homer catalogue jointly issued by the National Gallery and the Metropolitan in connection with the recent retrospective exhibition of Homer's work.

There have been writers who are indubitably American, writers whose essence stands apart from European influences, which if absorbed at all, were, in the work of these men, transmuted. We catch the first glimpse of this quality in the autobiography of

Benjamin Franklin; we find it in Cooper and Hawthorne, but not in Poe; it is strong in Emerson and Thoreau, and in Parkman, in Whitman and Mark Twain; it was absent in Henry James, who was never able to understand his own country, and vibrant in his brother William. Henry Adams lacked it as much as it was possessed by Theodore Roosevelt. Sinclair Lewis had it; so does Marquand, and, in his twisted fashion, so has Faulkner. It is stronger, I think, in Robert Frost than in any living writer of comparable accomplishment. I shall not attempt to define this quality; it is elusive, but I know that it exists.

Winslow Homer had it beyond any other American painter of excellence, with the possible exception of George Bellows. It was the possession, of course, of Remington and Charlie Russell, but these were not artists of equal caliber. I called the quality elusive because it does not depend entirely on the choice and use of native themes (Longfellow used them, yet he was not distinctly an American writer). Winslow Homer had it in spite of the fact that, as Mr. Gardner is at pains to demonstrate, he found himself as an artist only after he had absorbed, and adapted to his own uses, the art of the great Japanese print-makers. Whistler was affected by them too, yet Whistler—a rather unfair comparison because of his English residence—showed in his work no sign of his American origin.

To me, as to many others, Homer is by a wide margin the greatest painter the United States has yet produced. I know that my admiration for him is in part the product of his choice of subject-matter, for I too love the sea, the North Woods and the homely but endearing features of American rural life. But his devotion to these subjects does not make the sum of my reasons for placing him above all other American painters. It gave me great delight to see crowds flocking to the Homer exhibition at the Metropolitan, and I could not forbear hoping that exposure to those magnificent pictures might temper their appreciation of the empty, confused and emasculated work of which so much is foisted on a rightly bewildered public when it visits the Fifty-seventh Street galleries, or even, the Whitney Museum and the Museum of Modern Art.

I have seen abstractions I liked, though not many, and I still feel disinclined to buy a three-legged horse when I can get one with four legs. The most that non-representational painting can give you is pleasure in color, form, and design; usually you get but one of these. In Homer and in other men of his stature I get these three and a fourth quality besides, which is meaning, and which can be poetry. The abstractionists work on a lower level; theirs is definitely a more restricted art, and one devoid of human content.

Their emptiness has its parallel in a great deal of contemporary writing—in the work of the frantic symbol-hunters, in the sterile criticism, divorced from human life and from understanding of human beings, with which our more esoteric quarterlies are crowded, in the dull and meaningless repetitive descriptions of the sexual act —the essence of which, when informed by love, no writer has yet been able adequately to convey—which reduces to tedium the recent long novels of such a naturally gifted writer as John O'Hara, or the fumbling insistence of a misdirected talent like that of Jack Kerouac. This inconsequentiality was the base of my objection to Nabokov's *Lolita,* which is not a pornographic book. It is merely meaningless, judged from the viewpoint of universal human experience, and not worth the effort expended on it, unless Nabokov wrote the whole thing with tongue in cheek, in which case it still remains a trifle. Of those commentators who found the book hilariously funny I can only wonder what has happened to the American sense of humor.

We could do with more writing of a creative kind which is rooted in a sense of American identity. The writer who does not know and understand his own country cannot hope to reach that universality which every good writer craves.